WILD
IRELAND

A TRAVELLER'S GUIDE

BRENDAN LEHANE

WITH PHOTOGRAPHS BY
MARC SCHLOSSMAN

SIERRA CLUB BOOKS
SAN FRANCISCO

Published in the United States by Sierra Club Books, San Francisco, 1995

Designed and produced by
Sheldrake Press,
188 Cavendish Road,
London, SW12 0DA

Copyright © 1995 Sheldrake Holdings Ltd

Library of Congress Cataloging-in-Publication Data

Lehane, Brendan
  Wild Ireland/Brendan Lehane.
    p. cm
  ISBN 0-87156-427-0
  1. Natural history—Ireland—Guidebooks. 2. Natual areas
—Ireland—Guidebooks. 3. Ireland—Guidebooks. I. Title.
CH143.L43   1996
508.415—dc20   95-34011
                                                    CIP
Printed in Spain

EDITOR: Simon Rigge
Art Direction: Ivor Claydon
Deputy Editor: Tracey Beresford
Map Editor: Malcolm Day
Researcher: Sarah West
Editorial Assistants: Giles Clare, Charles Dietz, Ingrid Karikari, Chrisoula Petridis
Line Illustrations: Syd Lewis
Production Manager: Geoff Barlow
Typesetting: Cameron Typesetting
Maps: Arcadia Consultants
Index: Indexing Specialists

Front cover: a glen stream rushes through mossy boulders in the hills above Glengarriff, on the Beara peninsula.

THE AUTHOR

BRENDAN LEHANE comes from an old Irish family and has lived for long periods in Ireland. He has written, among other books, *The Companion Guide to Ireland, Dublin, The Compleat Flea, Natural History*, an introduction for children, *The Power of Plants*, a survey of the influences of plants on human life, and *The Quest of Three Abbots*, a view of life and spirituality during the golden age of Irish Christianity. He has travelled in Africa, America, the Middle East and continental Europe, and has written articles for the *Telegraph Magazine* and many other publications.

THE PHOTOGRAPHER

MARC SCHLOSSMAN contributes to many national newspapers and magazines in his native United States and in Britain, including *The Independent, Harper's and Queen* and *BBC Wildlife Magazine*. In his travels he has climbed Mount Kilimanjaro, lived with head-hunters in the jungle of the Philippines and canoed into the North-West Territories. His love of Ireland takes him there as often as possible. He travelled 7,000 miles, walked, climbed, camped on location and got soaked and chilled photographing the landscape of Ireland for this book.

THE GENERAL EDITOR

DOUGLAS BOTTING was born in London and educated at Oxford. He has travelled to the Amazon, South Yemen, the Sahara, Arctic Siberia and to many European wild places.

Douglas Botting's travel books include *One Chilly Siberian Morning, Wilderness Europe, Rio de Janeiro* and, in this series, *Wild Britain*. He has also written a biography of the great naturalist and explorer Alexander von Humbolt.

THE CONSULTANTS

JOHN BURTON is a natural history and wildlife conservation writer and consultant. Formerly secretary of the Fauna and Flora Preservation Society, he is the co-founder with Douglas Botting of the Wild series.

ELEANOR MAYES is an ecological consultant. She works in ecological research and survey, and in conservation policy, and provides planning and management advice.

THE CONTRIBUTOR

SUZANNE SCOTT, who contributed most of the fact packs, has travelled widely in Europe and North America and works as a travel journalist.

CONTENTS

ABOUT THE SERIES

What would the world be, once bereft
Of wet and of wilderness? Let them be
   left,
O let them be left, wildness and wet;
Long live the weeds and the wilderness
   yet.

        Gerard Manley Hopkins: *Inversnaid*

These books are about those embattled
refuges of wildness and wet, the wild places
of Europe. But where, in this most densely
populated sub-continent, do we find a truly
wild place?

Ever since our Cro-Magnon ancestors
began their forays into the virgin forests of
Europe 40,000 years ago, the land and its
creatures have been in retreat before *Homo
sapiens*. Forests have been cleared, marshes
drained and rivers straightened. Even some
of those landscapes that appear primordial
are in fact the result of human activity.
Heather-covered moorland in North
Yorkshire and parched Andalucian desert
have this in common: both were once
covered by great forests which ancient
settlers knocked flat.

What then remains that can be called
wild? There are still a few areas in Europe
that are untouched by man – places
generally so unwelcoming either in terrain
or in climate that man has not wanted to
touch them at all – and these are
indisputably wild.

For some people, wildness suggests
conflict with nature: a wild place is a part of
the planet so savage and desolate that you
risk your life whenever you venture into it.
This is in part true but would limit the
eligible places to the most impenetrable bog
or highest mountain tops in the worst
winter weather – a rather restricted view.
Another much broader definition considers
a wild place to be a part of the planet where
living things can find a natural refuge from
the influence of modern industrial society.
By this definition a wild place is for wildlife
as well as that portmanteau figure referred
to in these pages as the wild traveller: the
hillwalker, backpacker, bird-watcher, nature
lover, explorer, nomad, loner, mystic,
masochist, aficionado of the great
outdoors, or permutations of all these
things.

This is the definition we have observed in
selecting the wild places described in these
books. Choosing them has not been easy.
Even so, we hope the criterion has proved
rigid enough to exclude purely pretty
(though popular) countryside, and flexible
enough to include the greener and gentler
wild places, of great natural historical
interest perhaps, as well as the starker, more
savage ones where the wild explorers come
into their own.

These are not guide books in the
conventional sense, for to describe every
neck of the woods and twist of the trail
throughout Europe would require a library
of volumes. Nor are these books addressed
to the technical specialist – the caver, diver,
rock climber or cross-country skier; the
orchid-hunter, lepidopterist or beetle-
maniac – for such experts will have data of
their own. They are books intended for the
great outdoor traveller – including the
expert outside his own field of expertise (the
orchid-hunter in a cave, the diver on a
mountain top) – who wishes to scrutinize
the range of wild places on offer in Europe,
to learn a little more about them and to set
about exploring them off the beaten track.

One of the greatest consolations in the
preparation of these books has been to find
that after 40,000 years of hunting, clearing,
draining and ploughing, Cro-Magnon and
their descendants have left so much of
Europe that can still be defined as wild.

Douglas Botting

WILD IRELAND: AN INTRODUCTION

Nothing sudden triggered the race. A hefty mantle of ice, which had cloaked most of Ireland and the rest of northern Europe for millennia and made the living of any life beneath it more or less impossible, began during a new wave of warmth to melt. From southerly latitudes opportunist organisms began creeping, swimming, flying, drifting, blowing, walking and trundling in. They crossed the dry land which would in due course become the English Channel and some colonized Britain-to-be. A good many more went on to cross the dry land already beginning to be covered by what would be known as the Irish Sea and St George's Channel. Beginning 10,000 years ago, the period of melting lasted about 2,000 years, causing the sea to rise more than 300 feet (100 metres) – though part of this increased depth was due to a sinking of the floor of the Irish Sea. Many plants and creatures won this race to arrive before the last of the Irish-British land bridges flooded, but in species-counts, Britain, with only one water-barrier between it and Europe (and anyway not cut off for another couple of thousand years), did considerably better.

When all that could do so had settled down, Ireland had not much more than two-thirds the number of Britain's wild plants and insects, about four-fifths of the birds, a third of the amphibians and a quarter of the reptiles. Britain, moreover, is not, relatively speaking, well off. In terms of vascular plants, for example, Ireland today has 815 native species; Britain 1,172. But France, whence many of them came, has 3,500.

Not all this can be put down to Ireland's early insularity. Birds fly thousands of miles, some seeds float similar distances without harm, others are carried by flying birds, many animals swim. There are indeed wild plants in Ireland which do not grow in Britain at all and come from sources much further off. Compared with other countries Ireland was short of habitats as well. Absence of mountains as high as Scotland's, of England's chalk downs and lowland heaths, meant that many British plants, birds and animals, even if they had made it to Ireland, would have found no home there. When humans moved in and flexed their muscles, they tamed – because it was so tameable – a much larger proportion of the land than was the case in most other countries. Limited in size, habitats and species, Ireland might seem a poor bet for those in search of wilderness.

In fact, it is one of the world's more beautiful countries: a land of greens and purples and dramatic shapes and contours under a changing canopy of blue and white, blown in from the Atlantic. With a third of the area of Great Britain it contains no more than a fourteenth of the population. It does, it is true, spread its people more thinly and widely than Britain (Irish country people preferring the homestead to the village). But there are few places outside towns where numbers become oppressive, except perhaps in summer and on well-trodden tourist paths. Old tradition has for generations made it possible for travellers to walk almost anywhere (though a fencing frenzy financed by Europe is curtailing this privilege). Ireland's size makes it easy to get anywhere, except to islands in bad weather. Mountain and moorland come cheek by jowl with lush river valley, lowland bog, steep cliffs and broad sandy beaches. Ireland lies athwart important bird-routes, providing wonderful seasonal spectacles of the migrations of (in particular) sea-birds and waders, and the frequent occurrence of rarities blown off their familiar routes, as well as the continual viewing of its native birds.

Ireland is rich in unexpected sites of wildness, often too small for detailed treatment in this book but fascinating all the same. Wildness of course begins as soon as humans turn their backs. Ants, mice, moths and other wildlife advance from the sidelines. A minute spider swings in like Tarzan on a rope of gossamer. Wildness pullulates under our eyes. In a mysteriously cheap Dublin flat many years ago I was to be so vexed by fleas that I turned to studying them as a therapy – *tout comprendre c'est tout pardonner* – and in due course published a book on them. In our towns, foxes scavenge among the garbage bags and peregrines nest on towers. Huge flocks of pied wagtails spend winter nights on bare trees in the middle of Dublin's central thoroughfare. A naturalist could keep busy well within city limits

Unless they had a pressing reason for doing otherwise, the Irish have generally left redundant buildings to rot and corners of old fields and demesnes to grow and teem and tangle according to nature's way. They have let hedges grow fat at the expense of pasture. They have lèft disused canals to breed their own aquatic populations; ancient barns and monasteries and churches and bridges and Anglo-Irish mansions to drape themselves in ivy and offer homes to innumerable owls, swallows, bats, squirrels, frogs, toads, fungi and lichens.

I use the past tense here not because these things are no longer true but because they are less true than they used to be. At a time when most people acknowledge that a stop has to be put to the poisoning and squandering of natural resources, the Irish – with the help of the EU – seem to be squandering, polluting, fouling, spraying, ripping up and hacking back more than ever before. You see miles of hedges cut with disfiguring mechanical cutters (often at a season when birds are nesting inside them), prematurely bare and savagely ruined choirs, where evicted birds have no more cause to sing; you see barbed-wire fences where once all could roam freely; you see mile upon mile of flat muddy rock from which ten feet of peat has been gradually lifted. Less harmful but quite out of keeping with the spirit of the wild, it is necessary to mention the doings of the Irish equivalent of the Indian baboo, the normally deskbound functionary who cannot see a blade of grass without wishing to attach an explanatory label to it. There seems at times to be hardly a hill or lake or pass or valley they have not ringed with signposts – 'The Tain Trail', 'The Comeraghs Drive', 'Sarsfield's Route' – so much so that you find yourself choosing roads bare of these baubles, not so much to escape the signs as to find out what exceptional qualities can cause a route to be left without them.

I have to be very careful in saying all this. There is a strong tendency among writers about the country to thrash Ireland for doing things other countries have been doing with impunity for years. Ireland for some reason brings out the old-fashioned parent or pedagogue in the people of other nations. You can fancy you hear them saying – perhaps you can even hear yourself saying – very late and quite without penitence, 'Don't do as I did, foolish child. Do as I say'.

The truth is that Ireland's record, while not stainless, is considerably better than those of Britain and other European countries. Ireland may be small, but it is still quite big enough to offer huge and magical tracts that have escaped so far the hand of polluter and bureaucrat. There are the mountains, many of them (especially in the south-west) wild enough to pose problems to the most experienced climber, even if they may have quite easy alternative routes to the top. There are inland ranges and inland lakes and rivers, some of which have retained the rugged air of wilderness. Most of all, there is the west coast, the startling, varied sequence of sliced mountain, lone islands, long façades of spume-splashed cliff, bird-packed stacks, snaking promontories and stiletto inlets, golden strands, blue lagoons, deep, clear, rocky bays – and an ancient people who have graduated from the harshest buffets of climate and history to become as friendly and kind and hospitable as any on earth.

THE KEY TO IRELAND'S WILD PLACES

THE SHAPE OF THE WILD

Ireland consists of a generally flat, limestone-based interior, rimmed disjointedly by mountains or lesser uplands. The mountains in Donegal, Mayo and north-west Galway go back to the so-called Caledonian orogeny (or mountain-birth) of some 400 million years ago, whose south-west to north-east foldings and upthrusts also created the Highlands of Scotland. Some of the central ridges of these mountains consist of granite. The ranges in the southern part of the country are predominantly formed of old red sandstone and tend to lie in an east–west direction. They resulted from the Hercynian orogeny, which erupted about 300 million years ago, and created over to the east what have become the Harz mountains of Germany. The long peninsulas in the west of Counties Kerry and Cork are also of sandstone. The Wicklow mountains of the south-east, another huge granite outcrop hemmed by durable metamorphic rocks, came about through the upheavals of 500 million years ago. In the north-east the Mourne mountains are another, far more recent, granite intrusion, dating from about 65 million years ago, at the end of the age of dinosaurs.

Limestone is not confined to the low-level midlands where it underlies the great but diminished bogs and the lush pastures of Ireland's richest dairy farms. It also rises up to form grass-topped mountains in Sligo and Leitrim; distinctive rock overhangs, dramatic cliffs and gorges in Fermanagh and Cavan; and the uncanny landscape of the Burren in County Clare.

All these things happened while Ireland drifted wherever the tectonic plates of which she forms part took her: from near the Antarctic, where all the world's land masses were once concentrated, over the Equator (with long periods of submergence and a time of division which carried one half of the country hundreds of miles from the other and back again), to her present location a little closer to the North Pole than to the Equator. This is 99 per cent of Ireland's history. In the most recent moments of geological time – a million or so years ago – came the Ice Age, which periodically covered parts or all of the country in a mile or more of ice. An instant ago came humans.

The movement of ice wore down rock, scraped rough surfaces smooth, dug out valleys and blocked them with stony litter so that many became lakes. People removed the forests that sprang up when the ice receded, turned land to pasture and crops, dug away much of the peat that came after the tree-felling, drained marshes, dammed rivers, and made reservoirs, towns, highways.

WILD HABITATS

All of these stages in their varied ways provided homes, temporary or permanent, for all kinds of flora and fauna. Many of the species of the past have disappeared for ever, such as the great auk and giant Irish deer (*Cervus giganteus*). Others like the hippopotamus and elephant have moved to more sympathetic climates. Plenty remain and most of them survive in habitats which still qualify as wild.

The coast: the battle between land and sea is at its most relentless on the west coast, where Atlantic might is flung, most days and most nights, and with real if imperceptible effect, at massive cliff-faces like those of Slieve League, Croaghaun and Moher, or the toppling defences at the ends of the peninsulas of Cork and Kerry. Most of the rest of the coast is rocky, too, but lower-lying, less stark and bluff: rock coves, rock stacks, rock islands. More kinds of bird inhabit the coastal features of Ireland than any comparable habitat. Where rivers meet the sea there are, in many cases, deep broad estuaries, emptying and filling with the tides, fringed with mud-flats, sand-dunes or salt marshes and attracting thousands of wading birds and wildfowl. Seaside pastures such as the Wexford Slobs are used by wintering geese, swans and ducks, sometimes in flocks of many thousands, making some of the most impressive spectacles Ireland has to offer.

Mountain and bogs: most of Ireland's raised bogs have been lost to peat exploitation but a handful remain, mostly as nature reserves. However, together with the coast, the highlands occupy the greater part of Ireland's wild places and most, on their upper levels, are covered by blanket bog, which developed after the Ice Age. The plants supported by the bog must be acid-lovers, either needing a minimum of minerals or able to supplement the soil's meagre supply.

Inland waters: with its miles of coastline, its tracery of rivers, its ubiquitous lakes, its marshes, callows, canals, lagoons, rias and heavy rainfall, Ireland is a watery fief. On her own, nature did not overload these waters with fish. Fresh-water natives are few in number. Since the Ice Age, which killed off all previous species, only migrant fish – salmon, sea trout, shad, smelt – and stickleback and lamprey were able to occupy the lakes and rivers. A surviving curiosity is the char, usually found in and close to the Arctic. A similar Arctic species is the pollan, found in Lough Neagh and in the lower Shannon.

Birds that eat them follow the fish but many more settle on rivers and lakes to graze or eat the seeds of the underwater and waterside vegetation – reeds, spike-rushes, pondweeds, mare's tail grasses and several kinds of algae – or excavate wet mud and pasture for invertebrates. Some choose this habitat as protection from predators. The heron is a solemn, still presence in almost all fresh-water habitats. Lough Neagh, the country's biggest lake, and Lough Corrib are the most important Irish lakes for birds, mainly because they are quite shallow. They attract huge numbers of duck and other waterfowl.

Low-lying riverside pastures which regularly flood in winter are known in Ireland as callows. Thousands of birds take advantage of the safety afforded by the floodwaters in winter and early spring. Callows are found on the Shannon river, on the River Suck in County Roscommon and on the River Blackwater in County Waterford. Turloughs or karst lakes provide protection for curlews, lapwings, some golden plovers and other waders and wildfowl.

Woodlands: the broadleaf forests, primarily of native oak, but including also native elm, ash, yew, hazel, birch, rowan, willow and alder which once covered most of the country have been reduced to patches and pockets by massive clearances. Irrepressible sycamore, beech, horse-chestnut and the one deciduous conifer, larch, are all introductions of recent centuries.

Woodland animals may include grey and red squirrels, pine martens, foxes, badgers, and in the fewer places where they occur, fallow, sika, red and red-sika hybrid deer. By far the largest number of woodland birds – up to 85 per cent, according to surveys – are robin, wren, blue tit, coal tit, chaffinch or goldcrest, the country's smallest bird, common in conifer woods as well as broadleaf. Treecreeper, jay, kestrel, woodcock, pheasant, sparrowhawk, chiffchaff, blackcap, song thrush and wood pigeon are also found.

PROTECTED WILD PLACES

National parks in the Irish Republic, as in most other countries but not in Britain, are entirely state-owned. There is therefore no clash between the interests of visitors and those of resident farmers and landowners. It means, however, that the space occupied by such parks is small, less than half a per cent of the country's area. The five existing national parks are Glenveagh, Co. Donegal; Connemara National Park, Co. Galway; Killarney National Park, Co. Kerry; Wicklow National Park; and Burren National Park, Co. Clare.

Natural Heritage Areas at present being designated, following a new survey, will cover much more of the country: some five to seven per cent. They are equivalent to Sites of Special Scientific Interest (SSSI) in Northern Ireland and in Britain.

Northern Ireland contains no National Parks but does have officially designated Areas of Outstanding Natural Beauty, SSSIs and National Trust land and reserves.

MAPS

For years the standard large-scale maps of Ireland for the use of walkers, climbers and other country-users were the 25 sheets of the Ordnance Survey of Ireland half-inch-to-one-mile set. They contained inaccuracies, as every frequent user discovered.

A few years ago the Ordnance Survey offices of both Northern Ireland and the Republic decided to supersede these old half-inch maps with a complete set in the metric scale of 1:50,000 or two centimetres to one kilometre. The Northern Irish 'Discoverer' series was completed in 1993 and is referred to in this book as the OSNI Discoverer Series. The Republic's 'Discovery' series (which is to cover the whole country) is due to be completed by the end of the century. The maps that have appeared so far are great improvements on what went before, but until the series is complete the old, inaccurate half-inch maps will in parts be the only options. Along with misspellings and omissions, these unfortunately show old-style road-numbers, too.

TO THE READER

Eagle symbols: the eagle symbols used at the head of some entries in this book indicate the wildness of the exploration zone to which they refer. This scale is based on a number of factors, including remoteness, ruggedness, spaciousness, uniqueness, wildlife interest, natural beauty and the author's own subjective reactions. Three eagles is the highest rating, no eagles the lowest.

Updating: while everything possible has been done to ensure the accuracy of the facts in this book, information does gradually become out of date. For this reason we would welcome readers' corrections and comments for incorporation in subsequent editions. Please write to The Editor, Wild Traveller's Guides, Sheldrake Press, 188 Cavendish Road, London, SW12 0DA.

Non-liability: both the author and the publishers have gone to great pains to point out the hazards that may confront the traveller in certain places described in *Wild Ireland*. We cannot under any circumstances accept any liability for any mishap, loss or injury sustained by any person venturing into any of the wild places listed in this book.

CHAPTER 1

Donegal and Sligo

Malin Head, a scatter of rock at the north end of Ireland, is better than most places to start pursuing Irish wildness. Wildness is what its name, location and character suggest. Europe stops here. Northward, across a thousand-mile gap of bleak ocean, lies the Arctic. The ghostly green of the northern lights is sometimes seen from these shores. Anyone who has heard years of shipping forecasts in Ireland or Britain knows of the frequency of Malin's gale-force 9s or storm-force 11s. The cliffs to its right and left glower out their resistance to the worst that north and north-westerly wind, tide, sleet and hail can do. It takes a lot of getting to, whatever means are employed. As wildness goes these days, Malin and the miles of mountain and moor and rock promontory that are its neighbours well deserve the epithet.

You can see this untamed landscape, dramatically, from an ancient elevated structure south of the peninsula and just five miles (eight kilometres) north-west of the city of Derry. The Grianan (pronounced greenan; it means 'sun-place') of Aileach is a restored circular stone royal palace, with much myth attached. It offers a telling preview of substantial parts of Counties Donegal, Derry and Tyrone. To the north is clearly seen Inishowen's great mass, and left of that, every bay and inlet of winding Lough Swilly, which the Fanad peninsula separates from Mulroy Bay and Sheephaven. To complete a circuit of the closer landmarks you can cast your

Sunset falls over Loughros Point on the Donegal coast. To the north lies Dawros Head, to the south the dramatic mass of the Slieve League Peninsula and to the west, America.

eye around anti-clockwise until, after the basalt bluff of Binevenagh across to the east and the simple, shapely outline of Lough Foyle, you come back to Inishowen again. Further off to the west a receding series of domed, coned and elongated outlines takes the view almost to the limits of this north-western section of Ireland, to the west and south of Donegal and the nearer heights of Counties Sligo and Leitrim.

For me, and many others I think, this coastline of Donegal was once the most romantically wild of all. You thought of the battered galleons of the Armada, the great rebel Gaels sailing away from all their ambitions, or Wolfe Tone cutting his throat when his last great hope turned to despair. Thirty years ago, neither nature nor man had done much to mar the setting of these pictures. Eagles and wolves had gone since Tone's time, it is true, but most of the rest would have at least looked unchanged. In recent years, however, something has happened which has removed the essentially wild personality from large tracts of land and coast.

Anyone looking for the wildness of Ireland nowadays has to adopt an attitude to bungalows. Their presence here is as intrusive as it is anywhere in the country, and although I never thought I should use the remotest coast of Donegal to discuss a rampant rash of bourgeois construction, it now seems the most sensible place. I shall look very hard for balance.

I used to think a symbol of Ireland was the explosive bush. If you walked close to almost any tangle of briar, bramble, thorn, furze or broom, in almost any field, on almost any summery day, your approach triggered a buzzing firework of insect life: flies, bluebottles, greenbottles, bugs, ladybirds, cardinal beetles took off in all directions – a

wonderful precipitation of colourful motley. Years before, England had the same thing, but stripping fields for monoculture crops or grasses did for it there, and many parts of Ireland have gone the same way since. But there are still yards and in some places acres of these knotty shrubs, left because farmers like them or cannot be bothered to smooth the bumps or clear the stones or claim the soil they occupy.

One of Ireland's major crops must, in consequence, be the blackberry, and I must have removed tons of the fruit myself. I have seldom seen anyone else picking it. The Irish like blackberries, for sure, said my Irish cousin years ago. They will buy tins of blackberries with pleasure. They will buy frozen blackberries with delight. But they will not pick blackberries. Picking blackberries is what their grandparents or great-grandparents had to do to stay alive, and they would sooner avoid that association.

I say all this to stress that until recent years the country Irish were forced and accustomed to concentrate on necessities, and to work hard and long to acquire them. It was not a life – least of all in the barren west – that offered much time for refinements. It is difficult now to recall how hard life was in the west only thirty and forty years ago. There was no tourism, and farming offered no more than subsistence. All the young went to England or America. For the rare visitor, such as myself, it was very picturesque and appealing: there were thatched hovels and courteous peasants with leathery skins and charming turns of phrase, and transport by horse and cart, and fortunes under mattresses from mistrust of banks, and much porter and poteen and smiles and nasal song and the music of fiddles and some noisy drunkenness. A few people still spoke as they speak in the plays of Synge, who after all got much of his dialogue from listening to kitchen girls through the cracks in the floor of his rented room on Aran. For all the hardship, human life seemed congruous with nature.

But it is, and would have been then had one bothered to ask, perfectly clear that the peasants themselves did not think so. Those who could do so with ease escaped. Islanders gladly left lovely islands in which scraping a living took a heavy toll on health and time. They gladly forgot the Gaelic language that tied them to these harsh ways. But many of them could barely afford to do so. On the mainland too, life was a struggle.

Quite suddenly, the things the Irish coveted in Britain and the USA became available to them at home. Huge investments in tourism paid off. The European Common Market brought a range of subsidies, skills and opportunities that could not have been dreamt of ten years before. There were jobs, grants, buoyancy. To hell, the collective voice of western Ireland might have gone, to hell with your blackberries. From now on we buy them in syrup, in cans. To the devil, they said, with your Donegal thatched cottages, that you came to admire and patronize for a couple of weeks and never had to live in. They were damp and dark and cramped and dirty. We hated them. We wanted spreading bungalows with glowing white walls and pedimented porticoes as in *Dallas* and *Dynasty*. We wanted big picture windows with views over the sea and the cliffs; wall-to-wall carpeting and central heating and swishing curtains with fancy pelmets; satellite television, fitted kitchens, en-suite bathrooms and lavatories, car ports, patios, balustrade boundaries and lions and pineapples on the piers of our garden gates. And now we can have them, and by Jesus, Mary and Joseph we will, say

what you dare. And our old houses can rot and go to the devil.

In an amazingly short span of years the bungalows were there. Revisiting parts of the west coast after long intervals, I got the impression that it had all happened, slyly, while my back was turned, as in a game of grandmother's footsteps. There is no other option but to see the inhabitants' point. Some of them can be rather touchy on the matter. If you say, 'Yes, but is it not a pity to abandon perfectly sound and agreeable two-storey houses to the winds?' they may sense the opposition they have heard often enough before, and bristle slightly. If you mention that the many new bungalows in Northern Ireland are at least subject to stringent planning laws, and kept in clusters rather than spread piecemeal about the most conspicuous eminences of the landscape, they will think you have gone far enough and their eyes may start to narrow. They may suggest that you would prefer to see them back in their cabins, ten to a room and the pig in with them, and a hole in the roof to let the smoke out. Or that you would have objected, twelve centuries ago, to the mass construction of the so-called beehive huts for monks on the Kerry promontories, claiming they spoilt the view (I probably should have done). The houses are there, occupied, giving deep satisfaction. Mr Jack FitzSimons, author of *Bungalow Bliss*, which outsells the Bible and provides plans for hundreds of such homes, has made his fortune amid the grateful thanks of his fellow countrymen. In this short time the country has undergone the greatest change of its whole existence. Bungalows have not brought the tourist numbers down. Quite the contrary. They are here to stay.

It is what they have done to the nebulous ideal of wildness which is our

13

concern here. You trudge round a windswept cape to be confronted by a pyramid pattern of bungalows. Like fairy lights, glossy white bungalows shine over the former desolation of a broad peat bog. There are bungalows beside the quiet meanders of tree-lined stream, or on the shores of a lake that is otherwise the private haunt of birds and fish. But they are not everywhere. They are most numerous on the west coast, a large proportion serving as holiday cottages, to let or not as the case may be. A lot of Donegal's bungalows are owned by citizens of Northern Ireland. Inland, which has always been unfairly neglected by visitors, is relatively – but not entirely – free of them. Mountains are mercifully spared, and there are mighty tracts of unspoilt wilderness. Above a certain height, bungalows, like trees, do not flourish. We may soon be talking of the bungalow line. Otherwise they can spring on you anywhere, without warning. I recommend a bungalow blind-spot, a knack of looking past, over or around them without actually noticing. So far it has eluded me.

I have put the worst of it. I believe it needed saying, but it is certainly not the last word on this or indeed any part of modern Ireland. Small it may be by comparison with its neighbours, but Ireland could sustain a lot more blemishes without losing its beauties, or its wildness. Up and down the north-west and west coasts are those wild habitats which draw huge numbers of sea-birds to breed every spring and summer: mile upon mile of cliff for the auks and others who lay and guard their solitary eggs against all perils and dangers; countless sea-girt rocks and islands whose grazing attracts vast numbers of wintering geese; broad mud-flats for long-legged, long-billed waders; cliff-top grasslands for puffins and nocturnal

shearwaters. Ireland's abundance is not in numbers of species but in the numbers of individuals within a species – including spectacular breeds like gannets – which fill the available spaces.

Not only the coast teems with wildlife. Donegal's interior – Errigal and Muckish and other mountains, the deer-stocked parklands of Glenveagh, the Poisoned Glen, Lough Dunlewy and the rest – is as dramatic as anywhere in Ireland: primevally beautiful. Further south, in County Sligo, are the picturesque mountain formations of Ben Bulben, the stunning waterscapes of Glencar and Glenade, and the wealth of plants their limestone substrate induces. And not a bungalow in sight.

ST PATRICK

Most places associated with St Patrick, Ireland's patron saint, are in the northern half of the country, although most information about him is rather vague. He was born in Britain, perhaps Wales, perhaps Cumberland, possibly Dunbartonshire. A piratic Irish chief – ancestor of the O'Neill family – kidnapped him and he was put to work as a shepherd. A few years after escaping (to England or the continent) he saw visions calling him back to Ireland and he went in 429, or 430 or 431. He was not the first Christian or missionary, but he was clearly very successful. In other countries of Europe the establishment of Christianity took much longer and cost martyrs' lives. Ireland took to it readily.

Patrick generated more stories than most. On the summit of Croagh Patrick, where he was spending Lent, he exiled all snakes from the country. He explained the idea of the Trinity by means of a three-leafed flower, the so-called shamrock, and thereby converted a king. When he died, in 461, at Saul, near Downpatrick in County Down, the country was more or less converted. The day of his death was 17 March, St Patrick's Day, and the most important date in the Irish calendar.

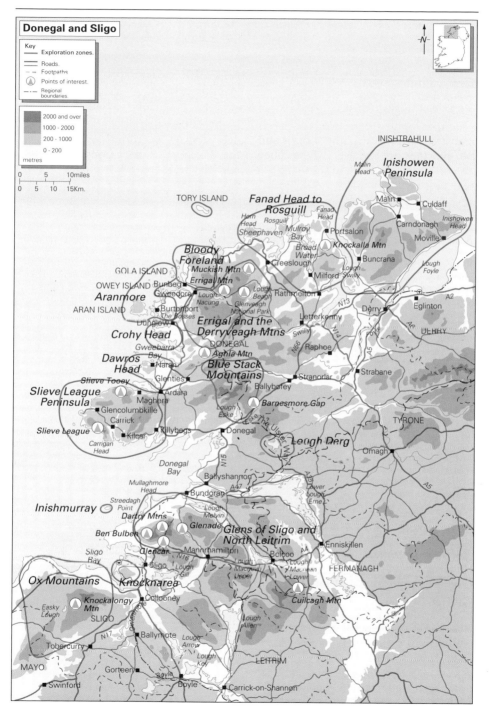

Donegal and Sligo

Key
— Exploration zones.
═ Roads.
- - Footpaths
Ⓐ Points of interest.
-·- Regional boundaries.

2000 and over
1000 - 2000
200 - 1000
0 - 200
metres

0   5   10 miles
0 5 10   15Km.

-N-

INISHTRAHULL

Inishowen Peninsula

Malin Head

Malin ■ Culdaff

TORY ISLAND

Fanad Head to Rosguill

Fanad Head

Inishowen Head

Horn Head

Rosguill

Carndonagh

Moville

Sheephaven

Mulroy Bay

Portsalon

Broad Water

Knockalla Mtn Ⓐ

Lough Foyle

Bloody Foreland

Muckish Mtn Ⓐ

Creeslough

Buncrana

GOLA ISLAND

Errigal Mtn Ⓐ

Milford

Lough Swilly

OWEY ISLAND

Bunbeg

Gweedore

Lough Nacung

Lough Beagh

Rathmelton

Derry

Eglinton

A2

Aranmore

Glenveagh National Park

Ⓐ Ⓐ

Letterkenny

N13

DERRY

ARAN ISLAND

Burtonport

The Rosses

Errigal and the Derryveagh Mtns

Dunglow

Crohy Head

DONEGAL

Aghla Mtn Ⓐ

Swilly

N56

Raphoe

Strabane

Gweebarra Bay

Blue Stack Mountains Ⓐ

N14

Dawros Head

Naran

Glenties

Ballybofey

Stranorlar

Slieve Tooey

Ardara

Lough Eske

Barnesmore Gap Ⓐ

TYRONE

Slieve League Peninsula

Maghera

Glencolumbkille

Carrick

Donegal

Lough Derg

Omagh

Slieve League Ⓐ

Kilcar

Killybegs

The Ulster Way

Carrigan Head

Donegal Bay

N15

A5

Mullaghmore Head

Ballyshannon

Lower Lough Erne

A5

Streedagh Point

Bundoran

A47

Inishmurray Ⓐ

Dartry Mtns

Lough Melvin

Glenade

Glens of Sligo and North Leitrim

Enniskillen

Ben Bulben Ⓐ Ⓐ

Ⓐ Ⓐ

Glencar

Manorhamilton

Belcoo

A4

FERMANAGH

Sligo Bay

Lough Macnean Upper

Lough Macnean Lower

Ox Mountains

Knocknarea

Sligo

Lough Gill

Easky Lough

Knockalongy Mtn Ⓐ

Collooney

Cuilcagh Mtn Ⓐ

Lough Allen

SLIGO

Tobercurry

N17

Ballymote

Lough Arrow

Lough Key

LEITRIM

MAYO

Gorteen

Swinford

Boyle

Boyle

Carrick-on-Shannon

15

GETTING THERE

By air: regular international services to Belfast, Dublin and Shannon airports. There is a small airport at Carrickfinn in north-west Donegal, with services from London and Glasgow; internal flights from Dublin connect with Sligo. Flights also serve Eglinton Airport near Derry city from Glasgow and Manchester, and Knock Airport in Co. Mayo from London throughout the year.

By boat: from Britain, the closest ferry routes to the north-west run from Holyhead to Dun Laoghaire and Dublin, from Liverpool to Belfast and from Stranraer (Scotland) to Belfast and Larne (near Belfast). Visitors from continental Europe can travel by ferry from Le Havre and Cherbourg to Rosslare, near Wexford.

By car: when travelling by car to the north-west, take care if your route crosses the Northern Ireland border. Traffic is not permitted on any but the authorized border crossings marked on road maps. If you are hiring a car in the Republic, ask whether the insurance covers you for Northern Ireland; you may have to pay an extra premium.

By rail: Irish Rail (Iarnrod Eireann) offers services from Dublin to Sligo, and Northern Ireland Railways connects Belfast with Derry. For information on Iarnrod Eireann, T:Dublin (01) 366222. For details of Northern Ireland Railways, T:Belfast (01232) 899411.

By bus: Irish Bus (Bus Eireann) routes connect Sligo and Letterkenny in Co. Donegal with Dublin and many points in between. Express services also operate from Donegal to Belfast, Derry and Enniskillen. For timetable information for the Republic and Northern Ireland, T:(01) 836 6111.

WHERE TO STAY

The Irish Tourist Board (Bord Failte) produces a yearly *Accommodation Guide* listing approved hotels, bed and breakfasts, Irish homes, hostels, and caravan and camping parks. Local Bord Failte offices operate a nationwide accommodation reservation service for personal callers. They will find you inspected accommodation for a nominal booking charge. There is also plenty of accommodation which is not tourist-board approved, and is not necessarily inferior.

ACTIVITIES

Walking: access to some of the coastal paths can be difficult, and there are few tracks on Irish mountains, so a good map and compass are essential. The Long Distance Walking Routes Committee at Cospoir, 11th Floor, Hawkins House, Dublin 4, gives useful information and Bord Failte produces information sheets with recommended walks. The Ulster Way, essentially a Six-County affair, sends out a Donegal offshoot from Pettigo to Gortahawk on the north coast of Co. Donegal. The 30-mile (48-km) Leitrim Way provides a good, varied walk with dramatic views of lake and mountain.

Riding: organized post-to-post trail rides are offered in Counties Donegal and Sligo, and there are numerous riding centres, some of them residential. Bord Failte's *Equestrian Ireland* brochure has details of activities offered at the Stracomer Riding School, Bundoran, Co. Donegal, T:(072) 41685/41046, and at Horse Holiday Farm, Grange, Co. Sligo, T:(071) 66152.

Climbing: the Derryveagh mountains in Co. Donegal are one of the finest areas in Ireland for rock climbing. The three main crags offer long, high-quality routes on granite. Rock climbing in Co. Sligo is mostly on limestone. Information from Bord Failte.

Fishing: Ireland's north-west is renowned for fresh-water and sea fishing, with catches including river trout, salmon, brown trout and sea trout. The annual *Anglers' Guide*, published in association with Bord Failte, offers information on species, seasons, competitions, regulations and local accommodation.

Cycling: popular routes cross mountain ranges at up to 864 ft (270 m) or follow the rugged coastline. Bicycle rental shops are common, and many offer mountain bikes. The Bord Failte *Cycling Ireland* brochure gives details of routes.

Sailing: yacht charters are available on the north-west coast. Contact the Irish Yachting Association, 3 Park Road, Dun Laoghaire, Co. Dublin, T:(01) 280 0239.

Surfing: the north-west coast offers some of the world's most challenging surfing conditions, with equipment available for hire at selected resorts. Information from the Irish Surfing Association in Co. Donegal, T:(072) 51261.

FURTHER INFORMATION

The region's major tourist office is in Sligo at Aras Reddan, Temple Street, T:(071) 61201. It opens all year, as does the Letterkenny tourist office on Derry Road, T:(074) 21160. There is a smaller office in Donegal town, T:(073) 21148, which opens May–Sept, and seasonal information centres in Bundoran and Dunglow in Co. Donegal and Carrick-on-Shannon in Co. Leitrim.

Inishowen Peninsula

Rugged country of mountain and blanket bog edged by tall cliffs and sweeps of sandy beach. The road round it is known, from its length (in miles) as the 'Inishowen 100'

This fist of mountain, bog, cliff and rock, thrusting so far seaward that its northernmost headland, Malin, is also the northern extremity of Ireland, clung on more obstinately than other parts to its link with Britain. The last land-bridge to unite the two islands probably ran from Inishowen to Jura, Islay and the western Grampians. There were other bridges between the east coast and Wales, but they did not survive quite as long.

Across these bridges, as the ice receded and the land warmed, animals, birds and plants returned, by the multifarious methods they have evolved. But access was of limited duration. Melting ice gradually raised the sea-level. This in turn submerged the land-bridges. By perhaps 9,000 years ago most of the forms of wildlife that characterize Ireland today were in position. Only those species which wind, waves, birds or humans would bring in, deliberately or otherwise, were still absent.

In historical times the peninsula has been known not for international links but for remote inaccessibility, barely affected by the insistent claims of tourism. The transatlantic liners which called in the late-nineteenth century at Moville, on the east coast, were simply removing suffering surplus population to America. Like the earlier flight of the earls – a bowing out of the scene by rebel leaders at the end of the reign of Elizabeth I, which took place from the opposite shore of Lough Swilly across to the west – it was a one-way traffic.

Inishowen was O'Neill territory from earliest times. O'Neills built the Grianan of Aileach, the massive circular stone fort which, heavily restored in the nineteenth century, still commands all approaches to the peninsula, from Inch island to Derry.

This was a family of lasting influence. Niall of the Nine Hostages, its founder, was a pirate-prince among whose captives, taken on raiding trips to Wales, was the youthful Patrick, patron-saint-to-be. Niall's successors became high kings of Ireland (a title of little meaning but high prestige), and the clan thrives to this day, rich in lands and titles. Not so long ago it produced a prime minister of Northern Ireland, when there still were such things.

Some towns on the east side offer what is still called good crack (by which the Irish mean nothing more sinister than good talk and high spirits) to young people driving out from Derry at evenings and weekends, but for the most part this square block of land is desolate and scantily peopled. The highest peak is that of Slieve Snaght (2,019 feet/615 metres), centrally placed south-west of Carndonagh, the area's main market town. The mountain can be climbed without excessive exertion from the road running along its south-eastern perimeter. There are fine views from the top, of Lough Swilly and the Donegal mountains to the west, and Lough Foyle, Antrim and even the Scottish coast to the east.

The most picturesque scenes are along the west and north coasts, with their bays and beaches. Here are the great headland bluffs of Malin Head, Glengad Head and Inishowen Head. North of Buncrana the road nearest the coast makes for Dunree Head, then turns right up the bleak Owenerk valley to the Gap of Mamore. On either side the heathery terrain rises to heights (Croaghcarragh, 1,250 feet/381 metres; and Mamore Hill, 1,361 feet/415 metres) from which the alternations of promontory and inlet along the crenellated coast of Donegal show up wonderfully, the more so in afternoon or early evening light.

There are good walks along the ridge from the Gap, south-west into the Urris Hills or north-eastward towards Raghtin More. Good walking is also to be had between Malin Head and Glengad Head. Around Malin, for all its exposure to Arctic storms and western breakers, the country is quite gently contoured, while the coast itself is rich in beaches, but as you move eastward the ground rises to successions of cliff, with labyrinthine tracks and deep chasms. Malin is an important staging post for birds migrating southward in the autumn, when north-westerly winds bring sooty shearwaters, Leach's petrels and Sabine's gulls in large quantities, and a long list of rarities over the years. A few miles south, the broad mud-flats of Trawbreaga Bay and adjoining meadows and dunes of Doagh Island attract large populations of geese, ducks and waders. Winter brings flocks of brent and barnacle geese. In summer there are at least three kinds of tern – common, Arctic and little – laying their eggs without defence (but with effectively camouflaged shells) on the pebbles of beaches. Eiders are to be seen all the year round.

BEFORE YOU GO
Maps: OS Discovery Series maps Nos 1 and 3.

GETTING THERE
By car: from Letterkenny take the N13 (north-east) till you reach the R239. The R239 leads north on to the R238. For Malin Head, take the R242 at the northern end of the peninsula, through Malin.
By bus: Lough Swilly Buses run eight buses a day from Derry that stop at Muff, Carndonagh and Strove, T:(01504) 262017.

WHERE TO STAY
Hotels: there are hotels and bed and breakfasts at or near Moville and Culdaff on the east coast of the peninsula and Fahan, Buncrana, Clonmany, Ballyliffen, Malin and Malin Head on the west. Among the more far-flung, northerly establishments are the Strand Hotel at Ballyliffen, T:(077) 76107, a bed and breakfast in Malin, T:(077) 70645, and one at Malin Head, Mrs Doyle, T:(077) 70184.
Outdoor living: campers can pitch their tents in the grounds of the Muff Hostel.

Youth hostels: the Muff Hostel, situated 6 miles (10 km) north of Derry, T:(077) 84188, is one hostel on the peninsula.

ACTIVITIES
Walking: the tourist offices in Letterkenny and Donegal have leaflets and maps describing possible routes.
Riding: the Lenamore Stables in Muff organize hacks and treks and are open all year, T:(077) 84022.
Bird-watching: Lough Swilly, on the western side of the peninsula, has large autumn arrivals of whooper swan, wintering greylag geese and other wildfowl. The best localities are to be found between Buncrana and the southern end of the lough.
Fishing: Moville is a sea-angling centre where there is shore fishing for pollack, wrasse and mackerel. The main angling grounds outside Lough Foyle provide cod, dogfish, pollack, coalfish, ray, ling, tope and haddock.
Cycling: bikes can be hired at the Muff Hostel, T:(077) 84188.

FURTHER INFORMATION
Tourist offices: the nearest Bord Failte tourist office is in Bishop St, Derry, over the border, T:(01504) 369501. This and the Bord Failte office in Letterkenny, T:(074) 21160, are open all year.

A newcomer to Ireland in 1911, the fulmar, an elegant glider with a strong but superficial similarity to a gull, now nests all round the Irish coast, generally on narrow ledges set in sheer cliffs.

Fanad Head to Rosguill

Sandy beaches like this one, hidden in a deep cove beneath Raghtin More, decorate the rugged west coast of the Inishowen Peninsula. The nearest town is Ballyliffin.

These peninsulas confine their heights inland. Seaward, they share mild contours and their rims are low, sandy and sinuous, punctured by the dents and penetrations of long, angular bays

From the heights above Lough Swilly you can snatch a visual geography lesson before engaging with County Donegal's northern coastline. What shows up best is the jigsaw of land and water of which the lough and the inlets to its left are part, a pattern of islands, a layout of lagoons and dunes, white foam-fringes, brown-purple heather, chequerboards of pasture and marsh and clusters of hill and low mountains spread out beneath a huge sky, not necessarily blue, nor always recognizably a sky at all, but for most of the year a lively expanse of white-blue variations. In Ireland, there is more to be had from remembering to look at the sky than in most other countries.

The Donegal coast is holiday country for Irish northern and southern. In this part of the county, the contortions and curlicues of the coast mean there are innumerable separate sandy beaches, often with sand-dunes and machair grassland on the landward side, and it is still quite possible to have one to oneself, even in the summer. But it is no longer possible, as it was a few years ago, to (almost) guarantee it. The dilemma is one that recurs constantly down the west coast: wilds may cease to be wild when overrun by tourists, but many of them revert when the tourists leave. If we are set on seeing wild country, and have to come in peak holiday times, do we simply avoid the parts we should hurry to if they were unpeopled? Or go, and make the best of it? Nevertheless there are certainly places which it would be silly – so it seems to me – to miss.

Along the western shore of Lough Swilly, north of Rathmelton (sometimes spelt, as it is pronounced, Ramelton), are a number of nice old fishing villages and quays, rich in

19

history. The rocks on the seashore are strewn with seaweeds and shells by the million from minuscule to mussel-sized, the latter tight-shut when the tide is out and presumably edible. Oystercatchers pick and peck among them, and a curlew flies by with its musical gargle. There is a good walk on this peninsula, from end to end of Knockalla Mountain, set amid miles of gently undulating bog. This knobbly ridge is known as the Devil's Backbone, though to me it suggests a knuckleduster. At its north-eastern end, Saldanha Head gives spectacular views over Lough Swilly, the golden sands of Ballymastocker Bay and the bulky humps of Inishowen over the water.

It would be sad to miss Mulroy Bay with its pretty bony and angular islands, some of them covered in conifers. The whole area has good, changing bird populations; ducks and swans are in evidence here all the year round, and the elegant Sandwich tern breeds on the islands. But the fish farms strike a discordant note of human interference.

After Fanad Head you need to go 14 miles (23 kilometres) inland before you can start on your way to the sprawling sandy head-land of Rosguill, and to go thence to Horn Head requires a detour of similar distance around Sheephaven, which unfortunately is seldom seen because the road is set well back. Horn Head is a grand sight, though it would be a great deal grander from the sea, for the north-facing 600-foot (180-metre) cliffs hold at times, and especially in winter, impressive numbers of kittiwake, guillemot and razorbill – some four thousand of each – and many other sea-birds.

A narrow lane, lengthened in recent years to include a circuit of Croaghnamaddy, takes the driver close to a concrete viewing post. All habitations and pasture have been left behind, but not human activity. Turf is cut here and some of the local young, I imagine, use the abundant stones to form large names, nicknames and obscenities visible for hundreds of yards. All the same, these cannot detract from the intense drama of the place, with diminishing promontories, besieged by white foam, receding into the distance right and left. Out to sea, to the north, lies Inishtrahull, an island formed of Ireland's oldest rock, Lewisian gneiss, and a breeding ground for eider duck.

BEFORE YOU GO
Maps: OS Discovery Series Map No. 2.

GETTING THERE
By car: Grianan of Aileach is reached from the city of Derry by taking the A2 as far as Bridge End on the Northern Ireland border; Grianan is to the left of the N13. For the Fanad peninsula, follow the N13 to Letterkenny, then take the the R245. At Rathmelton, follow the R246 for the western side of the peninsula and the R247 for the eastern side. The 17-mile (27-km) Fanad Scenic Drive is signposted.
By bus: The privately operated Lough Swilly bus service runs twice a day from Letterkenny round the peninsula, T:(074) 22400.

WHERE TO STAY
The area is dotted with bed and breakfasts and small hotels, and there are camp-sites open generally Apr–Sept. Rosguill peninsula has a youth hostel, T:(074) 55374.

FURTHER INFORMATION
The tourist office at Letterkenny, T:(074) 21160.

Bloody Foreland

The north-western corner of Donegal is a scrawny, stony land bounded by a rocky coast

It is not the colour of Atlantic sunsets that gives Ireland's north-west corner its name, Bloody Foreland, though there are days when you might think it was. A red mineral has at some geological period stained the bands of quartzite inlaid among the granite, and the effect can be a blood-red glow. It is a place to inspire awe: the hill running down to the rocky coast and the sea, and over the horizon Iceland, Greenland, and the land – so people once believed – of perpetual youth. It produced poignant legends. While you grew not a day older during your stay, the world you had left went on as before; and if you returned and touched ground, you acquired all the years you had till then deferred. The poet and warrior Oisin (pronounced Usheen) rode there over the waves with his lover; but on returning for a visit, dismounted and found his skin wrinkled, his beard long and grey, his back bent. Worse, the pagan life he had known and loved was being ousted by the mission of St Patrick. Before dying, he made a nice

heathen attack on the new pieties, and Patrick in particular.

When I came here a generation ago, this kind of thing worked a magic on me. I loved the Irish way of identifying mythical sites: the mountain-top beds slept in by eloping Dermot and Grania, the fields of great battles and, a few miles over the sea from here to the north, Tory Island, home of Balor the giant, a glance from whose single eye killed those it fell on, till his grandson pressed a red-hot iron into the eye and finished him. There was the magic of the view as well. Standing on the hill slope and looking down the west coast you saw – and still see – a succession of lateral lines, made up of tongues of land, elongated islands and islets, shingle spits, strip after strip of white foam in fidgetty motion, and the intervening bands of grey sea. But you cannot any longer entirely lose yourself in contemplation of natural grandeur, for on the landward side there has been a huge and amorphous burgeoning of bungalows. Had Oisin delayed his return to now, I think he might have accelerated death by cutting his throat. Balor might have put his one eye out voluntarily.

Before you go *Maps:* OS Discovery Series map No. 1. *Guidebooks: The New Irish Walk Guides: West and North* by Tony Whilde and Patrick Simms (Gill and Macmillan, 1991), or *Great Walks: Ireland* by David Herman (Cassell, 1991).
Getting there *By car:* from Letterkenny follow the N56 to Falcarragh; 3 miles (5 km) on, turn right on to the R257 for a coastal route to Bloody Foreland. *By bus:* Feda O'Donnell Coaches from Gweedore to Letterkenny, T:(075) 48114. McGinley,

T:(074) 35201, operates a service between Annagary, Gweedore and Dublin. The Lough Swilly bus service stops at Dunfanaghy on Mon and Fri mornings and evenings, T:(074) 22863.
Where to stay: there is one hotel, Foreland Heights, T:(075) 31785, at Bloody Foreland and plenty of other possibilities around Falcarragh and Dunfanaghy: Corcreggan Mill Cottage Hostel, T:(074) 34609, the Shamrock Lodge Hostel, T:(074) 35859, and Ballyconnell House, T:(074) 35363. Self-catering accommodation is widely available. **Activities:** the area is home to a variety of sea-birds, including puffins, kittiwakes and guillemots.
Further information: the nearest year-round Bord Failte tourist office is at Letterkenny, T:(074) 21160.

Aranmore

Off-shore islands, including the largest, Aranmore, which ascends from east to west and has a fine curve of cliffs in the north-west

The boat from Bunbeg sails north at scheduled times, weather allowing, to Tory Island, which with its village and native artists is perhaps the most thriving, if bare and windswept, of Ireland's off-shore islands. Along this stretch of the Donegal coast, where Bunbeg itself is situated, a boat can deliver delights. It opens up views of long winding inlets, which become sculptured mudscapes at low tide and are thronged with sea-birds at all times. Out to sea it allows you to explore a straggling archipelago of islands great and small, some occupied and cropped by sheep, some lone and rocky and seemingly forgotten. On an ocean-facing sandy beach, of which there are hundreds, you can believe yourself deserted by mankind, though grey seals may keep you company.

The Rosses, opening out to the south of Bunbeg, is a low-lying mainland area, six or seven miles across, of heath and grass, spattered with farms and rocks and more than a hundred lakes. From Burtonport, on its western edge, boats cross regularly to Aran Island, winding first among a jigsaw of islands. (Aran Island is sometimes called Aranmore, not to be confused with the more famous Aran Islands off County Galway, the largest of which, since *mor* means big, is also called Aranmore.) The high ground of this island, which rises to 750 ft (229 m), is composed of quartzite, hard enough to survive the originally overlaid granite which climate has worn away. Aranmore, too, has long sandy beaches and fine cliffs in the north-west where sea-birds breed, and also mountain lakes and good climbs. The thousand people living on it tend to keep themselves, their cars and shops near the east side, where the quay is.

Before you go *Maps:* OS Discoverer Series Map No. 1.
Getting there *By car:* the N56 and R257 pass close to all the departure ports for Tory Island. For Burtonport turn off the N56 at Gweedore or Dunglow and on to the R259. *By ferry:* Tory Island is accessible by boats from Bunbeg, T:(074) 31991, and Magheraroarty, T:(074) 35061, from June to Sept, with less

frequent services operating out of Meenlaragh and Port na Blagh. Bikes are carried free. The 20-min. ferry service to Aran Island operates from Burtonport year-round, with more frequent services in summer, T:(075) 21532.
Access: Tory Island is inaccessible in poor weather, and difficult to reach in winter when there is the likelihood of being stranded.
Where to stay: Tory Island has very limited accommodation, mostly involving sleeping on the floor in your own sleeping bag. Aran Island has bed and breakfasts, including the Glen Hotel, T:(075) 21505, and Mrs A. Bonner, T:(075) 21532, and a youth hostel (no telephone) open May–Sept. A variety of accommodation is available in Dunglow on the mainland.
Further information: the nearest tourist office is in Dunglow, T:(075) 21297.

Crohy Head

A bulbous projection into Gweebarra Bay, the peninsula hides dramatic lakes and tough climbs in its hinterland, but is prodigal with marvellous sea views from its peripheral road

Here is a quartzite peninsula, bulking up over the widespread granite of the area. Discounting bumps and appendages, it is about 3 miles (5 km) across, and Croaghegly, something south of centre, reaches 808 ft (246 m). Aware of its scenic splendours, the

From Horn Head, with its dizzying drops to rock and ocean, you can look back across Sheep Haven to Rinnafaghla Point and Rosguill with its promontory tapering to Melmore Head (upper left).

Tourist Board has caused the road which used to end at a hamlet halfway round, to continue and complete the circuit.

Maghery Bay, at the north of the promontory's seaward side, is prized by geologists for the variety of its rocks. More obvious to the layman are the mats of kelp (*Laminaria*), known locally as sea rods, which are strewn over the sandy beaches, especially after rough weather (when strong currents can make these beaches dangerous). Its ruddy, bull-pizzle stems often remind me of classical serpents and bring out my Laocoon complex. They are collected in huge numbers and dried over fences and walls for months before being sent to Greenock in Scotland to be manufactured into an antibiotic.

Grandeur is higher up. You leave the nicely scruffy village of Maghery and climb steeply. Crohy Head discloses good views of the series of headlands to the north, the Dawros peninsula just to the south, and of Aghla and the Blue Stack mountains, away to the south-east across a pretty inlet of Gweebarra Bay. Heady permutations of the marine panorama are to be had during steep walks and climbs over the blanket bog of Croaghegly.

Dawros Head

Unlike the promontories to north and south, Dawros is a gentle expanse of hills and lakes, its deeply indented shoreline providing sandy coves and beaches and long ranks of cliff

Robert Lloyd Praeger is the patron saint of Irish naturalists. He lived from 1865 to 1953 and distinguished himself as botanist, geologist and archaeologist: a polymath in an age that still tolerated them. He knew all the scholars of his day – it was an age when that too was possible, in a country the size of Ireland – and was always going on missions of discovery with them. He loved the outdoors and even in old age never missed the chance, when tramping over the countryside, of bathing in pond, lake or river. He makes hikers of our own time seem namby-pamby, never seeming to let safety considerations, as of mist on mountains or soft patches of bog or rough seas, discourage him.

If he wanted to get somewhere he strode off (or cycled in extremes; cars he loathed) and usually got there, an hour or eighteen later, soaking wet, utterly cheerful, and full of some unexpected plant he had encountered up the mountain. He wrote, apart from more scientific work, a memoir of travels in Ireland called *The Way that I Went*, which has never been bettered, even by one of Ireland's latter-day great geologists, Frank Mitchell, who in a gesture of homage called his own memoirs *The Way that I Followed*. In fact, almost everyone who has written since Praeger's time about the Irish outdoors has pillaged his work, and I am no exception. He had a soft spot for the Dawros, with its rather subtle attractions. 'Not lofty,' he wrote, 'but full of little heathery hills and lakes, with a sandy or cliffy shore – a particularly attractive area.'

Attractive it is, though its appeal is not as dramatic or stupefying as that of the Slieve League a few miles to the south. No mountains are to be found here, but there are a few nice cliffs, some good long sandy beaches (at Naran and Rosbeg), quite a few lakes, birds, rocks and inspiring antiquity. Off Naran, on the north coast, is Inishkeel. The name means 'narrow island', and so it is at high tide, but it is joined to the mainland at low tide by an exposed reef of sand. It has the ruins of two churches on it, and the memory of a sixth-century monastic retreat founded by St Conall Caol, in whose honour there is an annual May pilgrimage. Other ancient remains are scattered over the promontory: a huge unrestored round fort of stone from the ninth century, built on a lough island; a 20-ft (6-m) dolmen; cairns, crosses and other survivors. Every so often along this farthest coastline, north and west, there are signs

Several species of the seaweed *Laminaria*, known as kelp, are collected, as they have been for centuries, when the ebbing tide exposes them. Once dried, kelp can be used in various culinary preparations. Nowadays it is exported to Scotland for factory processing.

of human activity, dating from two, five, even – as the discovery of mesolithic remains under peat testifies – ten thousand years ago. Usually we know peoples so distant from ourselves only through their pots, weapons, knives and needles; as if we ourselves were to be identified aeons from now only by the salvaged contents of a branch of Woolworths.

There is one other element here, which always mystifies and awes me: the force that drew them to the edge of a world which was not crowded, to subsist on the begrudged gifts of rock and air and hostile sea, and on beliefs and aspirations we shall never know. Would we recognize this force, from traces left in our myths and religions, or would we have to admit the existence of wholly alien sentiments in people who were, give or take a gene, our own flesh and blood?

There are far more ancient remains. Among the gnarled hummocks, bumps, hollows, lynchets and sullen black cattle lies an untidy sprinkling of granite core-stones, remains of an outflow from inland Donegal. Contrary to reputation, granite (often permeated by cracks which admit water and chemicals in solution) can break down easily. Faultless cubes are often left, which in time are worn into the spheres we see here.

Before you go *Maps*: OS Discovery Series map No. 10. **Getting there** *By car*: take the N56 (south) to Maas, join the R261 then follow local roads out to Naran, Portnoo and Dawros Head. **Where to stay:** bed and breakfasts at Naran, Portnoo and Ardara. Dunmore Caravan and Camping Park at Portnoo, T:(075) 45121. **Further information:** Dunglow tourist office, T:(075) 21297.

Slieve League Peninsula

A massive promontory whose interior pattern of mountain and glen is upstaged by the dramas of the coastline and Slieve League, one of the tallest, grandest expanses of sheer cliff in Europe

Seen from a distance, as it is from many angles, the Slieve League is of a deeply satisfactory shape: an utterly enormous hump or mound or hedgehog or guinea pig or upturned hulk or bisected egg. Somebody has perhaps worked out how many Empire State Buildings or *Titanics* or tankers of Guinness would fit into it but, whatever the number, there are few places which give me such a sense of mass and solidity. It has other distinctions. It is 30 miles (18 kilometres) long and at its widest, 12 (19 kilometres). Round most of its edge it falls from a height straight, or steeply, down to the sea. Most of its summits are in the range of 1,000 to 1,500 feet (300 to 500 metres) with the highest, Slieve League, 1,970 feet (600 metres). In half a dozen places, hardly more, estuaries of the tumbling rivers which drain its plateau give access to boats arriving from the sea, but for the most part it opposes sheer wall to wave.

Glencolumbkille on the west side of the peninsula and Carrick and Kilcar on the south are substantial villages, but elsewhere the population is a thin smattering. Most of the hamlets formed at river mouths are abandoned; distance, gradient and the tightly winding approach roads priced contact with the outside world too high

Slieve Tooey is the northerly summit of the peninsula. You can drive to Maghera, at sea-level to its east, or Port or Glencolumbkille to its west, and walk part of the way along a rudimentary and treacherous sheep-path close to its cliff edges, with exhilarating views of coastal Donegal and the Atlantic.

A close relative and often associate of the jackdaw, the chough confines itself chiefly to the rockiest, ruggedest cliffs, headlands and islands of the West.

Ten o'clock on a raw, windy morning, and a fisherman is out in his boat (*previous page*), a mere speck beneath the southern flank of the Slieve League Peninsula. To the east, across the inlet, lie Muckros Head and the inner reaches of Donegal Bay.

Below you are vertiginous drops (down which less than a century ago nerveless natives were lowered on ropes to collect sweet grass), fanciful and contorted rock shapes, knife-edge ridges from one pinnacle to another, rocky bays and spindly rock stacks. There are loughs inland and rather poignant descents to the lonely habitations.

For all its magnificence the north is outclassed. The southern seaward face of the peninsula where Slieve League peak abuts the shore is one of the grandest sights in Ireland. Not many years ago you had to go to sea to appreciate it, but now a spiralling road takes you up the south-eastern spur beside Carrigan Head to a tarmac park where you can admire the view from inside a car. The only time I used this facility (and after looking furtively all round in case of human company), I moved my car back from where I had first parked it to a more sheltered spot. I have never known such wind. I pictured an exceptional gust followed by an encapsulated fall to the rocks below. Soon after this I was hypnotized by the nearby movements of gulls, choughs and jackdaws, who seemed to have discovered the perfect distraction for such weather. Looking down 1,500 feet from where I stood, tethered to posts by both

IRISH PLACE NAMES

English place-name element (Irish-language source or equivalent), *meaning*

agha, augh (achadh), *field*
ard (ard), *high place, hill*
ass (eas), *waterfall*
ath, augh (ath), *ford*
ballagh (bealach), *pass*
bally (baile), *townland*
bar (barr), *top*
barna (bearna), *gap*
bawn (ban), *white*
beagh (veagh), *birch tree*
beg (beag), *small*
bel (beal), *river mouth, ford*
ben, ban (beann), *peak*
bo, mo (bo), *cow*
boher (bothar), *road*
bohreen (botharin), *little road or track, originally for cows*
boola, boley (buaile), *summer hill-settlement*
brack (breac), *speckled*
cahir (cathair), *stone fort*
cairn (carn), *pile of stones*
cappagh (ceapach), *tillage plot*
carrig, carrick (carraig), *rock, stone enclosure*
carrow (ceathramhadh), *quarter of land*
cashel (caiseal), *ring-fort*
clare (clar), *expanse of land, plain*
clogh (cloch), *stone, stone place or building*
cloghan (clochan), *stone hut,*

beehive hut
cloon, clon (cluain), *meadow*
cor (corr), *round hill*
cork (corcaigh), *marsh*
coum (com), *corrie*
croagh (cruach), *steep hill*
darrig (dearg), *red*
derry (doire), *oak wood*
donagh (domhnach), *church, especially an early one*
doon (dun), *promontory or conspicuous fort*
drum (droim), *ridge*
duff, doo (dubh), *black*
eask, esk (eisc), *cliff, rock gully*
emlagh (imeallach), *marginal land*
faha (faiche), *lawn*
fin (fion), *white, clear*
freagh (fraoch), *heather*
glash (glas), *stream*
glass (glas), *green*
glen (gleann), *valley*
gort (gort), *tillage field*
green (grianan), *sunny place*
gwee (gaoith), *wind*
illaun (oilean), *island*
inish, inch (inis), *island*
inver (inbhear), *river mouth*
ken (ceann), *headland*
kill (cill), *church*
knock (cnoc), *hill*
kyle (coill), *wood, grove*
lack (leac), *flagstone*
lackan (leaca, leacan), *hillside*
lag, leg, lig, lug (lug, lag), *hollow*

law (lagh), *hill*
lea (liath), *grey*
lis (lios), *ring fort*
lough (loch), *lake*
mace, mas (mas), *thigh, low hill*
magha (macha), *cattle-field*
maghera (machaire), *plain*
maum (mam), *pass*
money (muine), *grove*
more (mor), *big*
mullagh (mullach), *summit*
mweel (maol), *bare hill*
oughter (uachter), *upper*
ow, owen (abha, abhainn), *river*
poll, pool (poll), *hole*
rath (raith), *ring fort*
reen, ring (rinn), *point, headland*
roe (rua, ruadh), *red*
ros (ros), *burial ground, wood*
scarriff (scairbh), *ford*
see (suidh), *seat*
shan (sean), *old*
shee (sidh), *fairy hill*
skellig (sceilig), *rock*
sker, skerry (sceir), *rock, reef*
slee (slidhe), *road, track*
slieve (sliabh), *mountain, mountain range*
tagh, ty (teach), *house*
tave (taobh), *hillside*
teer, tir, tyr (tir), *land*
temple (teampall), *church*
tor (tor), *tall rock*
tra, tray (traigh), *strand, beach*
tubber (tobar), *well*
tully, tulla (tulach), *low hill*

hands, I saw them begin to rise, one by one, from a point close to the sea. Their ascent brought them close to me and then high above, above me and the land – all in one vertical rise. They paused for seconds, and began a slow but accelerating swoop towards the sea on the far side of the headland, behind me. This must have been more than half a mile. Approaching the water they levelled off, swerved round and glided towards the start-point, completing an aerobatic triangle. It was mesmerizing, but one thing surprised me more than any other. Such was their mastery of their element, I do not believe they ever moved their wings by more than a few adjusting degrees.

This was, however, the side-show. Behind the birds and in front of me, placed as I was on my raised wing as in a theatre box, stretched a two-mile wall of 2,000-foot (600-metre) cliff, ranged above little bays with narrow stone beaches and a sea of deep blue growing paler as it approached the land. The grain, faults, knots and jointings of the cliffs made me think of a gnarled old log split open, but as the sun appeared and hid in turns, far more showed up. All over the place, among projecting rocks and vertical patches of grass and sprawls of grey scree were areas of glinting pigmentation, like much used and smudged palettes. One would comprise shades of red ochre and terra-cotta and raw sienna – a spectrum of reds and browns – while another changed from deep grey through cobalt to white, and another from pale sulphurous yellow to green and coppery verdigris.

From various angles Slieve League can be climbed, none of them presenting great difficulty, although on one approach there is an (avoidable) two-foot shelf with a steep drop beside it known as One Man's Path. I must climb it one day, but if, as before, time makes me choose between the view from it and that sweeping seaward view of it, I shall again choose the latter.

BEFORE YOU GO
Maps: OS Discovery Series map No. 10.

GETTING THERE
By car: follow the N56 south until you come to the junction with the R263 a couple of miles north of Killybegs. To reach Slieve League turn off this road towards Bunglas at Carrick.

WHERE TO STAY
Hotels: there are several bed and breakfasts in Glencolumbkille and one hotel, Glencolmcille, T:(073) 30003; and a larger selection in Killybegs, including the Bay View, T:(073) 31950, and Cope House, T:(073) 31834. **Youth hostels**: there is a hostel in Glencolumbkille, The Dooey Hostel, T:(073) 30130.

ACTIVITIES
Climbing: there are a number of good sea-cliff climbs at Malin Beg, south of Glencolumbkille. For more information contact Rory Boyd, The Mountaineering Council of Ireland, 25 Cranford Court, Stillorgan Road, Dublin 4.

FURTHER INFORMATION
There is a small information office at Carrick which is open June–Sept, T:(073) 39007, and others at Ardara and Donegal. The nearest year-round Bord Failte office is in Sligo, T:(071) 62101.

South-West Donegal

Errigal and the Derryveagh Mountains

The central fastness of County Donegal, an area richly varied in scenery and wildlife at every level, from the waters of Dunlewy and Nacung to the dominating quartzite cone of Errigal

To understand the work of geologists, I have sometimes imagined a madman going berserk in a room. He pushes tables over, throws down other bits of furniture, hauls books off shelves and rips them apart, turns on taps, opens windows to smash porcelain, empties files, heaves the carpet off the floor and dumps it among the debris. That is to represent the effects of geological time, the eruptions, earthquakes, ice, weather and so on over 2,500 million years. The geologist must now examine the nature of everything in the room and the way it lies and has been damaged. He must deduce from all this its original position and state; and when, and by what route, however violent and precipitate, it arrived where it is. If I am right, then Donegal imposes special demands. Reading Donegal calls out for the Sherlock Holmes of geologists.

No other part of Ireland has experienced such seismic surges, tugs, stretchings and tumblings. Its deepest foundations have been rolled over by subterranean power, subjected to inconceivable heat and covered for hundreds of thousands of years by moving, mile-thick carpets of ice. The earth's crust has been sliced in two and then sliced again and again, and the sliced parts have slid miles out of their original alignment. All this has left a landscape of unique form and variety: a seaboard riddled with indentation and hemmed by islands; and behind, a wall of mountain, an interior of chasms, lakes, vertiginous heights, boulder-strewn valleys and broad heathery plateaux, which for many people make Donegal the most beautiful county in Ireland.

What is most noticeable is the south-west to north-east orientation of the central features. The county is bisected by a long tear-fault that includes Glenveagh and the Owenbeagh river, and from either side of which rise parallel mountain ranges of granite. The part of the county to the north-west of this line, including most of the spectacular coastline, is virtually islanded by the divide, connected only by main roads close to the sea at either end. The mountains are an extension of the Caledonian ranges in Scotland, and were formed with them, around 400 million years ago, during the Lower Palaeozoic. The cause of this phase of orogeny, or mountain formation, was the eastward movement of what is now North America across the so-called Proto-Atlantic ocean towards Europe, squeezing deep strata of rock until they folded upward into mountain ranges. The same movement created America's Appalachian mountains, and also the Scottish Highlands, which accounts for the frequent

Flowering cotton grasses catch the evening sun on the slopes near Poisoned Glen.

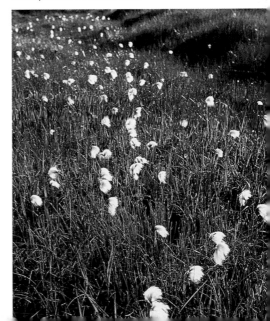

Above Poisoned Glen in the Derryveagh Mountains a small lake lies tranquilly between two marshy ridges. This secret eyrie may be reached by 45 minutes of long, squelchy walking from the nearby minor road (R254), itself deserted.

Herds of red deer, the only indigenous Irish deer (other species having been introduced in Norman and later times), occur in Glenveagh, County Donegal, Killarney National Park and the Wicklow mountains.

comparison of Donegal with the Highlands.

Errigal mountain is 2,466 feet high (752 metres). It has twin pointed conical tops but from west and south only one can be seen, which makes Errigal look like the perfect mountain-shaped mountain, and renders it recognizable from any angle. In any wanderings round Donegal its unmistakable shape keeps reappearing from behind trees or other mountains or hills. The climb, if the height is no deterrent, is an easy one. The summit really is pointed, with scarcely room for a person to lie down. The view, with every feature and contour of north-west Ireland laid out below, is quite simply one of the best in the world. A narrow ridge, without room for two people to pass, leads to the second summit, and a filling of any gaps in the previous view.

Apart from the distant vistas of coast and sea and mountain range, there is a fine view of the surrounding hinterland. South-west are two adjoining lakes, Nacung and Dunlewy. The long line of the granite Derryveagh mountains, with Slieve Snaght and Dooish especially prominent, blocks the horizon south-east. Errigal's northern slope

dips down dangerously – owing to the quantities of loose scree – into the long cold forbidding crescent of Altan Lough, from whose further shore rise directly the two Aghlas, More and Beg.

The whole region, for some miles around, offers some wonderfully striking walks and climbs and sights. People walk from Muckish to Errigal in a day, taking in the Aghla peaks on the way. Eastward and out of sight behind the Derryveaghs is Glenveagh Castle, a romantic Victorian reconstruction of an imagined medieval fortress – all towers and arrow-slits and battlements and lacking only a distressed and captive damsel – given to the nation a few years ago by the American owner. With the castle went gardens (a triumph of refinement in a hostile setting), a huge railed-in red-deer park and the rest of a colossal estate, over three miles long, which has now become the Glenveagh National Park and includes much of what we can see. At the centre of the whole region is Lough Beagh, scoured out of the granite by a glacier during the last Ice Age. Its steep granite walls, pendant streams and waterfalls and overhanging mountains covered in blanket bog make it an awesome sight.

A hundred years ago, golden eagles nested here but they have not been seen since. Gulls, peregrines, ravens and ring ouzels nest on high rocky shelves, curlews and red grouse on the floor of the moorland. There are a few sleek red-throated divers and goosanders nesting on the lakes, and a large variety of woodcock and smaller birds can be found in the oak woods among the hills.

By a ruined Protestant church, a lane turns off the main road and curls round the lake to the little village of Dunlewy. From here a path leads south-east, along a small stream, into the mountains. The valley is U-shaped with a broad floor between steep slopes, which reveals its glacial origins; for the infinitely slow sweep of the receding glacier gouged out channels of this shape.

Three miles on, deep down among a brotherhood of huge, shadowy, round-shouldered mountains, lies the Poisoned Glen, an awesome, marshy place but very beautiful and intriguing. The name is thought to derive from the former presence of Irish spurge (*Euphorbia hyberna*), still known in east Donegal, south-east Galway and Cork and Kerry, whose poisonous sap might have contaminated the water. Smooth walls of pink granite tower above, often glinting with recent rain water, but there are kinder gradients to the east. One of the finest walks in Donegal takes you up from here, over the Ballaghgeeha Gap to the Owenbeagh valley, and down through the heather, with glimpses of red deer, to the romantic castle of Glenveagh.

BEFORE YOU GO
Maps: OS Discovery Series maps Nos 1, 2 and 6.

GETTING THERE
By car: take the N56 from Letterkenny (north) to just past Kilmacrenan. Then take the R255 (west) till it meets the R251. Keep heading west, past the Derryveagh Mountains and Errigal mountain. When visiting the Glenveagh National Park you must leave your car at the entrance, but a free shuttle bus service takes you further in and drops you at the visitor centre.
By bus: Bus Eireann services from Derry, Dublin and Sligo stop in Letterkenny. Local bus services are operated by Funtrek, T:(01) 73085, and McGeehan's, T:(075) 46101.

WHERE TO STAY
Hotels: there is a good selection of hotels in Letterkenny including Clanree, T:(074) 24369, Mount Errigal, T:(074) 22700, and Gallagher's, T:(074) 22066. O'Hagan's provides facilites for disabled persons, T:(074) 21137. Bed and breakfasts in Letterkenny include Castlegrove House, T:(074) 51118, and Gleneany House, T:(074) 26088. There is one bed and breakfast in Kilmacrenan, Angler's Haven, T:(074) 39015.
Youth hostels: An Oige runs the Errigal Hostel, Dunlewy, Gweedore, T:(075) 21950. There are also two independent hostels in Letterkenny, the Letterkenny Tourist Hostel, Mansion Apartments, High Road, Letterkenny, which is open Feb–Dec, and the Rosemont Hostel, 3 Rosemont Terrace, Letterkenny, T:(075) 26284.

ACTIVITIES
Walking: there are trails around the Derryveagh mountains and from Glenveagh National Park and Muckish mountain to Errigal mountain. You can lose yourself quite easily in the vast forested areas hereabouts. For your safety the authorities have marked trails within the national park that head off from the castle, near the visitor centre, and there are guided nature walks in the summer, as well as the chance to see the largest herd of red deer in Ireland.
Climbing: the Garton Outdoor Education Centre, Garton, Churchill, Letterkenny, runs week-long climbing courses, T:(074) 37032/37254.
Fishing: both Gweedore and Glenveagh lakes have good trout fishing. For more information contact the Northern Regional Fisheries Board, T:(072) 51435.
Cycling: *Cycling Ireland*, a pamphlet produced by Bord Failte, has a suggested cycling route that runs right through the middle of the Glenveagh National Park.

FURTHER INFORMATION
The visitor centre inside the national park is open from Easter to Oct, 10.30 am to 6.30 pm, all week, T:(074) 37088/37090. The Bord Failte tourist information centre in Letterkenny is open all year round, T:(074) 21160.

Blue Stack Mountains

A neglected range of rounded mountains, webbed with good walks, hanging above the scenic splendours of Lough Eske

From the town of Donegal, tucked firmly into the north-eastern corner of Donegal Bay, the broad and fertile valley of the River Eske rises on a gentle incline to the pretty, tree-lined expanse of Lough Eske. At the lake, the battlemented tower of a ruined nineteenth-century castle peers over a dense cushioning of conifers; islands and tiny islets, the bigger among them supporting a gorse bush or thorn tree, decorate the water, which is home to swans and grebes. Beyond the kempt green foothills whose scattered upright evergreens suggest Tuscany is a broad backdrop of granite mountains.

Those north of Lough Eske are the Blue Stack mountains, rising over the heather of the lower slopes to 2,219 ft (676 m). To the east the range culminates in Barnesmore (1,491 ft/454 m), isolated on the far side of the Lowerymore river and the road (and formerly the railway) from Donegal town where they pass through the spectacular Barnesmore Gap. The name is one of those many tautologies generated by the mixing of languages: Barnesmore means big gap, so Barnesmore Gap repeats itself, as – elsewhere – do River Avon and Combe Vale. Shining walls of pink granite, stained by feldspar and polished by the infinitely slow passage of ice, rise a thousand feet either side of the pass.

Too close to the dramas of the coast, the Blue Stack have not detained many travellers, and inhabitants have always been few, except for the highwaymen who preyed on travellers through the gap well into the last century. On the lower land to north and east the uniform spread of mountain bog has a loneliness and desolation in it. But the heights offer good walking – much of it tough going, and without tracks – with fine views displaying the picturesque and intriguing effects of the last Ice Age. There are interesting plants: ferns usually associated with the south of the country, and the whorled caraway (*Carum verticillatum*), which has chosen to grace a very few select locations in Ireland.

During the Ice Age, a glacier seems to have centred on Lough Eske and moved across the mountains, scouring deep grooves and *roches moutonnées* (solid masses of rock, their long backs smoothed to an upward slope, the hinder end left rough and shaggy), depositing erratic boulders and gouging out huge basins which have now become in many cases rather formidable, sunless, north- or east-facing mountain tarns with tall sheer crescents of rock as backdrops. A walk which starts and finishes at the rough road beside the Reelan river to the north of the range and takes in the five peaks over 2,000 ft (600 m) high, passes all these features and more. There are granite crags where eagles once nested, webs of stream and cataract, fragments of a Sunderland aircraft which

34

crashed here in 1944, and Lough Belshade pocketed among sheer cliffs.

A stratum that underlies every inch of Ireland but eludes the most diligent geologist is that of myth and legend. Plenty are concealed hereabouts: of Aonghus Og, a god who fell in love with a maiden in his dreams, learned that she lived in the form of a swan on this lake and was promised she would be his if he picked her out from a flock of 150. He did, naturally, and took her away to bliss in his palace by the Boyne. There is, too, a crock of gold within the lough. As tends to be the case, it is guarded; in this instance by a ferocious black cat. I am not sure whether it or the temperature of the water affords the greater deterrent.

Before you go *Maps:* OS Discovery Series maps Nos 10 and 11.

Guidebooks: The New Irish Walk Guides: West and North by Tony Whilde and Patrick Simms (Gill and Macmillan, 1991).

Getting there *By car:* from Letterkenny take the R250 (SW) to Glenties, passing Aghla mountain, then the R250 (E), passing north of the Blue Stack mountains to Ballybofey, and finally the N14 (S), through the Barnesmore Gap, towards Donegal, passing Lough Eske on the way.

By bus: Bus Eireann run services from Donegal to Letterkenny, via Lough Eske. The service that connects Portnoo and Killybegs stops at Glenties. The local bus company is McGeehan's, T:(075) 46161.

Where to stay: there are hotels and numerous bed and breakfasts in Donegal. A few country homes and farmhouses provide bed and breakfast, including Mrs N. McGinty, Arches, Lough Eske, T:(073) 22029. There is also the

independent Campbell's Holiday Hostel, Main Street, Glenties, T:(075) 51491.

Activities: there is good hill-walking in the Blue Stack Mountains (see guidebook listed above). The Co. Donegal extension of the Ulster Way follows the east shore of Lough Eske and continues over the east end of the mountains. Salmon fishing in the nearby River Finn and horse-riding facilities at the Finn Farm Hostel, T:(074) 32261.

Further information: the nearest year-round Bord Failte office is in Letterkenny, T:(074) 21160.

Lough Derg

Lake known for pilgrims and a reputed path to Purgatory

Praeger calls it the 'dreariest of Donegal waters' and it has not improved since his time, though the land about has been altered by the large-scale planting of conifers, set amid miles of almost featureless black bog. Lough Derg has about 25 islands, one of which is made top-heavy by an ugly and amorphous range of buildings rimming a basilica of 1930. Hell on earth, you could call it; and in the opinion of perhaps millions you would be near the mark. Since the Middle Ages this island, called Station Island, and another called Saint's Island further to the north, have been visited by

On the north side of Glencar Lake, between Sligo and Manorhamilton, a beautiful, mossy, ferny glen provides the setting for Yeats's Waterfall. The poet is buried at Drumcliff churchyard, beneath the peak of nearby Ben Bulben.

innumerable pilgrims intent on earning those visions of purgatory and hell which were vouchsafed to St Patrick when he came here for a retreat during the fifth century. He sat in a cave on Saint's Island and saw a succession of the punishments delivered to the wicked after death, and got a glimpse of the entrance to paradise.

All this was described in a twelfth-century account, since when people have flocked here in large numbers every summer, prepared to undergo various mortifications and deprivations for a number of days (two in our time). Authorities from popes to English governments have tried to suppress the whole thing. Despite or perhaps because of this it thrives now as never before. A new transit area beside the quay on the mainland, possessing every conceivable facility, has been completed recently.

Station Island (which refers to the Stations of the Cross) is open only to bona fide pilgrims. For those who do not cross the water the options are limited. The surrounds are flat, monotonous, cheerless and without colour, unless you consider conifer plantations a refreshment. There is a reasonable walk on the east side which takes in the hills of Crokkinagoe and Grousehall, some 2 miles (3 km) away. From the first of these, you can see the islands and the basilica, and, in the distance, the peaks of Tyrone and Donegal. Ferry boats ply the lake continually during the pilgrimage season from 1 June to 15 August.

There are temperaments for which drear melancholy and dour wilderness have a certain appeal. I urge you to check yours is one of them before making the detour.

Before you go *Maps:* OS Discovery Series map No. 11. *Guidebooks: The New Irish Walk Guides: West and North* by Tony Whilde and Patrick Simms (Gill and Macmillan, 1991) and *Walking the Ulster Way* by Alan Warner (Appletree Press, Belfast, 1989). **Getting there** *By car*: from Enniskillen, take the A32 then the A35 (N) to Pettigo, passing Lower Lough Erne and crossing the border. From Pettigo the R233 travels right up to the shores of the lake, and ends in a car park. *By bus:* a Bus Eireann summer-only service runs from Sligo to the shores of Lough Derg, stopping in Pettigo, once every morning. During the pilgrim season in the summer a special service operates from Dublin each day, T:(01) 366111. **Where to stay**: there are two bed and breakfasts in Pettigo: Mrs McVeigh, T:(072) 61565, and Mrs O'Shea, T:(072) 61535. **Access**: anyone over the age of 14 can obtain a pass and travel to Station Island to join the other pilgrims. **Activities** *Walking*: the Donegal extension of the 435-mile (700-km) Ulster Way, a way-marked route, passes Lough Derg on its way to the north coast. For more information contact the Field Officer, Sports Council for Northern Ireland, House of Sport, Upper Malone Road, Belfast. *Fishing:* Lough Derg provides fine brown-trout fishing, mayfly time only. For more information contact the Manager, Northern Regional Fisheries Board, Station Road, Ballyshannon, Co. Donegal, T:(072) 51435. **Further information**: the nearest Bord Failte office is in Bundoran and is open June–Sept, T:(072) 41350.

Glens of Sligo and North Leitrim

A region rich in wild glens, plateau-capped mountains with concave sides, water cascading and water at rest in long wood-edged lakes

Fifteen miles (24 kilometres) east of Sligo town lies the little town of Manorhamilton, impressively sited at the hub of a wheel of mountains whose five spokes are formed by valleys and glens radiating outwards. To the north-west is the chunky sector, bounded by Glencar and Glenade, which ends in the strange formations of Ben Bulben, famous for its shape and beauty, its plant-life, its myths and the remains of Yeats in a graveyard at its feet. Northward rises the peak of Crocknagapple and other pinnacles ending in the broad, fish-rich span of Lough Melvin. North-east is Dough mountain, south-east an area of highlands pocked with little lakes, and west-south-west, between the Ben Bulben range and the valley of the Bonet river, is Benbo and a further lean line of peaks, dropping sharply towards Sligo. South of here, between the main heights and the north bank of Lough Gill, there lies a fascinating little area of lakes and minor peaks which is known as the Doons.

These ranges boast almost every outline a mountain is capable of taking: cone, basin, ridge, bun, loaf. I do not know why it should seem remarkable when something made by nature resembles something made by man, as if nature would ever bother itself with imitating art, or need to be congratulated on getting it right. Nature's designs – eye, ear, orchid, humming bird, crystal, whirligig beetle, oak tree – are cleverer than the cleverest of ours. Nevertheless I think it is true that part of the appeal of this area comes from the almost unnatural, the positively manmade look of it: the semi-abstract impression (depending on angle of view) of a colony of Saracen castles, tiered cakes, table tops, high-heeled shoes or, in the case of the ridge north-east of Ben Bulben, a particularly vicious-looking rotary blade for gouging holes out of something very hard. It is an area of geological freaks but there is nothing in the least ugly about it. Quite the contrary. In my opinion this is one of the most beautiful and intriguing parts of Ireland.

The region owes its nature to the earth's stirrings 350 million years ago, when a warm sea covered this part of the globe. The expended shells of minuscule animals floated down and laid a thick foundation of carboniferous limestone over its bed. Sand was swept in and, under the sea's weight, compacted first into sandstone and shales, then into millstone grit. When the sea retreated, the subsequent growth of plants led to the formation of coal. Now weather began its work. Rivers formed and their channels were readily deepened because all the rock they cut through was of this sedimentary kind and relatively soft. Much more recently, the ice scoured through, rounding the channels into the present-day shapes of the glens. The high plateaux, whose vertical substructures stand out so starkly, were left, and remain, grandly distinct.

Judging from the number of their burial chambers and other memorials surviving in elevated places, our Stone Age ancestors saw grandeur here too, but where we reach for kitchen comparisons, they saw perhaps spiritual meaning and significance. The place became imbued with legend, more it seems

than other parts of Ireland, which has everywhere been fertile in myth-making. One of the greatest of these tales reaches its climax here, on the summit of Ben Bulben. Dermot, a beautiful youth who had eloped years before with a girl, Grania, destined for the ageing hero Finn, comes with Finn to hunt a magic wild boar. Dermot kills it, but not before it has lethally gored him. As he lies dying, Finn gloats over him, refuses to use his healing powers, and lets the water Dermot craves slip through his fingers.

The two star glens, Glencar and Glenade, seem to crack the hills asunder to disclose an enchantment of long lakes fringed with trees, thick woods, waterfalls. At the north edge the many-islanded Lough Melvin rests the eye with its vast flatness. To the east, straddling the national border, are Loughs Macnean (Upper and Lower), with Cuilcagh mountain and its descending line of caves, made easily accessible at Marble Arch, rising to the south of the lower lake. In the south of the region there is Lough Gill, a contrast: its steep wooded sides sometimes too forbidding for the epithet pretty, a touch Scottish with its castles and rocks and innate romance. And there, a mile above the eastern end of the lake, rise the Doons.

They are smaller than the surrounding mountains, these flattish-topped, vertical-collared remnants of marine reefs pressed

Giant of the crow family, the all-black, thick-billed raven is often seen among mountains or coastal cliffs: a strong flier and skilled aeronaut, keen on aerial tumbles or flying on its side for long stretches.

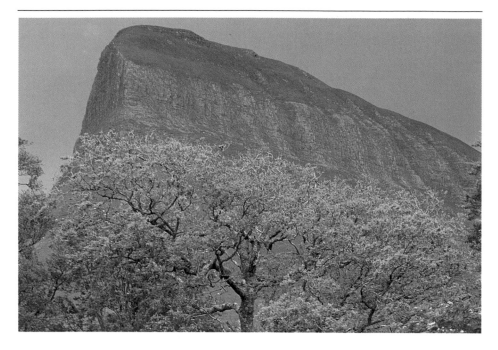

From the south Ben Bulben reveals the sawn-off tip of its massive peak, celebrated by Yeats in the epitaph he wrote for himself, describing his resting place 'Under bare Ben Bulben's head'.

into a lasting firmness by the regular wash of currents, and surviving long after less densely packed rock around them was eroded away. They stand up like prows from the slopes and valleys about them, and for my money offer some of the most rewarding walks: crisp, quite tough, with amazing views. High on the ascent, with a doon or two below and another, bigger one to overcome, you can look across a broad sweep of valley, hear a sheep's bleat or cough or a raven's churr come from the other side with the clarity of a bell, gaze over to the opposite hillside with its greens, browns, gaps of grey rock and wavy contours, and view the giant doodles worked unconsciously by men cutting peat in the past. 'I'd niver notice it. I suppose I was cradled to it,' a farmer down below said, curiously canvassing my opinion (which is patchy and covered with rust) of Churchill and Chamberlain, rather than talk of the land which is his life. Up here,

though above the world, there is something Parnassian, with every ridge revealing some splendid picture of mountain, lake, wood or broad panorama.

There are orchids, violets, daisies, primroses among the heather and grasses of these hills and mountains, but there are rarities too. Alpines, usually found on north-facing cliffs and surviving here from the time the ice left, include the very rare, pretty, white-flowered fringed sandwort (*Arenaria ciliata*), Arctic saxifrage (*Saxifraga nivalis*) with its spherical cluster of flowers held high over a whorl of basal leaves, and chickweed-leaved willowherb (*Epilobium alsinifolium*), an inconspicuous creeper.

Cast a cold eye
On life, on death
Horseman, pass by.

W. B. Yeats, 'Under Ben Bulben' (the epitaph on his grave at Drumcliff, beside the mountain)

BEFORE YOU GO
Maps: OS Discovery Series map No. 16.

GETTING THERE
By car: take the N16 (east) from Sligo to Manorhamilton, passing Glencar Lake and Forest on the way. From Manorhamilton go left and north-west towards Bundoran on the coast along the R280, through Glenade. A right turn at Kinlough on to the R281 takes you down the west side of Lough Melvin. To reach Ben Bulben, take the N15 (north) from Sligo. There are several small tracks that run from this road to the mountain. To reach Lough Gill, take the R286 towards Dromahair, passing the north of the lake.
By rail: the nearest train station is in Sligo, and the service runs daily from Dublin Connolly.
By bus: Bus Eireann, in conjunction with Ulsterbus, runs a daily service between Galway and Belfast that stops at Manorhamilton. There is also a once-a-day express service between Dooagh and Belfast that stops at Manorhamilton, and a local Bus Eireann service between Sligo, Manorhamilton and Enniskillen that runs four times a day. Bus Eireann also operates direct daily services to Dublin, Derry, Sligo and Galway from Bundoran. The Feda O'Donnell Bus Company, T:(075) 48114, operates a service from Crolly to Galway that stops at Bundoran.

WHERE TO STAY
Hotels: there are a few bed and breakfasts in Manorhamilton, including Maguire's Teach Cluainin, T:(072) 55201. There is a better selection, and some hotels, in Sligo and several more bed and breakfasts in Bundoran, including Bayview, Main Street, T:(072) 41296.
Youth hostels: there is an independent hostel near Bundoran, the Homefield Activity Centre, Bayview Avenue, Bundoran, T:(072) 41288.
Outdoor living: camping is available just outside Bundoran at the Dartry View Caravan and Camping Park, East End, Bundoran, T:(072) 40794, which is open Easter-Sept. There is another camp-site at the eastern end of Lough Melvin, near Garrison.

ACTIVITIES
Walking: the 30-mile (48-km) Leitrim Way, a way-marked route, starts in Manorhamilton and heads south-east to Dowra and Drumshanbo, joining up with the Cavan Way en route. For more information contact Leitrim County Council, Courthouse, Carrick-on-Shannon, Co. Leitrim, T:(078) 20005.
Riding: the Stracomer Riding School, T:(072) 41787, operates saddle-tours of Donegal town and the surrounding coast and countryside.
Caving: there is a great deal of pot-holing activity in the area. All clubs operate out of Manorhamilton.
Fishing: salmon and brown-trout fishing is available at Lough Melvin. The Lough Melvin Trout Wet-Fly International takes place 17-19 Jun. Contact the Kinlough and District Anglers' Association.
Cycling: Cycling Ireland, a pamphlet available from Bord Failte, suggests a route that runs from Sligo up to Bundoran and down through Manorhamilton to Blacklion.

FURTHER INFORMATION
There is a Bord Failte tourist office in Bundoran, T:(072) 41350, which is open May to mid-Sept. The nearest office open all year is in Sligo, T:(071) 61201. The private tourist office in Manorhamilton is situated behind Maguire's Bar and is open Apr-Sept.

Knocknarea

A cairn-capped peak west of Sligo town, on a promontory bisecting Sligo Bay and seen from five counties

Twenty-five years ago I bought a day-return railway ticket for me and my bicycle from Dublin, where I was writing a book, to Sligo. The book was about the early Celtic Church in Ireland, and one day I felt an overwhelming desire to visit the mountain-top grave of one of the characters, Queen Maeve. Her remains are supposed to lie under the 40,000 tons of stones that form a cairn, visible on a good day all over the county of Sligo and beyond, on the broad flat surface of Knocknarea.

From the station in Sligo town I cycled the five or six miles to the foot of the hill, hid the bike under a bush, and climbed, admiring the wonderful views over sea and land. I considered the unscrupulous monarch whose jealousy and greed led (in legend, anyway) to a desperate and tragic war between Ulster and her own Connacht, and whose remains now shared this mountain-top with me alone. She is one of those many historical figures who have taken on the attributes of a mythical namesake – a figure which in this case has given us the personage of Queen Mab. The grave has never been excavated – and an old tradition that visitors carry up a stone to add to the cairn makes it all the time more difficult to contemplate. Such chastity in a remarkable tomb is rare, and adds to the awe of the place.

I came down again after a couple of hours or so. A man approached.

'We saw ye hidin' yer bike,' he said. Was he, I wondered, going to warn me to be more careful, or complain that I had not asked permission? His house, it seemed, was a hundred yards or so away.

'We saw ye,' he went on, 'and now ye're sure to be needin' a cup of tea.'

That was true. He led me to his cottage. Inside, his wife stood beside a table laid with plates of potatoes, Limerick ham, boiled eggs, salad, trifle, bread, cheese and a quart-sized pot of tea. I almost cried with pleasure. In addition I heard more about Maeve than I have heard or read ever since.

I cannot guide you to the cottage. When I went back after twenty years I was not sure which it had been, or whether it had been replaced by a new one, and inquiries failed to find my benefactors. But I can recommend the climb, the view, and epics of Irish myth in which Maeve figures.

Before you go *Maps:* OS Discovery Series map No. 25. **Getting there** *By car:* take the R292 from Sligo. This road goes right round Knocknarea mountain and cairn. *By rail:* there are trains from Dublin Connolly to Sligo three times a day and four times on Fridays. *By bus:* Sligo is well served by Bus Eireann routes from Belfast, Dublin and Derry. **Where to stay:** there is a very good selection of hotels and bed and breakfasts in Sligo and Strandhill, but they can get overcrowded, especially during the Yeats International Summer School in mid-Aug. Camping is available at Strandhill, T:(071) 68120, and there is an An Oige hostel in
40

Sligo, the Eden Hill Hostel, T:(071) 493204. **Activities**: apart from walking up Knocknarea to see the grave of Queen Maeve, Bord Failte have a suggested cycling route round the base of the mountain. **Further Information**: the nearest Bord Failte office is in Sligo, T:(071) 61201, and is open all year.

Inishmurray

A low, flat, wind-swept, now deserted island in the middle of Donegal Bay, rich in ancient remains, wintering geese and breeding sea-birds

One kind of wildness – the ferocity of weather and the bleak animosity of land or sea – is usually avoided these days. More often than not, we stay indoors. This was an option closed to the torn remnants of the Spanish Armada when, having rounded the north of Scotland from east to west, seeing one after another of their vessels swallowed up, three frigates in the vicinity of Inishmurray, off the north-west coast of Sligo, were pounded by storms on to the opposite strand at Streedagh. Next day 1,100 bodies were counted.

Until 1948 Inishmurray was inhabited by a community of a hundred or so who knew a way of avoiding such catastrophe. Three drops of water from a particular island well sprinkled on the sea always ensured a calm crossing. They had other ways and rituals that sound strange or wonderful to us. Turning certain stones widdershins ensured the success of a curse; clockwise, of a blessing. They could cure

disease by water and faith. They buried their men in one graveyard, their women in another far apart. But for nearly half a century now, such practices have been discontinued. The island is left to its wealth of ancient ruins – many of them from a monastery first founded in the fifth century by Muiredach, a follower of St Patrick – and to the birds which were doubtless there before humans came.

In winter, barnacle geese – distinguished from the rapidly proliferating Canada geese by their shorter neck, white face and grey rather than brown plumage – fly in from their breeding grounds in Greenland and elsewhere in the Arctic Circle to graze on the two hundred or so acres of the island, the majority of which is bog. In spring it becomes the breeding ground for some gulls, the Arctic tern, which may have spent the winter in Antarctica, eiders – easily recognized by their white upper and dark lower plumage – and storm petrels, traditionally known to sailors as Mother Carey's chickens. The petrels' eerie calls may be heard from their rabbit-hole nests at night, but they are unlikely to be seen in the vicinity since they pass the day on and over the sea.

True to ancient belief, the first chronicler of the Anglo-Norman invasion of Ireland, Giraldus Cambrensis, thought that barnacle geese were born from logs of fir lying in sea-water. Other cultures have them growing on trees. Until they were strong enough, Giraldus asserted, they clung by their beaks to seaweed attached to the logs. For these birds, mating had no connection with procreation. So close were they to the life of the sea that they could be eaten, according to a useful Irish tradition, on fast days.

Today the weather is still as

wild as it ever was, and the low flat terrain is short on defence and shelter. The land is poor – the former inhabitants' income came from fish – and access is no simple matter. Antiquities and bird life can, however, be rewarding. The best hope of a lift across is at Rosses Point or Mullaghmore, on the mainland 4 miles (6 km) away.

Before you go *Maps:* OS Discovery Series map No. 16.

Getting there: there is no regular boat service to the island of Inishmurray, but trips can be arranged through Lomax Boats, from Mullaghmore, T:(071) 66124. At least six people need to travel to make the crossing economical. **Where to stay:** there is no accommodation on the island, although there is a large selection of hotels and bed and breakfasts in Sligo and Bundoran. **Further information:** the nearest Bord Failte office is in Sligo, T:(071) 61201, and is open all year.

Ox Mountains

A long granite ridge of wood and moorland with an isolated lake, tying County May to Sligo

People are rather patronizing about the Ox Mountains, a long low wall (rising at its highest point, Knockalongy, to 1,786 ft/544 m) which almost divides Counties Mayo and Sligo, and which can seem from some angles and a fair distance to be short on features and character, especially in comparison with the sculpted peaks of north Sligo and north Leitrim. The Ox mountains are a quite different affair: much older (consisting of igneous

and metamorphic rocks, mainly granite and gneiss, built up by the great Caledonian upheavals 400 to 500 million years ago), much harder, and of much gentler outline. But they are rich in the remains of ancient cultures. Cairns and other megalithic monuments abound. Probes of the peat have revealed well developed field systems worked much later by Bronze Age people. Fossil forests under the peat also show that the blanket bog which covers much of the range and extends over most of the neighbouring county of Mayo has increased at the expense of widespread conifer forests. One of the commoner ancient plants was the rhododendron. This too was to die out. Spreads of rhododendron seen now in the middle and west of Ireland come from the re-introduction of the plant in the eighteenth century.

The centre of the range, not spectacular, still has the appeal of the big, broad, strong and self-assured. The glen that cuts across the middle and contains Easky Lough, though dully afforested in the foothills, rises slowly about the banks of the Owenaher river through a broadening valley – among scatterings of massive, Attic rockiness – to the mile-long shallow basin of rock-fringed lake where the only sounds are the lapping of water, the wind and an occasional bleat. (Sheep, of an impressively fearless kind, are everywhere.) It feels like the world's summit, or the roof of Tibet. I have seen lakes like this in Iceland, which leads me to expect to hear, though I have never heard nor found evidence that others have, the carrying calls of the great northern diver or whooper swan. The nearest I can get is the common gull, which nests around the edge of the lake and bravely swoops to

frighten away human intruders, and the pert and ubiquitous common sandpiper.

Near the mountain's eastern end, and west of Collooney, gneiss rock gives way to quartzite, whose hardness here and elsewhere means that it often stays stubbornly upright when later rock accretions have been worn off its surface by wind, ice and water. The result is a silhouette unlike that of the rest of the range – a knobbly dinosaur-back which stands out vividly as a landmark and supplies more varied walks than other parts.

Before you go *Maps:* OS Discovery Series maps Nos 24, 25.

Getting there *By car:* from Sligo take the N4 (S) to Collooney and Tobercurry. Turn right here on to the R294 which crosses the Ox Mountains. Access to the north coast is by means of innumerable roads off the N59 between Ballysadare, 5 miles (8 km) south of Sligo, and Ballina in Co. Mayo. *By rail:* Sligo station has three daily services (four on Friday), from Dublin Connolly. *By bus:* Bus Eireann runs services between Sligo and Ballina. Private bus companies also operate in the area; Treacy's, T:(096) 70968, runs a daily service from Ballina to Sligo.

Where to stay: there is plenty of accommodation in Sligo and a few bed and breakfasts in Ballina and scattered along the north coast. Camping is available just outside Ballina at the Beleek Camping and Caravan Park, T:(096) 71533.

Activities: Bikes may be hired from Gerry's Cycle Centre, Ballina, T:(096) 70455. Gerry's is closed for two weeks in July. **Further information:** the Bord Failte office in Ballina is open May-Sept, T:(096) 70848. The nearest tourist office that is open all year is the Bord Failte in Sligo, T:(071) 61201.

CHAPTER 2

The West

About 600 million years ago, almost all lands and continents were clustered far to the south of the Equator. North America (as it would in time become), distantly detached from South America, looked as if it had keeled over clockwise, its present east coast facing south. Between that coast and the South Pole lay the British Isles, a quarter turn clockwise from their present orientation. The sea bounded on the north by North America and on the south by Britain, known as the Iapetus Ocean, contained an east–west line of islands which would become a number of different things. They and the two land masses were the more prominent features of two huge plates of earthcrust – there are seven major ones today – floating on the molten magma of which the earth's interior consists.

These two were moving inexorably together and, at the incomprehensibly drawn-out pace of geological time, they eventually collided in what would seem to us impossibly slow motion – a yard or metre or two a year. Nevertheless the effect of their clash was cataclysmic. One end of the American plate slowly, imperceptibly, nudged, scraped, and was eventually forced under the European plate. All prominent features, including the intervening islands, were now squeezed (I imagine) in a prolonged sequence of searings, crashings and seethings, creating mountains, valleys and every other conceivable physical feature, as well as heat and steam clouds like those from nuclear

The north shore of the lake at Delphi is an oasis of woodland amidst the highlands of south Mayo. Not unlike its Parnassian namesake, it is hemmed in by rocky mountains, with the shoulder of Ben Creggan thrusting in from the right and the Sheefry Hills rising steeply in the background.

explosions. After a hundred or so million years the clash was about complete. The islands had been changed into the prominences which after eras of erosion by weather would become the central range of Connemara (the Twelve Bens), the Maumturk mountains to the east and several of the peaks of County Mayo to the north, all quartzite-hearted and consequently resistant to the depredations of climate.

Other, lesser ranges – Joyce's Country, the Partry mountains – were at the same time pushed up from surrounding sedimentary rocks, which had been fused by heat into schists and marbles. The recipe for the delicate pairings of green and black in Connemara marble is to be found in the infernal convulsions of this era. But the heat generated by these movements moved downwards too. Far below the earth's surface it melted solid rock into a magma which burst up and spread over the south of Connemara (the broad coastal strip) in the form of an uneven but never very high blanket of granite.

Still united, the American and Eurasian plates were all the time floating northward, away from the original cluster around the South Pole. Three hundred million years ago Connemara and the rest of Ireland were covered by sea: a warm sea because the part of the sea-bed destined to become Ireland was at that time passing over the Equator. A rich sediment of tiny marine shells coated Ireland with the carboniferous limestone which still underlies the major part of the country. For the most part, though, it has been washed off the Galway highlands.

Something under 200 million years ago, the two plates began to separate again. The division, after what had occurred, could not tidily replicate what went before. Bits from each plate stuck to the other. As it happens, half of modern Ireland – the half that includes Ulster, Louth, Sligo, Mayo and much of Galway and the northern midlands – having been part of the western, American continent, clinging to what is now Newfoundland, stayed this time with the European. The join seems to have occurred along a rough line from Clogher Head in County Louth to Connemara. (It might be tempting to read political significance into these changes – to try to see allegiance in alignment – but they predated humans and all human aspirations by rather too long a period for that.)

The greatest geological dramas in the formation of this part of Ireland were over. There was some volcanic activity to follow in the last 60 million years, the so-called Tertiary age. Doon Hill, beside Bunowen Bay on the way to Slyne Head, comprises a volcanic plug, a bolt of lava that cooled within the core and was in due course partially exposed by erosion. The Ice Ages changed much, but in the manner of a plastic surgeon, modifying and altering features without breaking the underlying mould. There are mountain lakes in carved-out corries, scree-hung valleys, slopes of rock scraped smooth, moraines, eskers, a colony of drumlins and here and there erratic boulders left by ice in its several comings and goings.

Plants moved in as the ice receded. Dwarf birch and hawthorn served as curtain raisers until oak and pine established themselves over large areas. Then man came, as thorough and nihilistic as the ice itself. To get land for animals and crops he felled and burned trees on an Amazonian scale. The fires he lit, and the many which began naturally, created charcoal. Charcoal clogged the soil, making it more or less impervious, a process assisted by the leaching of minerals through the soil to form a compacted layer below. Rain fell and lay on the surface. Plants lived and died and sank into the acid, increasingly airless water, which greatly slowed down their decomposition. Bog was being created, and as it took hold it curtailed the number of plants able to survive. The only trees to come from the bog are the stumps and boles of those ancient oaks and pines which preceded it. Connemara – mountain and coast – is for the most part singularly bare of trees, though there are entrancing exceptions to the rule.

For want of forests, of course, modern man has been destroying the peat that developed slowly in the bog, not just in Connemara but over much of the country. Burning it in his grate made little impact, but selling it to bulk out the soil in suburban gardens in other parts of the world, and to be converted to energy in power stations, and leaving nothing much in its place, has gravely changed large parts of the West, not least the bleak boggy wilderness of north-western Mayo known as the Barony of Erris. Equally jarring change has come from the conifer plantations that here and there spread a dull green domestic velvet over the former grand desolation of moorland.

Yet the West and the South-West of Ireland retain between them by far the largest share of the country's wildness. For most visitors, the West is not the easiest part of the country to reach. You arrive on the east coast or the south, and wherever you start and however you travel, getting to Counties Clare and Galway and Mayo loses you at least half a day, unless you arrange to fly to Knock, Shannon or Farranfore. But if wildness does not take some getting to, it is hardly worth the name.

Remoteness, though, is a relative word, and it is not at all what it used to be. Not long ago I stayed at an inn in the north of County Mayo, and imagined what it would have been like at the beginning of the century. Getting away once darkness fell would have been unthinkable. You would have been thrown on the company and hospitality and catering skills of the innkeeper, his wife and a handful of local peasants, and bad weather would have kept you here for days. Your companions' conversation would have been limited in scope to their experience, mostly local. But I dare say everything about it would have been memorable. As it was, when I was there, the television dominated the bar. Locals asked for international-sounding things like Bacardi and tequila with Coke, and talked about cars and sex. I had telephone conversations with people hundreds of miles away in Ireland or England. If I had had the right sort of computer I could probably have linked up with the Library of Congress catalogue in Washington, DC.

Then I walked out into the twilight air. It was a sepia print of a view: sepia moorland all about, low sepia hills, breaking now and again to show vees of sepia sea, and behind me mountains too dark to be called anything but black shadows against a deep-violet sky. The only sound was of regularly spaced stonechats, uttering their indignation at (I suppose) my presence at this time of night. It was easy to forget the world I knew; but nonetheless a pity not to know it was utterly out of reach, as it would have been from an uninhabited offshore island.

To reach wildness a bit of getting away is always necessary, from the town, perhaps, or simply from the road. In the parts of the West that are best to see and walk in, there are singularly few of either. In Erris you can walk all day and cross only one road. The Twelve Bens, the central glory of Connemara, are surrounded by a respectable road, but only one or two single-lane tracks lead into their central precinct. Coastal Connemara has easier road access and a great many people to take advantage of it. Few, however, go to the uninhabited islands; to get to these involves a deal with a fisherman which might cost dear. The Burren draws crowds in cars and coaches, and in season they clog the roads, especially at places the brochures make much of. Leave them behind, trust to two feet, and humanity becomes a memory. It is still amazingly true that two districts of world fame – Connemara and the Burren – can, in great part, be so free of people.

The component areas of the West are, in the Irish way, very different in character. Elsewhere you would have to travel hundreds of miles to cover such a range of landscapes. The Burren is a pavement of stone wherein every dip and crack and crevice capable of carrying a teaspoon of soil supports plants of kinds that draw botanists from all over the world. In central Connemara and to its east, brotherhoods of mountains rise in conclaves, challenging the climber and botanist to scramble up their hunched shoulders. Salmon breed in the rivers that start in tumbles down their sides, and there are broad fish-rich lakes in the dells of Joyce's Country and the Partry mountains. Connemara's periphery is a belt of flat-lands sequinned with small lakes and hemmed by sea. There are festoons of spring flowers here, too, and many that are rare and far from their normal homes: America or Spain. A botanist's Mecca, the author Robert Lloyd Praeger called the country near Roundstone. A hedonist's too, he might have added. And then, a few miles away, are the monotone bog-lands of Mayo, and a few miles further still, the wild cliffs of Achill, a fist of resistance held out to the battering Atlantic.

GETTING THERE

By air: the majority of overseas travellers enter Ireland via Dublin, T:(01) 379900, and Shannon, T:(061) 61444, airports. There are regular scheduled flights from Dublin to Carnmore Airport in Galway, T:(091) 55569, and Knock Airport in Co. Mayo, T:(094) 67222. Flights are operated by Aer Arann, T:(091) 93034, to all three of the Aran Islands from Minna, near Inveran west of Galway. The flight takes about 10 minutes; a connecting bus to the airport runs from Galway.

By boat: there are no ferry services to the west coast, but Swansea Cork Ferries, T:(01792) 456116, sail their car ferries between Cork and Swansea every one or two days (depending on the season).

Several companies, including Stena Sealink, T:(01233) 647022, and B&I Line, T:(0171) 499 5744, operate services to the east coast from UK ports such as Stranraer, Holyhead, Fishguard, Swansea and Pembroke. Ferries also operate from Galway, Rossaveel and Doolin to the Aran Islands.

By car: good main roads link all ports of entry with Galway and other destinations in the West. An enjoyable benefit of sailing overnight by Swansea Cork Ferries is the full day it allows for the drive.

By rail: the rail link from Dublin to the West splits at Athlone. Travellers bound for the north of the region should go to Westport or Ballina. Travellers for the southern area should go to Galway. The journey takes around 3 hours from Dublin to Galway and all trains have snack or buffet cars. The service runs about four times a day. Contact Iarnrod Eireann, the Irish railway service, for timetable information, T:(01) 36333.

WHERE TO STAY

There is no shortage of campsites, bed and breakfasts, hostels and hotels in this part of Ireland. Bord Failte produces an invaluable accommodation guide which lists registered and approved establishments. The Irish YHA, An Oige, publishes a directory of hostels, and can be contacted on T:(01) 304555. The approved Irish Independent Hostels are privately owned and require no registration card. Their headquarters are in Doolin, T:(065) 74006.

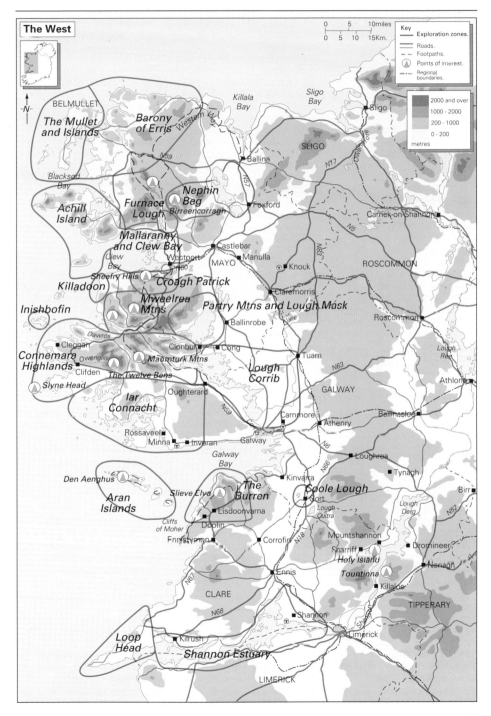

The West

Key
— Exploration zones.
═ Roads.
--- Footpaths.
⌂ Points of interest.
-··- Regional boundaries.

0   5   10miles
0   5   10   15Km.

2000 and over
1000 - 2000
200 - 1000
0 - 200
metres

BELMULLET

The Mullet and Islands

Barony of Erris

Killala Bay

Sligo Bay

Sligo

Western Way

N59

SLIGO

N17

Blacksod Bay

Ballina

N57

Achill Island

Furnace Lough

Nephin Beg

Birreencorragh

Foxford

N5

Carrick-on-Shannon

Mallaranny and Clew Bay

Castlebar

Manulla

ROSCOMMON

Clew Bay

Westport

MAYO

Knock

N60

Sheefry Hills

Killadoon

Croagh Patrick

Claremorris

Inishbofin

Mweelrea Mtns

Partry Mtns and Lough Mask

Roscommon

Lough Ree

Ballinrobe

Clare

Dawros

Cleggan

Clonbur

Cong

Tuam

N63

Connemara Highlands

Owenglin

Maumturk Mtns

Athlone

Clifden

The Twelve Bens

Lough Corrib

GALWAY

Ballinasloe

Slyne Head

Oughterard

Iar Connacht

Carnmore

Athenry

N59

Rossaveel

Galway

N6

Minna

Inveran

Loughrea

Galway Bay

N65

Tynagh

Den Aenghus

Kinvarra

Coole Lough

Birr

Aran Islands

Slieve Elva

The Burren

Gort

Lough Cutra

Lough Derg

N52

Lisdoonvarna

Cliffs of Moher

Doolin

Corrofin

N18

Mountshannon

Scarriff

Dromineer

Ennistymon

Holy Island

Nenagh

Tountinna

Ennis

Killaloe

Loop Head

Kilrush

CLARE

N67

N68

Shannon

TIPPERARY

Shannon Estuary

Limerick

LIMERICK

ACTIVITIES

Walking: the Western Way is a 120-mile (190-km) way-marked route divided into 6 main stages varying from about 10 miles (16 km) to 40 miles (65 km). Some stretches are still being developed. Starting from Oughterard, the Way follows Lough Corrib, then curves round the west of the Maumturk mountains, the east of the Sheefry range, through Westport to the mountains and moors of the Barony of Erris in County Mayo, finishing (at present) at Ballina. For further information, see *County Mayo – The Western Way* by Joe McDermott and Robert Charman (Mayo County Council).

Riding: the Connemara and coast trails are suitable for riders of all standards. Contact W. Leahy, T:(091) 41216. Trails can be undertaken from the Milchem Equestrian Centre, Tynagh, T:(095) 76388. The Cashel Hotel, T:(095) 31001,

and Hazelwood House, T:(091) 94275, offer week-long and weekend residential packages.

Climbing: Ben Corr in the Twelve Bens has a quartzite crag with good routes up to 1,000 ft (300 m) which provide choices for climbers of different standards. Maumtrasna in the Partry mountains has shorter, easier climbs on sandstone. Bord Failte produces a hill- and rock-climbing guide.

Fishing: salmon rivers include the Bundorragha, Clare, Corrib, Dawros, Erris and Owenglin. Loughs Feeagh and Furnace have salmon. Lough Corrib has brown trout and salmon. Lough Mask is better known for its trout. The Lakeland Country Home School of Casting on Lough Corrib, T:(091) 82121/82146, provides seasonal instruction in all aspects of trout angling.

Cycling: three lengthy circular routes in the region are recommended by Bord Failte. The plains of Galway and

Mayo are least demanding while Connemara and Killary are more rugged. The Mountains of Mayo route is the longest of the three at 194 miles (312 km) and offers cyclists the chance to explore the breathtaking cliff scenery of one of the least populated parts of Ireland.

Sailing: Little Killary Adventure Centre, T:(095) 43411, has a wide range of activities, including sailing and wind-surfing. Both Galway and Westport have sailing clubs.

FURTHER INFORMATION

The main tourist office is in Galway, T:(091) 63081, where accommodation can be booked. There are further information offices in Westport, T:(053) 23111, and at Knock Airport, T:(094) 67247.
Further reading: The New Irish Walk Guides: West and North by Tony Whilde and Patrick Simms (Gill and Macmillan, 1991).

Barony of Erris

A fretted coastline of cliffs and some fishing harbours, and inland the vast unpeopled peatlands of north Mayo

Mayo is as wild a county as Ireland possesses: a big county which imprints itself on the visitor's mind as a carpet of bog interrupted by some stately mountains and contained within a coastline of frenzied indentations and a quite uncountable number of islands. Among the hard acid terrain of the interior there are in fact some rich alkaline lands, most of them once colonized by the Anglo-Irish, who could usually tell good soil from bad. These lands tend to be around Killala Bay, Lough Conn and Lough Mask, and east of Clew Bay between Westport and Newport. One of the great

Ascendancy houses that has found its feet as a tourist draw in modern times is Westport House, home of the Browne family, marquesses of Sligo, of whom twelve generations have lived here since Tudor times. Another family possessing lands in the county for four centuries is the Binghams, earls of Lucan. The last earl disappeared after the murder of his children's nanny in London several years ago, and is generally assumed to be dead. But as long as there was serious doubt, I have been told, tenants on his lands around Castlebar decided without overmuch distress that it would be inappropriate to pay rent to his heir and best to pay nobody. This could, of course, be groundless gossip.

The less kempt demesnes of the old Anglo-Irish landlords are often places where a certain wildness can be found. The Irish people are not inclined to gut or clear away deserted buildings. Ruins of all kinds – defensive, ecclesiastical, domestic – remain

48

from all the eras of Irish history. Beside the shell of some eighteenth-century or earlier mansion, abandoned or burnt by accident or design, there will often be woods and an uncontrolled growth of shrubbery and weeds replacing what was garden or decorative parkland. Such areas may well have become unofficial nature reserves, havens for birds, ringing with morning and evening song. All such lands are private. Many are jealously guarded by a rump of the landlord family who may in some cases be carrying on their lives in an unrecognizably intact corner of a house which is otherwise ruinous. Care and courtesy are called for in what can be a rewarding approach.

St Patrick, calling a blessing on Ireland from the summit of Croagh Patrick, is traditionally supposed to have missed out Mayo's more characteristic surface: the blanket bog of the great Barony of Erris in the north and the Nephin Beg range along the southern edge, in parts heavily planted with monotonous forestry trees. You would not explore it for richness of scenery or flora or fauna – though the familiar little Pickwickian stonechat, with its buff chest and white collar, light cheep followed by cicada's churr, is a common attraction, as is the graceful wheatear – visiting for the summer – with its mottled shawl and white rump. Golden plover, snipe, woodcock, merlin and the amphibious dipper are pleasing to see but not to be counted on. The red grouse is uncommon and clever at camouflage. The expansive brown or purple of the bog, with mountains of like colours as backdrop, is less scenery than tone, or mood; something not to comment on or describe but to feel one's way into a kind of communion with. According to taste and temperament, you can be serenely in tune with the landscape or bored out of your mind.

Where bored, I suggest you home in and narrow the focus. The bog was not daubed by an impressionist, to be loved or not for its general depiction. It was painted lovingly by an early Flemish or Italian artist, disclosing more and more precise detail to the inquisitive eye. The Wildlife Service's Knockmoyle Sheskin nature reserve in the middle of the Barony of Erris is an excellent place to put this claim to the test. (You are advised not to go without a qualified guide because of the danger of walking into a hollow, pond or swallow-hole.)

It is, simply, a well-maintained 3,000 acres (1,200 hectares) of blanket bog, endowed by nature with streams, pools, wet hollows and so-called flush areas rich in minerals and supporting their own tally of plants, including birch and willow trees. What man has done to much of the surrounding bog – a third afforested by means of European Union money; substantial parts mechanically removed for fuel or to bulk out the flower-beds of millions of suburban gardens; part chomped up for drainage schemes – has been prohibited here for good.

You can identify bog grasses, rushes, mosses, red worm-like liverworts, bogbean, crowberry, ling and bell heather and many others, discerning the soils they like and companions they choose. You can see a sinister threesome of bog plants reversing nature's normal procedure of animal eating plant. The sundew traps the unwary insect with glue-tipped red tentacles rising from its whorl of reddish leaves. It folds them over and slowly squeezes and digests nutrient juices from the cadaver. The yellow-green leaves of the butterwort ooze adhesive, trap and dissolve their prey, while the aquatic Greater bladderwort (*Utricularia vulgaris*) wafts hair-triggers from its roots in the water. When touched, the hairs open up a small round bladder whose interior vacuum sucks in the victim. The flowers of all three

The strikingly spotted, furry-bodied emperor moth lives among the heather, which provides its food during June and July. The male can detect a female well over a mile away.

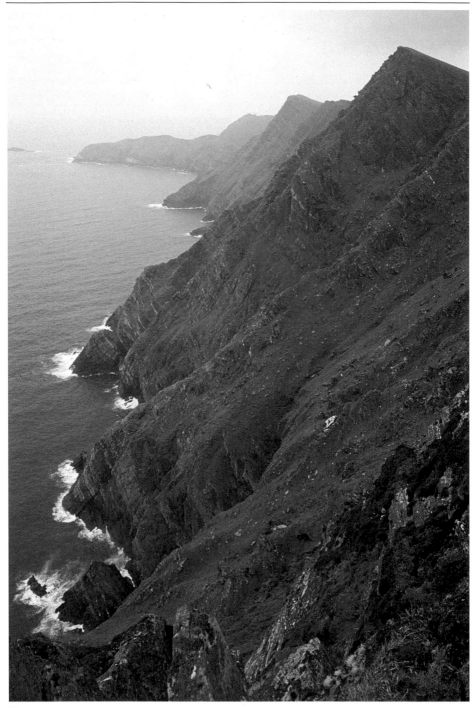

carnivores wave innocently atop leafless stems, while the carnage is conducted by leaves below.

The north coast is as different as can be from this insulating bog; here the landscape is clearly more specific and variegated, but wild too, and awesome in high winds and racing clouds. Much of it consists of cliffs, the grandest being Benwee Head in the county's north-west corner, but this is only visible in full splendour from the sea. (There are, of course, stupendous views from its summit.) There is a good walk from close to Porturlin harbour eastward to Belderg, after which the road runs along and sometimes almost next to the coast. The distinct trio of small islands known as the Stags of Broad Haven are a couple of miles out to sea. About halfway along the 10 or 11 miles (16 kilometres) of the walk, cliff-top positions give views of the island of Illanmastir where two thousand pairs of puffins nest and breed, one of the more important Irish colonies. With unquestionable wisdom, the Irish Wildbird Conservancy bars access, but no harm is done by a distant scrutiny with binoculars. The second, eastern half of the walk, with a couple of sweeping descents and the steep climb to Glinsk, is more dramatic than the first.

BEFORE YOU GO
Maps: OS Discovery Series map Nos 22, 23, 30 and 31.

GETTING THERE
By car: the Barony of Erris is bisected by and easily reached from the N59 from Ballina to Bangor.
By rail: Iarnrod Eireann run three services a day from Dublin Heuston to Ballina, the nearest station.
By bus: a Bus Eireann service runs from Ballina to Blacksod Point and stops at Belmullet. For local services enquire at the travel agent's on Main Street, Belmullet. Services run into Ballina from all over Ireland. Treacy's, T:(096) 70968, runs a daily service to Sligo, and Barton Transport, T:(01) 6286026, runs a daily service between Ballina and Dublin.

WHERE TO STAY
Hotels: there are quite a few bed and breakfasts on the main road approaching Belmullet,

including Mrs E. Cosgrove at Bangor Erris, T:(097) 83494, and plenty of hotels, guest-houses and bed and breakfasts scattered about, though there is a huge almost unpeopled area in the south of the barony. Among bed and breakfasts in and near Ballycastle are Hilltop House, T:(096) 43089, and Mrs B. Kelly, T:(096) 43288.
Youth hostels: there is an independent hostel at Bangor Erris, the Owenmore River Lodge, T:(097) 83477, situated south of Carrowmore lake.
Outdoor living: there is a camp-site in Crossmolina by Lough Conn.

ACTIVITIES
Walking: good walks can be had along the cliffs towards Ceide Fields. Walks across the moorland and in the mountains, including the Western Way, can stray miles from habitation and should not be undertaken lightly or alone.
Fishing: the River Oweniny is one of several good salmon rivers in the area.
Cycling: *Cycling Ireland*, from Bord Failte, suggests a route that takes in Ballina, Ballycastle and Belmullet, following the road along the coast.
Ecology: the Knockmoyle-

Sheskin Nature Reserve, north of the Bangor–Crossmolina road, is an area of lowland blanket bog with interesting flushes (no telephone). For further details contact National Parks and Wildlife Services, T:(01) 661 3111.

FURTHER INFORMATION
There are tourist information points at Ballycastle, T:(096) 43256, and Ballina, T:(096) 70848. Both these offices are open only during the summer.

From the cliffs beneath Croaghaun, Achill Island's second highest peak, knife-edge ridges continue north-west for nearly two miles (3 km) before tailing off beyond Little Saddle to the digital extremity of Achill Head.

The Mullet and Islands

Peninsula lying between the ocean and Blacksod Bay, with much sandy beach and machair on its western side and, off-shore, a number of uninhabited islands

The Mullet, a long thin peninsula hanging north to south from the mainland at Belmullet, has a rocky north-west coast with wintering and breeding bird-life. Nearby, areas of machair grassland and marsh provide the only breeding ground in Ireland for the red-necked phalarope. Most of the peninsula is windswept, treeless and largely cultivated, segmented by barbed wire and scattered with new bungalows. (This was once prime Bingham territory, as several place names suggest.) Further west are a number of islands of many shapes and sizes. On Inishglora, storm petrels nest on the stony beach. Inishkea North and South have been uninhabited since 1927 when storm-damage to the fishing fleet finally killed the traditional way of life. More seals breed here than elsewhere in Ireland, and barnacle geese (some 2,000 pairs) spend the winter, grazing on the rough grasses that proliferate over the windswept flats.

Reaching these and other islands is a matter of negotiating with fishermen, complicated nowadays by insurance considerations. There was no such thought ten, twenty and even fifty years ago, when the author of *The Once and Future King*, T.H. White, took a cottage on the Mullet and sailed from island to island looking for the magic image of St Mac Dara, thrown into the sea in the eighteenth century by a Catholic priest who believed it was encouraging idolatry.

The search took White to many islands because it had become inlaid with other islanders' accounts and with his own theories about fertility cults and phallic symbols. He did not discover the idol, which may for all I know remain where it was thrown, off St Mac Dara's Island, south Galway. But his inquiries brought him all kinds of knowledge about island beliefs and rituals, faith and religion, about Penal Days murders, about a giant's wife turned into a heron on Inishkea, about where to practise falconry and shoot geese or catch salmon, all of which he enjoyed. One night, on one of the islands, he came face to face with the Devil. It had a wicked face, horns, cloven feet. Of course, it turned out at dawn to be a particularly dark goat, innocently grazing, but the story White tells in his account of this quest, *The Godstone and the Blackymor*, is a wonderful evocation of the richness of life, history and tradition in islands which without such sources yield little of their past and can even seem to be hitherto untrodden by man.

Before you go *Maps:* OS Discovery Series map No. 22. **Getting there** *By car:* follow the R314 (west) from Ballina to join the R313. This leads north-west to Belmullet.

THE CHILDREN OF LIR

Lir was the god of the sea (related in myth to Shakespeare's King Lear) and by his first wife had three sons and a daughter. When his wife died he married her younger sister Aoife. She became the classically jealous stepmother. She took the children to Lough Derravaragh in County Longford and ordered a servant to kill them. When he refused she had them pushed into the lough and turned by magic into swans. (Men, women, gods and goddesses were often converted into birds in Irish myths, and birds were, for this reason, frequently protected by a ban on hunting or shooting.)

The swans were fated to spend 300 years of misery on the lake, 300 more on the waters of the Moyle (the icy strait below Fair Head, off the north coast of County Antrim) and a final 300 on the sea by Inishglora, west of the Mullet in County Mayo. Here they were at last restored to human form, only to die and be buried on the island. When he learned what his wife had done, Lir had Aoife turned into a wretched air spirit, to float homeless for the rest of time. The story is known as one of 'the three sorrowful tales of Ireland', a gross underestimate. Celtic gloom recurs constantly in the old literature.

The great Gaels of Ireland
   Are the men whom God made mad;
For all their wars were merry,
   And all their songs were sad.

By bus: Bus Eireann runs a local service from Blacksod Point to Ballina that stops at Belmullet.
By rail: The nearest station is in Ballina, where services run to Dublin Heuston.
Where to stay: there are a number of bed and breakfasts in Belmullet and several on the island, including Mrs Cafferty at Carne, T:(097) 81270. The nearest hostel and camping is at Owenmore River Lodge, T:(097) 83497.
Activities: there is sea angling around the coast; information from the Belmullet Sea Angling Club, T:(097) 81195.
Further information: the nearest tourist office is in Bangor. McIntyre's Travel in Belmullet also has local information, T:(097) 82199.

Nephin Beg

A tall, handsome range of peaks and lakes stretching from the sea at Clew Bay far into the boggy interior of Mayo

You can still stand within the southern half of the Barony of Erris and look to north, south, east and west without seeing any land-surface other than blanket bog. A hundred years ago, and for a hundred years before that, you would have seen people too: bent, undernourished people whose little smoky cabins, home also to any sheep or goats or pigs they were fortunate enough to possess, crowded many of the valleys and lower hillsides. The unmistakable patterns of the lazy beds they constructed are still evident on the most unlikely slopes. But there are no more people. The population which peaked in the 1840s just

'When the airs is warming, in four months or five, it's then yourself and me should be pacing Neifin in the dews of the night, the times sweet smells do be rising, and you'd see a little, shiny new moon, maybe, sinking on the hills.'

J. M. Synge, The Playboy of the Western World

before the great famines, slumped, then rose, teetered at an impossibly high level for the rest of the nineteenth century and finally drained away to almost nothing in the twentieth.

This is the bleakest, barest, most brooding, most haunting countryside in Ireland, occupying about 400 sq miles (1,000 sq km) of plain from the centre of which rises the great Nephin Beg range: Slieve Car, Nephin Beg itself, Birreencorragh and the outlying Nephin, isolated and shapely across the valley of the River Crumpaun. Not that the bog has been left alone by meddling man. In the middle of the plain, north of Nephin Beg, the power station of Bellacorick has devoured miles of peat for the generation of electricity. What is left behind is an earth-scar which will last years. There are big forestry plantations of dull monotone evergreens. Around the base of Nephin Beg, they create quite a barrier to those wishing to climb the mountain.

The bog itself, of course, was probably man's doing, at least in part created by the wholesale tree-fellings carried out by Neolithic settlers. But that seems long enough ago to be sanctioned now as natural, certainly long enough to have attracted its own flora and fauna: black bog rush, bog asphodel, purple moor grass, cross-leaved heath and several other grasses and sedges, mosses and liverworts. Cotton-grass and white-beaked sedge are staple foods for the

Greenland white-fronted geese and also for golden plovers, merlins – the smallest of falcons, precision killers – meadow pipits, skylarks, snipe and many other birds.

The Nephin Beg mountains are of quartzite, heated to its present obdurate consistency by the same volcanic turbulence that created the Scottish Highlands and the mountains of Donegal. Resistance to erosion has given them a clear, sharp outline, and their silhouettes are impressive from most angles. Closer in, they offer good walks and climbs, with a number of icy lake-filled

The merlin is found all over Ireland, a small falcon that can fly close to the ground over lowland bog and (in summer) over high mountain with equal facility, snatching small birds from their perches or chasing them with uncannily accurate, twist-and-turn dexterity.

corries, tumbling streams and modest waterfalls. From their heights mighty panoramic views open out over the upland plains of Mayo, the distant line of the Ox mountains, Achill island and its massy peaks, Clew Bay with its shoals of drumlins, innumerable islands, the sculpted peaks of Connemara and the unbounded, hemming Atlantic. Robert Lloyd Praeger, considering the bare brown heather of these mountains, found them 'not lonely or depressing but inspiriting. You are thrown at the same time back upon yourself and forward against the mystery and majesty of nature, and you may feel dimly something of your own littleness and your own greatness.' It has to be said, in spite of this, that Tony Whilde and others who know the range well sound less than inspired by their climbs. There are,

moreover, dangers in hiking in parts which can be ten or more miles from the nearest tarred road. Sizeable patches of bright green sphagnum moss may indicate hidden pools, which can give way with dangerous consequences. Although tracks cross the range here and there, it would be rash to make a long lone foray into this territory. **Before you go** *Maps:* OS Discovery Series maps Nos 23, 30 and 31. **Getting there** *By car:* from Westport the N59 goes north and follows the coast of Clew Bay. The mountains lie to the north. *By rail:* several services a day from Dublin Heuston stop at Foxford and Castlebar, the nearest stations, and Ballina. *By bus:* Bus Eireann runs plenty of services to Ballina. A Bus Eireann Expressway service stops once a day at Foxford on its way from Ballina to Cork; another runs from Dooagh to Cork, stopping

at Pontoon. **Where to stay** *Hotels:* Mountainview Hotel, Foxford, T:(094) 26242. There are bed and breakfasts in and near Mallaranny, Ballycroy, Newport and Castlebar. *Outdoor living:* Hiney's Caravan and Camping Park, T:(096) 31262, at Crossmolina. Carrowkeel Caravan and Camping Park at Ballyvarry, outside Castlebar, T:(094) 31264. **Activities** *Walking:* the Nephins are not suitable for lone walking. *Fishing:* Lough Conn is a world-famous brown trout lake, open Apr–June. The Pontoon Bridge Hotel, Co. Mayo, has a purpose-built fly-fishing school and runs residential courses, T:(094) 5612015. *Cycling:* bikes can be hired from Robinson's in Castlebar, T:(094) 21355. **Further information:** the tourist office at Castlebar is open May–Sept, T:(094) 21207.

Achill Island

A large remote island, its central flat-lands densely inhabited, its coastal periphery rising, especially on the west and south-west, to huge and spectacular walls of cliff

Achill, Ireland's largest island, is only 20 feet (6 metres) away from the mainland. Indeed Ireland and Achill are joined by a bridge. (When the first bridge was constructed in 1888, foxes crossed over and islanders found it necessary to protect their poultry.) To get to this island you have to pass the stony hem of Corraun, a mountain which is all but an island itself, attached to the mainland for a short half-mile or so just to the west of Mallaranny.

West of the Mweelrea Mountains, and south of Killadoon, broad white beaches alternate with massive sand dunes. At mid-afternoon, the water's edge on this strand beneath Mweelrea is at least 400 to 500 yds (350–450 m) out from the shoreline.

The southern coast road to Achill has the best views. If you can judge mountains, as they say you can people, by the company they keep, then both Corraun and Achill are sensational. The haze that so often rises off the water of Clew Bay colours each distant plane a slightly different shade of blue, and it is these degrees of distinction, as well as the variety, stature and shapes of the features seen, that makes progress such a pleasure. A slow sweep of the view from Corraun takes in the slant backs of the drumlin islands cluttering Clew Bay, the faded blue of the distant Partry mountains, the darker cone of Croagh Patrick, the hazily withdrawn Sheefry hills, the huge shadowy wraith of Mweelrea and many other slopes, cones and curves of the Mayo and Galway mountains. Looming from the Atlantic as you round the coast comes the crouching sphinx of Clare Island, paws and head to the right, rising rump and long extended tail to the left. Then the road turns away, up the narrow sound to Achill bridge.

Another reason for enjoying the distant view is that when you come close things may

From the coast below Mweelrea the sea stretches westward, shallow but deepening, to a scatter of islands, a long curving projection of the mainland west of Killary Harbour and 3,000 miles of ocean.

not be all you expected. Achill once personified the deprived west. Before and after the famine too many people tried to live off a frugal crop of oats and potatoes. The exploitation of the one rich resource, fish, was far from thorough, though basking sharks (unfortunately for themselves, perhaps, not aggressive to humans) were netted for their oil, off Keem Bay. Before the famine, at a time when corn was still ground between stones, an Anglican missionary picked on the island to undertake a mass conversion of Catholics to his own faith. He built a settlement for the converts, acquired more than half the island's land and laboured restlessly, providing school, orphanage, printing works at Doogort, and a colony of homes on the slopes behind. Not for the first or last time in Irish history religions confronted each other. The Catholics, put on their mettle, began to match the mission's innovations and slowly recouped their

West Mayo

0 — 5 — 10miles
0 — 5 — 10 — 15Km.

Key
- - - Footpath.
▭ Exploration zone.
▲ Points of interest.

STAGS OF
BROAD HAVEN

Benwee Head ▲   Illanmastir   Belderg   Minaun   Downpatrick Head
                                              Harbour
                    Portulrin
        Broad   Harbour
        Haven   Glinsk
                                                      R314   Ballycastle
THE   Belderg
MULLET   Bellmullet
                    R314   R314
INISHGLORA   Barony of Erris
                    Carrowmore   Knockmoyle   R315
                    Lough   Sheskin
                    R313   ▲ Nature
                              Reserve
INISHKEA NORTH   Bangor
INISHKEA   Owenmbre
SOUTH   Crossmolina   Ballina
              Blacksod   Deel
              Bay   R316   R315
                                    Nephin Beg   Lough
        Slievemore Doogort   ▲ Nephin   Conn
Croaghaun   Dooagh   Beg   to
Achill Head ▲   R319   Nephin   Foxford
Moyteoge Head Keem Bay Keel Achill   Derreen
        Cathedral Rocks Island   Glen Nephin ▲   Pontoon
              R319   R317
        Achill Sound   Lough
              Corraun   Feeagh
              Mtn
        Corraun   Mallaranny   Furnace Lough   R312
        Peninsula   Newport   R311
        Mallaranny   Bay   Newport   Castlebar   N60
        and   R311
        Clew Bay Westport   Carramolly   N60   Manulla
CLARE ISLAND   Bay   Westport
        Ferry   R335   Westport   N59
        Louisburgh
                    Croagh ▲ Murrisk
                    Patrick Croagh   Western Way
INISHTURK   Patrick
        Killadoon
              Killadoon
INISHBOFIN   Sheeffry Hills
        Doo Lough   Mweelrea
        Pass   Mtns   Partry Mtns
        Mweelrea Mtns   Ben
        Killary   Gorm   Lough
        Harbour   Mask
INISHSHARK

---

losses. The Anglican colony is now a small ghost town, and philanthropy has turned to commerce. Thus the impression given by the three main centres, Dooagh, Keel and Doogort, is one of a rather brash prosperity. Roads that were almost impassable earlier this century are smartly tarred. The race on now is to win not souls but tourists. To this end, they have a few magnificent natural assets.

Achill, like much of the rest of west Mayo, consists largely of quartzite and schists, rocks that were chemically converted or baked by the convulsions of 400 to 500 million years ago into a hardness that stubbornly and more successfully than other rocks resists many of the attempts of wind and particularly water to erode it. Sudden, distinctly shaped mountains break from the Achill plain. The west-facing Cathedral Rocks and the nearby Menawn cliffs rise sheer out of the sea on the island's southern edge to a height of 1,500 feet (450 metres) and, when a rich red sun sets over the Atlantic ocean, they reflect its light in a rosy twilight glow of incredible beauty.

Slievemore (2,204 feet/672 metres), on the

north coast above Doogort, is the island's highest summit. The climb from Doogort is quite steep but follows a simple route and provides, of course, dazzling views of coast, mountains, ocean and islands. At the western tip of Achill, beyond Keem Bay, where amethysts produced by chemical action at the time of the great convulsions are often found, the land rises to one of those sights best seen from the sea: the broad face of dramatic cliffs under Croaghaun (2,192 feet/668 metres). But here the landward features are themselves among the finest natural scenes in Ireland. The slant of the land in parts suggests a board, heavily weighted in the middle, that has cracked, so that one of its halves has risen steeply to a great height. Its edge is narrow, even at times sharp, with the supporting cliffs dropping vertically away below. The knife-sharp ridge of the Little Saddle tails off to Achill Head on the western extremity. Among the heady uplands north-east of Croaghaun, a number of lakes appear, one of them, Lough Bunnafreeva, almost teetering on the edge of the cliffs. This whole western range offers a wealth of scenery but also real danger from the precipitous angle of cliffs. The sea eagle, which was described as common in the early nineteenth century, had gone by the beginning of the twentieth. But the rest of the outward views from heights which are not easy to reach are, quite simply, as beautiful and inspiring as any in Ireland.

BEFORE YOU GO
Maps: OS Discovery Series map No. 30.
Guidebooks: *The New Irish Walk Guides: West and North* by Whilde and Simms (Gill & Macmillan, 1991) covers the cliff-top walk which takes in Achill Head and Croaghaun.

GETTING THERE
By car: from Westport follow the N59 (north-west) to Mallaranny, then take the minor road (south) which runs along Clew Bay, curving north to Achill Sound.
By rail: the nearest station is Westport where daily services run from Dublin Heuston.
By bus: a once-daily Bus Eireann Expressway service from Dooagh to Belfast stops at Achill Sound, while a local Bus Eireann service from Dooagh to Ballina stops at Achill Sound five times daily in summer and three times in winter. In summer a local Bus Eireann service runs from Westport to Achill Sound.

WHERE TO STAY
Hotels: there is quite a large selection of bed and breakfasts and hotels. For self-catering contact Bord Failte's reservation service for the West of Ireland, T:(091) 63081.
Youth hostels: the Wild Haven Hostel, T:(098) 45392, is close to Achill Sound. In Keel, there is the Wayfarer, T:(098) 43266.
Outdoor living: Alice's Harbour Inn, near the bridge in Achill Sound, has camping next door. Lavelle's Golden Strand Caravan and Camping Park, T:(098) 47232, Seal Caves Caravan Park, T:(098) 43262, are on the island's north coast at Dugort. Keel Sandybanks Camping Park, is by the beach at Keel, T:(098) 32054.

ACTIVITIES
Walking: the highest peak is Slievemore and there are magnificent views from the summit. The walk can be reached from behind deserted Slievemore village. At the western end of the island, a ridge-back trail runs from Moyteoge Head to Achill Head (see Guidebooks entry above).
Climbing: there are routes on

Up to 30 ft (10 m) long, and one of the world's largest fishes, the basking shark is a resident of Irish as of most temperate seas. Capable of raising itself out of the water – it weighs up to four tons – it is harmless to man, surviving on a diet of sieved plankton.

Slievemore (2,204 ft/672 m).
Hang-gliding: hang-gliding is
available from the top of
Minaun.
Cycling: bikes can be hired
from the Achill Sound Hotel,
T:(098) 45245.

FURTHER INFORMATION
Tourist offices: there is a tourist
office at Alice's Harbour Inn,
Achill Sound, T:(098) 45384,
which is open July–Aug. There
is an activity centre just after
the Esso Garage near Keel,
where more information is
available on wind-surfing, rock-
climbing and hang-gliding,
T:(098) 47253.

With its slates glistening in the
rain, an abandoned cottage adds
a touch of melancholy to the road
leading north from wooded Delphi.
Ahead lie Doo Lough and the
Sheefry hills.

Furnace Lough

*A small lake in bumpy,
hillocky country, rich in
salmon and home of the
Salmon Research Trust of
Ireland*

Just to the north of the eastern
part of Clew Bay, a narrow
road leads off the main
Newport–Achill road. It takes
you quickly into a charming
little toytown lakeland,
climbing steeply, diving
precipitately, curving round
some rather hectic bends with,
feet away, drops of say 20 ft (6
m) and enough water at the
bottom to dunk a fair-sized car
in. The land between the lakes
is very rocky, supporting some
bracken, more heather and a
few diminutive trees. Suddenly,

if you take the right turns and
omit the wrong ones, you are at
Burrishoole Fishery, with
Lough Feeagh above, Furnace
Lough below, and the Salmon
Research Agency of Ireland
beside you.

Anglers come here for fish,
advice, information, and
various related services.
Germans come to restock the
Rhine, from which a quarter of
a million salmon might have
been fished a century ago but
which by the 1940s contained
none. In a most sportsmanlike
manner salmon continue to
come, in spite of the danger of
being caught in nets at sea, or
on the end of a line, legitimate
or otherwise, in rivers. The
Agency monitors numbers and
condition of salmon
throughout the country, and at
present is carrying out a
programme of restocking the
waters of Connemara. In fact,

all matters relating to salmon (and to a lesser extent trout and sea trout and other game fish) are subjects of the agency's active concern.

In spite of the management, restocking, monitoring and analysis, salmon remain an ingredient of wild Ireland. They follow a hazardous and still mysterious life-cycle, breeding in, and greatly enhancing, the value of many Irish rivers. Those of us who do not fish can be well educated by the agency's presentations, displays, aquaria and video, and are welcome to call during the summer months.

Before you go *Maps*: OS Discovery Series map No. 31. **Getting there** *By car*: the N59 from Westport runs past the lough and along Clew Bay. *By rail*: the nearest station is at Westport, where services run from Dublin Heuston three times a day. *By bus*: there are Bus Eireann services to Westport from Galway and Ballina. An Expressway service from Westport passes quite close to the lake and stops at Newport, as does a local Bus Eireann service from Dooagh to Ballina. **Where to stay**: among local bed and breakfasts are Mrs Leneghan, T:(098) 41202, and Nephin View, T:(098) 41481, both near Newport. There is an An Oige hostel, Traenlur Lodge, T:(098) 41358, above Lough Feeagh. **Activities**: bikes can be hired from Skerdagh Outdoor Centre, T:(098) 41647. Newport is good for fishing; Mary, T:(098) 41562, and Pat, T:(098) 41265, will organize angling trips. The Western Way runs nearby. **Further information**: available from a Portacabin, T:(098) 41116, and on Main Street, Newport, T:(098) 41895.

Wild salmon occur in rivers and lakes throughout Ireland, surviving nets, traps and skilled fly-fishers on their way to spawn in the rivers' upper reaches.

Croagh Patrick

One of the West's most distinctive landmarks, the quartzite peak draws crowds of pilgrims in late July (and other months), offering fabulous views of land, ocean and archipelago

Places which in other countries might be considered wild beyond argument may, in Ireland, be tamed and regulated for human purposes. The bleak islands in Donegal's Lough Derg and the storm-torn summit of Kerry's Mount Brandon were long ago adopted for religious purposes, a cairn or chapel raised on them like a territorial flag, and a regular pilgrimage established. Croagh Patrick (usually called the Reek) is the most famous and popular of such mountains. The path up it has been worn by the passage of millions of feet. All the same, this is not some rural equivalent of the department-store escalator. It is steep, exposed and, towards the top, a little dangerous.

In the past, pilgrims in their thousands climbed by night on the last Sunday of July to celebrate a festival with pre-Christian roots. They carried burning torches; when they reached the top – which consists not of the conical point you are led to expect from below but a half-acre plateau on which stands a small chapel – they walked long penitential circuits on the bare rock on their knees. But these traditions have been discontinued, and the main pilgrimage is officially confined to the daytime; for good or ill

the world has lost that annual night spectacle, a line of glimmering light moving upward, whatever the weather, in a harsh, backward (as it quite recently was) and remote territory of mountain and sea. It can still be hard, and, with wind or rain beating in from the Atlantic, seem desolate and hostile. To make it harder, some of the pilgrims still go barefoot.

Croagh Patrick occupies another key place in the story of wild Ireland. St Patrick, in the course of converting the country to Christianity in the fifth century, retired to this mountain, close to the probable site of his boyhood slavery, to spend the forty days and nights of Lent. During this time he summoned, by divine power, all the more noxious and repellent beasts of Ireland to the mountain and persuaded them to drop to their deaths down the sheer southern side. The result being that Ireland to this day has no snakes. Nor, for that matter, does it have any wild cats or moles.

Biologists explain things otherwise. Ireland's animals arrived from Britain after the retreat of the ice by means of a surviving land connection. Some were too slow, or failed to cross for other reasons. Of these some have since been introduced by man, not least those prizes of Lakeland, bream, rudd, pike and possibly perch. The status of frogs is argued about. The frog bones found among prehistoric remains in Sligo could, it seems, belong to animals which slipped through at a much later period. They are thought to have been released at Trinity College at the end of the seventeenth century. Of toads, only the natterjack exists in Ireland, in County Kerry and a few other places. They were introduced. Ireland possesses

only one reptile, the common lizard.

It has not, so far as I know, been suggested that the view from the summit went to the holy man's head, though it would not be surprising if it had. Clew Bay lies below, with its packed school of drumlins appearing to swim out from the inner shore. To the south are the Sheefry Hills and some of the Connemara Bens rearing up behind, while to the north, over the water, are the impressive peaks of Achill, Corraun and the Nephin Beg range. You do not necessarily require Christian convictions to find a spiritual boost here.

Before you go *Maps*: OS Discovery Series maps Nos 30, 37 and 38.

Getting there *By car*: from Westport take the R35 (west) to Murrisk, which lies below Croagh Patrick.

By rail: services from Dublin Heuston to Westport approximately three times a day.

By bus: there are plenty of services to and from Westport;

One of the plants whose tripartite leaves are worn as shamrock on St Patrick's Day, the lesser trefoil is a yellow-flowered relation of clover which grows commonly among grass from May to September.

SHAMROCK

As Irish as a harp, good luck or a pint of Guinness, the shamrock is also a mystery. St Patrick is said to have used its leaf to explain the three-in-one, one-in-three nature of the Holy Trinity, and the Irish put it in their buttonholes on 17 March, St Patrick's Day. However, plants displayed in this way may belong to any of several different species and there is no universal agreement on the correct one. The claims of several members of the pea family (*Leguminosae*) are well supported as are those of the white clover (*Trifolium repens*) and lesser yellow trefoil (*Trifolium dubium*), another clover, with small yellow flowers. A hundred years ago a collection of plants used as shamrocks and drawn from several counties produced, in addition to those already mentioned, red clover (*Trifolium pratense*), spotted medick (*Medicago arabica*), black medick (*Medicago lupulina*), watercress (*Nasturtium officinale*), wood sorrel (*Oxalis acetosella*) and several others.

The Irish word *seamrog* means clover, without distinguishing which of the closely related clovers, medicks or trefoils this might be. (A similar Arabic word is said to have the same broad definition.) Its use is not recorded, anyway, earlier than 1571. Seventeenth-century English writers often refer to shamrock as an important part of the Irish diet, and some call it bitter, which is true of wood sorrel but not of the rest. But many such writers were keen to dispossess or eliminate the Irish, and could be wildly inaccurate when holding forth about their nature and ways. To complicate the issue, many Irish claim the shamrock does not flower. It almost certainly does, but not, in all probability, by 17 March. After that date interest in it quickly wanes.

The incentive to pin shamrock down to one species comes from its place as a national emblem, which in turn stems from the link with St Patrick. It is, of course, possible that the saint used several of the plants mentioned, since the leaves of all of them are divided into three and would have served his purpose. However, since the Patrick connection is not mentioned in writing or print before 1727, in spite of numerous lives of the saint having appeared during the previous thousand years, it may be that the account is a late invention. On the other hand, clovers and trefoils had interesting reputations long before Patrick. Four-leafed clover could (and still perhaps can) help you discover treasure. The clubs of playing cards take their design from the trefoil. Pliny, writing in the first century AD, says that snakes never go anywhere near trefoils, and that the plant can be used to heal the stings of snakes and scorpions. This account predates Patrick by four centuries but nevertheless leads us straight back to him: the saint is, of course, famous for expelling snakes from Ireland. Possibly his association with the shamrock is thus explained. Specific identification remains impossible, though. Pliny does not help. And if you look closely at Irish buttonholes next 17 March you will doubtless see the mix as before.

In the North, by the way, and with neat Northern irony, the phrase 'shamrock tea' means weak tea. It tastes, the inference is, like tea brewed with no more than three leaves.

---

a local service to Louisburgh stops at Murrisk near Croagh Patrick.

Where to stay: there are a lot of bed and breakfasts and a few hotels in Westport, including Castlecourt, T:(098) 25444, Westport Woods, T:(098) 25811, and Grand Central, T:(098) 25027. There is a hostel, Club Atlantic, T:(098) 26644, and a few independent hostels in the area. Camping is available at the Club Atlantic Hostel; at Parkland Caravan and Camping Park, Westport, T:(098) 25141; and at the Old Head Forest Caravan and Camping Park, T:(098) 66021, quite near Louisburgh, just past Croagh Patrick.

Activities: sea angling is available in Clew Bay; for more information contact the Sea Angling Centre in Westport, T:(098) 25481/25182. Trails begin at Campbells Pub at Murrisk. Bikes can be hired from the Club Atlantic Hostel, T:(098) 26644, or from Breheny Bike Hire, Castlebar Street, Westport. The Bord Failte publication *Cycling Ireland* has a suggested route that runs south from Westport to Galway and back along the coast.

Further information: the nearest Bord Failte tourist office is in Westport, T:(098) 25711.

Killadoon

*Leading nowhere in particular, the road
down the west of the Barony of Murrisk
passes delightful seascapes and broad
beaches of white sand*

It was a place that invited deep speculation.
I sat on a rock and wondered what it would
be like to be a meat-eating animal stuck to
the floor waiting in vain for animals that you
wanted and needed to eat to enter your
mouth without compulsion. How would it
feel to function best submerged in salt water
and spend half your time – half of each day
– all but out of water, in the air, and much of
the rest of your day tantalizingly pummelled
and sluiced, as the tide went in and out, by
licks of water from which there was no
chance of extracting anything to eat at all.
This, it seemed from looking at it, was the
essential daily cycle of the small beadlet sea
anemone (*Actinia equina*), as it remained in
its rock pool assaulted by the flow and ebb
of the tide. Some anemones stayed open, the
pretty tassels that fringe their dark recesses
waving when there was water to wave in.
Others closed up and looked like wet
conkers, as if they were rather sniffily refusing to join in the waves' game.

There was no limit to the number of
things to be looked at on Killadoon beach.
The rock I was on was like a large vessel, 30
yards (27 metres) across, set in a sea of shining white sand. Its surface was pocked with
little pools, ranging in width from a few
inches to several feet across. The rock was a
grey limestone but it was mostly covered
with thin coats and stains of black and
yellow lichens, themselves obscured by
thousands of barnacles which collectively
had the texture of coarse sandpaper. Sprays
of seaweed of various kinds, innumerable
clusters of small mussels, from bead size to
about an inch across, colonies of limpets and
many varieties of shellfish filled in almost

The steep southern flank of Mweelrea mountain,
valued as a tough hike by climbers, stands bright in
the evening sunlight, above the creek of Killary
Harbour.

any available space. Terns flew about; a lone razorbill dived repeatedly a hundred yards out to sea. In the pools little fish darted into crevices when any shadow crossed the water.

I imagine anyone could spend the four hours or so that I did in such a scene, under a warm sun, watching the destinies of other beasts and plants played out, naming, identifying, theorizing, glowing with the entertainment and the warmth. Of course, my island in the sand became, as I watched and dreamed, an island in the incoming sea, but this was not to be a case for the air-sea rescue people. It was solved by the removal of shoes and socks, and the rolling-up of trousers and a pleasant paddle across to dry land. The sea almost followed me in, because the sand is very flat and the beach nearly half a mile across.

Killadoon beach lies towards the end of a road down the south-west coast of County Mayo, from Louisburgh to a point close to the opening of Killary Harbour, inaccessible here because the mountain drops flush into the water. The day I was there – in May – hardly anyone else was. There are other huge strands along the way – Gobis of warm white sand. On the other side of the road the Mweelrea mountains appear to present a soft lap into which to climb. North of the beaches is an isolated hotel – of no pretension, and pleasant – at Killadoon.

That evening I walked down to the sea past an inland lake in the middle of which is

Between Doo Lough and Sheefry Wood, a peat cutter digs winter fuel in the time-honoured Irish way, watched by his dog. Extraction on this scale is insignificant beside commercial exploitation of boglands for fertilizer and electricity generation.

a round island perhaps 30 feet (9 metres) across. On it were about 200 breeding terns, their number leavened by a few gulls. Here again, in spite of midges, was entertainment for an hour or two, for the terns had created the atmosphere of a barracks bathroom. Raucous gargles, belches, raspberries and fouler noises are pure tern, and when I went on to the beach there they were – two or three of them – buzzing and harrying me, like yapping terriers, to get me away. It shows the troubadour in me that I cannot reconcile these loudmouths' noisiness with their grace and beauty, like that of swifts made wholly white.

BEFORE YOU GO
Maps: OS Discovery Series map No. 37.

GETTING THERE
By car: from Westport follow the R335 (west) to Louisburgh. A minor road travels along the coast from Louisburgh to Killadoon.
By rail: the nearest station is in Westport, where services run to and from Dublin Heuston.
By bus: a local Bus Eireann service runs from Westport to Louisburgh and Killadoon, twice a day (Monday-Sat only).

WHERE TO STAY
There is a hotel at Killadoon, the Beach Hotel, T:(098) 68605; Mrs C. Heneghan offers bed and breakfast T:(098) 68730.
Camping is available at the Old Head Forest Camping and Caravan Park, Louisburgh, T:(098) 66021.

ACTIVITIES
There are plenty of walks along the empty sandy beaches.

FURTHER INFORMATION
The nearest tourist office is in Westport, T:(098) 25711.

Mallaranny and Clew Bay

The hump backs of drumlins crowd the eastern end of Clew Bay. Pleasant resorts cling to the land between sea and mountain

There is a Homeric grandeur to this wild west coast. Yet I choose with special affection an unremarkable village, a cosy and *déclassé* resort, stretched along a road too main for comfort, with two supermarkets, two garages and a huge hotel which, when I was last there (and following a change of ownership) was grotesquely empty, the glass in its ground-floor windows painted white, its extensive gardens turning to jungle.

In part, what appeals is nostalgia for an age and its ways; not my own ways, but missed all the same. In part it is what remains. Memory brings back annual family holidays of Irish and English at the Great Southern Hotel, with the railway itself just behind, or in rented houses; nannies and a maid or two brought along with the luggage. There were expeditions to the beach, to Achill, Newport and Westport, but mostly a routine of eating, sleeping, games and bathing, to ease which, a causeway had been built for passage from the hotel's ornamental lower gardens, over the extensive flats and dunes left by the ebbing tide, to the bathing beach.

The causeway is there, and the beach, and the dunes and acres of sand, covered twice daily by the tide; and the views across Clew Bay to the flotilla of motionless green porpoises – which are, of course, partly submerged drumlins – facing out to sea from Westport. I do not suppose the birds have changed either. The coastline lurches drunkenly with bays and inlets, and much of the shore is marshy and reedy. There are swans, terns, oystercatchers, ringed plovers, dunlins and the rest; the usual cheery, perky complement of companions for a beach walk. There is a woolly yellow moss that colours patches of sand and dune on which brent geese feed when they arrive for the winter, having

bred and summered on the tundra and estuaries of the Arctic. I have stood on the beach watching, and for bouts of a minute or two being watched by, a seal every time I have been to Mallaranny.

Everything that man did grandly is slowly falling away and decaying or being replaced, if at all, by tat. Perhaps the result is a little advance for nature – certainly trees are moving up the hill behind the hotel. Dissolution, birds, jungle greenery, the distant scrutiny of Croagh Patrick and the rest of its mountain brethren over the bay, and the twice-daily surge and retreat of the tide over the half-mile of almost level sand: all these make the place curiously irresistible for me. It is an enthusiasm in which I expect no support at all.

Before you go *Maps*: OS Discovery Series maps Nos 30 and 31.

Getting there *By car*: from Westport follow the N59 (north) round Clew Bay and on to Mallaranny.

By rail: the nearest station is in Westport, where services run from Dublin Heuston.

By bus: a local Bus Eireann service from Westport to Achill Sound stops at Mallaranny three times a day.

Where to stay: bed and breakfasts include Moynish, T:(098) 36116, and Breezemount, T:(098) 36145. There is a camp-site just outside Westport, the Parkland Camping and Caravan Park, T:(098) 25141. There are also a few camp-sites on Achill Island.

Activities: deep-sea angling is available in Clew Bay and walkers will find good routes along beaches, inland or on the Corraun peninsula and Achill Island.

Further information: available in Main Street, Newport, T:(098) 41895.

Mweelrea Mountains

Few roads penetrate the interior of the Mweelrea mountains, a grand volcanic range marking the southern boundary of County Mayo

The north of County Mayo is to a large (though unfortunately lessening) extent a roadless bog. The south-west of the county is an expansive range of almost roadless mountain. It comprises the Mweelrea mountains, Sheefry hills and Ben Gorm, three groups of immense inner beauty, any of which well repays the trouble of climbing. You will not see them otherwise. Distances are, for Ireland, long, and the boggy ground is often wet and always uneven. Care is advised in both the planning and execution of any long-distance walk.

Even the car-bound visitor who crosses this region from north to south will see some enchanting scenes. The road from Louisburgh to Leenaun cuts down between the Mweelreas on the west and the other two groups on the east. The northern part of this road-valley has a great and almost Scottish appeal, recalling the brooding broadness of the west Highland glens. The side of Mweelrea is sheer, much of it rock-grey with runnels and slipways of scree. Chutes of rock must often slide into the long low pouch containing Doo Lough. Steepness on all sides puts a heavy emphasis on falling, descent, precipitation. Gravity becomes an almost palpable feature of the landscape.

But just to the south comes the pretty oasis of Delphi,

named early in the nineteenth century by a young Marquess of Sligo whose lands, based in Westport, included most of this region, and who put a fishing lodge here. Now there is an adventure centre. Still further south, at Bundorragha, the road turns left short of Killary Harbour, a long deep inlet of ten miles by perhaps a half: the sunken channel of the River Erriff, which divides the Sheefry hills from the Partry mountains. From the north shore (not accessible by car) one of several routes up Mweelrea begins. You can also start from Delphi or Bundorragha, or indeed anywhere else on the perimeter, though some approaches call for rock-climbing skills. All ways take several hours because of the distances involved. You want to be sure the weather is settled and

that there is time enough and more before dark. Mweelrea is the highest mountain in the province of Connacht, which includes Connemara, and the views from the top are superb. It also has comforting, rather human contours, reminiscent of knees, a hollow chest, a lap.

Before you go *Maps*: OS Discovery Series map No. 37.

Getting there *By car*: from Westport follow the R335 (west) to Louisburgh and then south along Doo Lough Pass, along the east of the Mweelrea mountains.

By rail: the nearest station is at Westport, where services run from Dublin Heuston about three times a day. The journey time is about four hours.

By bus: Bus Eireann runs services to Westport and Louisburgh. Between the two

towns there is a service three times a day.

Where to stay: the Delphi Lodge, T:(095) 42211, is a fine hotel whose guests can fish several miles of river and lake. There are several bed and breakfasts at Leenaun, and one at Bundorragha, close to Killary Harbour and the Mweelrea mountains, the Ben Gorm Farmhouse, T:(095) 42205. There is camping near Louisburgh at the Old Head Forest Caravan and Camping Park, T:(098) 66021/66022.

Activities: water-skiing, wind-surfing and sea angling can all be enjoyed at Clew Bay. The Mweelrea mountains may be climbed from Delphi or from Killary Harbour.

Further information: the nearest Bord Failte tourist office is in Westport, T:(098) 35711.

Connemara Highlands

Wild and ancient region of bog and fish-rich river and lake, dominated by the central range of the Twelve Bens and surrounded by a jagged, varied coastline and countless islands of great beauty

Connemara is mountain, lake and electro-encephalographically ragged coastline. It is quite short on roads, so that a tour by car or bicycle follows one of a limited number of routes. It has marvellous beaches in such plenty that for much of the year it is easy to get out to yourself (though often enough someone fond of company will settle, a few minutes after you do, within yards). Beyond the shore, within and without the many big bays, lies a confetti of islands. In the middle of the region rise the hard, rocky slopes of the Twelve Bens, some bare, some peaty. These are arranged in the form of a mauled starfish with Benbaun rising to 2,395 feet (729 metres) at the hub, and the other eleven peaks distributed along the five ridges.

As so often in the new Ireland, you can no longer be sure of getting where you want from any point on the road because of the spread of barbed wire across the countryside. Still, you can get on to the Bens from little penetrating lanes and tracks, and there are some good, if taxing, mountain walks and very challenging climbs. Much of the ground is bare rock or stony scree. There are danger-ous cliffs but the Bens lack the high lakes that feature attractively in surrounding ranges. At the head of Glen Inagh, according to Tony Whilde, co-author of *The New Irish Walks Guide* (see page 216), are some of the longest rock climbs in Ireland.

If the uplands are short of lakes the periphery of the Bens is not. In parts it is moated: on the east by wood-fringed Loughs Inagh and Derryclare which divide the Twelve Bens from the Maumturk mountains and the plum-pudding peak of Knock-nahillion, and on the south by the lovely Ballynahinch lake. The MP Richard Martin built his grand home (now a hotel) on the banks of Ballynahinch; he also helped found what later became the Royal Society for the Prevention of Cruelty to Animals. Martin could boast of being able to walk the thirty miles to Galway without straying from his own land. Kylemore lake lies along the north rim of the Bens, overlooked on its northwestern edge by Kylemore Castle, a nineteenth-century Gothic affair lushly wreathed in rhododendron, fuchsia and good trees. The mountain behind the castle, Doughruagh (1,736 feet/529 metres), offers a steep, circular, bracing walk that can be over in two and a half hours, and fine views of mountain, sea and islands. There are, incidentally, lakes high in this small range in which insects – certain diving beetles, *Dytiscus* species, water-boatmen and others – have lived an isolated life since the Arctic conditions which originally suited them prevailed in postglacial times.

West of Kylemore two or three miles, and outside the village of Letterfrack, is what is called the Connemara National Park, rather less than ten square miles of land conserved to standards which would ideally apply to the whole region. The inevitable 'centre' shows a film and stages an exhibition which introduce the history and ecology of the area, telling of the eras which followed the

Ice Ages, and of the emergence of the flora and fauna to be found there. It also delves into the origins and growth of peat, shows the bird and plant life dependent on it, and the few scattered parts of our planet in which it is to be found. In Ireland, we learn, during the present century, more than 80 per cent of the peat, which has been five thousand years in the making, has so far been destroyed.

Out of doors there is a choice of nature trails, the higher of which may be extended to a climb up Diamond Hill (1,460 feet/445 metres). A useful guide points out the kind of birds, animals and plants which may be seen here and, of course, in the region at large. A feature which might puzzle travellers new to the West, and which, once understood, brings the historical past closer than any other survival, is the series of faintly separated vertical ridges running along the bases, and sometimes higher levels, of hillsides. These bear the quite unjustified name of 'lazy beds'. I do not know of ghosts more evocative than these faint ridge-and-furrow sites where hard-driven cabin-dwellers of one and two and more centuries ago, on slopes far too steep for anyone today to think of

BOG TYPES

Raised bogs and blanket bogs are the two main types of bog in Ireland. Raised bogs are characteristic of the central lowlands. They develop in former lakes, where underlying marl impedes drainage. Fen plants such as grasses, sedges, rushes and reeds fill the marshy lake bed and decompose, forming fen peat. Sphagnum mosses grow on top of this layer, and in turn decompose into sphagnum peat. Sphagnum is able to live on rain water and can therefore continue to grow well above the level of the underlay and its contained ground water. A bog will contain several different kinds of sphagnum moss, some of which prefer dips and wet places, while others form mounds known as hummocks. Two mosses in particular turn red in the autumn, creating what are known as red bogs. Ling heather commonly grows on the moss bed.

Round-leaved sundew, cranberry and bog rosemary will also be found.

Blanket bogs are widespread among the mountains of the West. They form where rainfall is so high and frequent (45 to 50 in/c. 1,200 mm a year) that peat can develop without the marshy conditions that promote the formation of raised bogs. Various sedges and grasses and other plants – bog cotton, black bog rush, purple moor-grass, bogbean, cross-leaved heath, and certain liverworts and mosses – form peat immediately above the soil or rock and spread over huge areas of plain and mountainside. Blanket bogs are the most widespread kind of terrain in large parts of Galway, Mayo and Donegal. Bilberry and crowberry are found at the higher levels. Like raised bogs, blanket bogs are broken up by pools, streams and sphagnum hummocks.

cultivating, grew their daily food. The ridges were built up of soil, seaweed, sand, peat and manure for the growing of the staple potatoes and oats. The furrows in between afforded drainage. Here, preserved like old scars on the surface of the land, are the historic work place and larder of the Irish peasant.

Across the way, over the broad curve of Glen Inagh and its lakes, the sprightly wraith of Robert Lloyd Praeger strides across the boggy uplands of the Maumturk mountains, also composed in the main of hard-wearing quartzite. 'A traverse of the whole ridge from Maam Cross to Leenane', Praeger wrote in *The Way That I Went*, 'provides a glorious day's walking, but the main interest will lie not in the hills themselves but in the striking and varied scenery on either hand. I followed that route one mellow October day, and shall not soon forget the lovely tints on hill and bog.' A day's walking it certainly is – 14 or so uneven miles (22 kilometres) and climbs totalling 7,000 feet (2,133 metres) or more – and mere mortals following in Praeger's steps in October might find, if the going on the bog were specially soggy, that they were pressing uncomfortably close to sundown after a start soon after dawn. More often than not during the walk they will be several miles from the nearest road. From the heights, of course, there are dazzling views of local lakes and neighbouring mountains framing the distant sea and islands in various dispositions.

Leenane consists of a long line of houses, shops, pubs, purveyors of bed and breakfast and a big centre whose educational theme – put across in films and displays – is sheep and wool. The air is thickly commercial: full of foreign cars, Gaelic muzak and the untiring, humour drained smiles of natives doing nicely. Beside the town is the eastern end of Killary harbour, a lovely ten-mile inlet of sea. It is also, looked at the other way, the drowned valley of the River Erriff, which drops picturesquely over its final falls a couple of miles away at Aasleagh. Here, in season, salmon fresh from Greenland waters are to be seen hurling themselves upward in their passage to upstream breeding grounds.

On a coast pocked by inlets, Killary is the one which can be truly described as a fjord: a valley of sea-water deeper than the sea-floor beyond and divided from it by a substantial underwater bar – the heap of moraine swept down by an ancient glacier. It goes down to 80 feet (24 metres) in mid-channel and has in the past accommodated fleets. Nowadays farmed mussels are more familiar than warships. It has greater distinction than the right to a Norwegian name, for it is both beautiful and in large part free of people. Apart from the road that flanks Killary at its eastern end, there is a track along the southern shore and nothing at all along most of the northern, which rises steeply out of the water and hardly pauses till it reaches the summit of Mweelrea, 2,688 feet (819 metres) above. Walking is not in fact difficult along this stretch, and it is the base for one of the popular ascents of the mountain. But the rarity of people enhances the chance of seeing wildlife. The philosopher Ludwig Wittgenstein, who spent long periods here late in life, escaping what he saw as the petty pother of university existence, found seagulls settled on his shoulders if he stood in silent meditation. So at least claimed his colleague Bertrand Russell. The shore also offers one of the better Irish opportunities to see otters.

Connemara is mountainy and flat in about equal measures, and the flatness tends to be close to the chaotic doodles of the coastline. North-west of Clifden (a pretty little Georgian town) the terrain has a bumpiness with a certain aesthetic appeal, but it must have been a cruel life that depended on fields where the stone count seems sometimes to exceed the number of grass blades. With Europe's intervention, though, quality of land and the status of its farmers no longer tally. There are big cars and bright white bungalows here to match those among the deep green pastures of Kildare.

South of Clifden a curious broad plain of blanket bog and lake, mixed in almost equal proportions and peppered with rocks, is overseen by the neat cone of Errisbeg (987 feet/300 metres). The area is full of natural curiosities. Pipewort (*Eriocaulon aquaticum*) grows at the edges of lakes: a long thin stem with white button-flowers at the top and a whorl of long thin leaves – underwater – at the bottom. It is found abundantly hereabouts, less so in other parts of western Ireland, here and there in the Hebrides, and in vast quantities in America. The idea that it was brought in by human agency (the first aeroplane to cross the Atlantic, for instance, which has been commemorated by a wing of stone north of Ballyconneely) is scotched by pollen evidence that it was here 6,000 years ago. Also found here are the insectivorous oblong-leaved sundew (*Drosera intumedia*), and bog pondweed (*Potamogeton polygonifolius*). Several other rarities are well described by Praeger, and by Tony Whilde in his exhaustive *Natural History of Connemara*. Connemara's wealth of orchids include the early purple, the spotted, the pyramidal, the green-winged (holding out here far better than in other parts of the country) and, in one or two restricted areas, the dense flowered.

There are good beaches along the coast, none better than the sheltered, west-facing Dog's Bay with its mile-long curve of white sand. Behind the bay is a substantial spit of sand broadening into a flat granite island. The sand of the bay is not sand in the normal sense of sea-bed and surrounding rocks ground to minuscule grains. Dog's Bay consists of *foraminifera* carried up by currents from the sea-bed to which they sank, after a brief lifetime as single-celled organisms contained within casings of shell. The shells are composed of calcium carbonate secreted by the organisms themselves or of granules of rock they have attached to themselves by an exuded glue. If you walked across the beach you might guess from the feel of each step that this was a different strand. You need a lens to appreciate the full difference. The shells are superbly decorative spirals, some flat, some round, many patterned by what look like pin-pricks. Different organisms have gone to make the so-called coral strands of Mannin Bay and other spots. They are not coral, which is of animal origin, but the petrified and pulverized remains of old seaweed.

In summer, on mountain and moorland, the trim, bold, buff-chested wheatear is seldom far away, fearlessly chattering its varied calls and song from flight or perch. Occurring on coasts too, it nests in holes in rock or wall.

BEFORE YOU GO

Maps: OS Discovery Series maps Nos 37, 38, 44 and 45.

GETTING THERE

By car: from Westport go south on the N59, which travels right down to Clifden among the Connemara Highlands. From Galway, follow the N59 (west) to Clifden, passing south of the Maumturk mountains and the Twelve Bens.

By rail: the nearest station is at Westport, with trains running from Dublin Heuston three times a day. The journey takes about four hours.

By bus: a once-daily summer Bus Eireann Expressway service runs between Westport and Clifden. A local Bus Eireann service runs from Galway to Clifden several times a day, passing some spectacular mountains, including the Maumturks and the Twelve Bens. Another local service also runs along this route once a day in summer.

WHERE TO STAY

Hotels: there are lots of hotels and bed and breakfasts to choose from in the vicinity of the central Connemara mountains. Grandest is the four-star Ballynahinch Castle, south of the Twelve Bens, T:(095) 31006. Clifden, Letterfrack, Recess and Leenaun offer cheaper options. **Youth hostels**: there are a few independent hostels in Clifden including Leo's Hostel, T:(095) 21429; Brookside Hostel, T:(095) 21812; and the Master House Hostel, T:(095) 44746. The An Oige Killary Harbour hostel at Rosroe, T:(095) 43417, north of Connemara, is where the philosopher Wittgenstein lived for a period in 1948. Access involves walking several miles. **Outdoor living**: there are several camp-sites near the Connemara Highlands, among them the Beach Caravan and Camping Park at Tullycross, T:(095) 43462, and the Connemara

Caravan and Camping Park at
Lettergesh, T:(095) 43406.

ACTIVITIES

Walking: take the Sky Road,
signposted to the west of
Clifden, for breathtaking views
from Clifden cliffs. The
Connemara National Park
south of Letterfrack, T:(095)
41054, has marked walks along
the hills, which are good for
bird-watching and observing
and identifying other wildlife.
Species include grouse,
Greenland white-fronted geese,
plover, snow bunting and corn
bunting. The Park is open from
10 am–6.30 pm, May–Sept. The
Western Way passes the
Maumturk mountains and
other peaks in the Connemara
Highlands. Doughruagh peak
offers a circular walk, which is
quite steep in places. Following
Praeger's route, described in
The Way That I Went (see
p. 216), along the Maumturk
mountains can take all day.
Bird-watching: the Connemara
coastline around the highlands
is a place to see the merlin and
many sea-birds.
Riding: for details of hacking
and treks in the area contact
Connemara Riding Centre,
Errislannon Manor, Clifden,
T:(095) 31134.
Fishing: Lough Corrib and the
Owenglin river are good for
salmon; contact Clifden
Anglers for further information,
T:(095) 21039/21164.
Cycling: bikes can be rented
from Mannions in Clifden,
T:(095) 21160; *Cycling Ireland*,
published by Bord Failte, has a
suggested route that runs from
Galway to Clifden through the
Connemara Highlands.

FURTHER INFORMATION
The Bord Failte tourist office
on The Mall in Westport is
open all year, T:(098) 25711.
There is also a tourist office in
Clifden, T:(095) 21163.

THE WESTERN WAY

OS Discovery Series maps Nos 37 and 38; OS half-inch map of Ireland No.˙ 6

Starting where County Sligo abuts County Mayo on the central ridge of the Ox mountains, the Western Way takes the walker west to Ballina, then northward and close to the coast of Killala Bay, from where it sweeps round to cross the forests, mountains and desolate peat bogs of the Barony of Erris. This is walking for the stalwart, though there are rewards for those who take time off to study the plants and fauna of the bog. South of the Nephin range, the path continues through wet, flat terrain to Westport, passes close to Croagh Patrick and the steep track familiar to millions of pilgrims, and on through the Sheefry hills to Leenaun on Killary harbour. The dramatic beauty of this part of the walk is a prelude to a traverse of Connemara by way of the Maumturk mountains, down Lough Corrib to Oughterard. All told, the walk covers some 130 miles (200 kilometres). Those who plan to trek from beginning to end should be sure to have good information on places to stay (if they are not camping) and to buy provisions. There are long, lonely stretches, especially in the region of Erris and Nephin, in north-west County Mayo.

Before you go *Guidebooks: County Mayo – The Western Way* by Joe McDermott and Robert Charman (Mayo County Council).
Getting there *By car:* from Westport follow the N59 south-west to Leenaun. To reach the Ox mountains, follow the R294 east from Ballina through the middle of the range.
By rail: the closest stations are Westport (Leenaun) and Ballina. There is direct service to Westport from Dublin Heuston three times a day. To reach Ballina, catch the Westport train and change at Manulla Junction.
By bus: In the summer the Westport–Clifden Bus Eireann Expressway service stops at Leenaun. Bus Eireann services between Galway and Clifden also stop at Leenaun. Plenty of Bus Eireann services run to Ballina from all over Ireland. Treacy's, T:(096) 70968, run a daily service to Sligo. Barton

Transport, T:(01) 628 6026, run a daily service between Ballina and Dublin.
Where to stay: plenty to choose from in Ballina.
Activities: The 130-mile (200-km) Western Way is split into 6 main stages: stage 1, Leenaun–Westport (27 miles/45 km); 2, Westport–Newport (10 miles/16 km); 3, Newport–Ballycastle (41 miles/67 km); 4, Ballycastle–Killala (10 miles/16 km); 5, Killala–Ballina (10 miles/16 km); 6, Ballina–Ox mountains (12 miles/18 km). The section between Newport and Oughterard completes the walk.
Further Information: Mayo County Council, The Mall, Castlebar, Co. Mayo, T:(094) 24444. Bord Failte tourist offices in Westport, T:(098) 25711, Newport, T:(098) 4116, Ballycastle, T:(096) 43256, Ballina, T:(096) 70848, and Killala, T:(096) 32166, are open during the summer.

Partry Mountains and Lough Mask

Less known than Connemara, the Partry mountains are spotted with lakes and penetrated by deep glens on the eastern side, sloping down to the huge wood-lined waters of Lough Mask

In modern usage the name Connemara is only vaguely defined, but it is generally agreed not to stray over the borders of County Galway. Mountains do, though. The highlands of Joyce's Country subside into the valley of the Fooey and Lough Nafooey, but start up again, even before the border, to begin the essentially Mayo range of the Partry mountains. In fact, several peaks are on the Galway side, including the Devil's Mother, a straightforward climb of rather more than 3,000 feet (900 metres), most easily made from the Erriff valley, which gives wonderful views of the lakes below and Croagh Patrick in the distance.

Further east a curious lip of County Galway – remnant perhaps of ancient baronial disputes and ambitions – laps up the mountainside and colonizes a few more summits. Whatever the historic reason for this, the border country is worth a visit. Here you have a region of heights, valleys, cliffs and a lovely long lake, which has still not attracted the tourist in huge numbers. I have driven along Lough Nafooey in summer without passing another car. The road is along one side; on the other the land rises steeply to the heights of Benbeg (1,788 feet/545 metres) and Bencorragh (1,539 feet/469 metres). Close to the water are the vertical stripes of ancient lazy beds (so-called), looking as if made by a comb with wide-apart teeth. Above, the land becomes a

wall of rock. In the north-west, the lough is supplied by a long white waterfall dropping beside angular trees that sprout from the sheer rock. It is a scene an old engraver could have reproduced without need of picturesque additions.

Below and east of Nafooey two long prongs of water from Lough Mask and the intervening upland make delightful scenery. North of them the River Owenbrin (technically a tautology, this; 'owen', like 'avon' means river) has carved a valley in the mountainside which affords a route for tackling the highest of the Partry mountains, Buckaun (2,046 feet/623 metres). This is not a heroic climb, with about 1,400 feet (425 metres) to ascend from the place at which a car can be left, though there are steep drops beside the topmost ridge. Four mountain

The Irish sky plays a favourite game, allowing shafts of light through moving keyholes in thick cloud to spotlight scenes on the gnarled hills rising from Lough Fee.

Killary Harbour, once a haven for ships of the Royal Navy, is nowadays left mostly to anglers, fish farmers, the odd solitary philosopher and enterprising yachtsmen with a taste for the remote and an eye for the picturesque.

loughs can be taken in. North of the Owenbrin, however, the Partry range becomes lakeless and flat-topped: a dull final fortress before the broad plains of Mayo and east Galway open up a fairly featureless view. Between heights and plains, though, are the most attractive Loughs Carra and Mask, continued to the south by the mighty expanse of Lough Corrib; the three of them making Galway into something approaching an island, with access only through the city of Galway, Cong or the few miles connecting the north of Lough Mask to the sea.

Carra, a shallow lake never more than 30 feet (9 metres) deep, is noted for its bird life. Shooting is prohibited. Up to fifteen hundred mallard and a number of tufted duck breed there. There are wigeon, teal, shoveler and pochard in considerable numbers, and, in winter, some goldeneye. Various gulls breed on the islands. The novelist George Moore, whose ancestral home is on the lake's eastern shore, had – or perhaps merely claimed – a wild side to his life. He was forever bragging about sexual conquests. When guests were gathered he would look at the fireside carpet and sigh, 'Such scenes of passion that rug has witnessed.' Or come back from the front door saying he had just seen off a woman seduced by him in Paris years before, who had come to demand money to educate the resultant child. Yeats and many others consumed hours arguing about the truth or otherwise of Moore's claims. He was a good novelist, and may have been exercising his talents for fiction.

BEFORE YOU GO

Maps: OS Discovery Series maps Nos 37 and 38.
Guidebooks: *The New Irish Walk Guides: West and North* by T. Whilde and P. Simms (Gill and Macmillan, 1991).

GETTING THERE

By car: from Castlebar take the N84 (south) to Ballinrobe, take the R334 to Neale and the R345 (west) to Cong and Clonbur, travelling south down the east side of Lough Mask. To reach Benbeg, Bencorragh and Buckaun, take the R345 (west) from Clonbur to Leenaun, then the N59 (north) towards Westport. These roads pass close to the peaks, but there are also some minor access roads on the west side of Lough Mask.
By rail: the nearest stations are at Castlebar and Westport. Services run from Dublin Heuston and all stop at Claremorris first.
By bus: a Bus Eireann Expressway service from Ballina to Cork stops at Ballinrobe, on the east side of Lough Mask, on Fri and Sun. A local Bus Eireann service from Galway to Castlebar stops at Cong, at the south end of Lough Mask, on Tues and Thurs, and at Ballinrobe once a day. A summer Bus Eireann service between Galway and Clifden runs daily and stops at Cong and Clonbur.

WHERE TO STAY

Hotels: there are a few bed and breakfasts in Ballinrobe and a few in Clonbur but there is a greater choice in Cong.
Outdoor living: the Cong Caravan and Camping park is open all year, T:(092) 46089.
Youth hostels: hostels in and around Cong include the Cong Holiday Hostel, T:(092) 46089, the Courtyard Hostel, at Cross, T:(092) 46203, and The Quiet Man Holiday Hostel, T:(092) 46511.

ACTIVITIES

Walking: good walks include the climbs up the Devil's Mother and Benbeg.

A diving duck with a rather peaked head, bright golden eyes and, in the case of the male, a large white patch behind the bill, the goldeneye winters in many parts of Ireland, coastal and inland. Some breed in the North.

County Galway

Key
- National Park.
- Footpath.
- Exploration zone.
- Points of interest.

0   5   10miles
0   5   10   15Km.

Riding: Ashford Riding Centre, Cong, T:(092) 46024.

Caving: there are quite a few caves in this area. The bridge near Monk's Fishing House, a mile to the west of Cong along the R345, takes you to Pigeon Hole, Ballymaglancy Cave and Teach Aille. Cave maps are available from all the hostels.

Fishing: Lough Mask is a good brown-trout lake and the World Cup Brown Trout Wet-fly Angling Championship is held here in late July. Contact John Nester, 10 Lakelawns, Ballinrobe, T:(092) 41174, for more details.

Cycling: bikes can be hired from O'Connor's Garage, Main Street, Cong. Cyclists can get a good view of Lough Mask and Lough Corrib from the top of Mount Cable.

FURTHER INFORMATION
The private tourist office in Cong is open June–Sept, T:(092) 46542. The main Galway office is on T:(091) 63081.

Iar Connacht

An austere region of granite rock, dappled with pond, lake and boggy stretches, between the north coast of Galway Bay and the esteemed fishing grounds of Lough Corrib

West of Galway city is a large, low-lying coastal area of stone and lake, beach and headland, with much bog and bare rock. People living in the region have always kept to the coast, leaving the interior uninhabited, and eked a living from fishing (to which hidden sandbanks and currents are hostile), peat (of which much of the land is now denuded), making tweed and growing staple crops on the thin soil, which they fortify with dried seaweed. The stone is granite, extruded through older rocks as a result of heat generated by the slow impact of two tectonic plates, the American and the European. But this is granite different in details of composition from that which created the Wicklow, Mourne and Donegal mountains. Only one peak in Iar Connacht tops 1,000 ft (304 m). The rock is of a variety more than usually prone to erosion. Over hundreds of millions of years it has worn low.

Like all hard, hostile landscapes, Iar Connacht has a peculiar gritty beauty to it, subject to strange variations as the weather changes, its thousand lakes reflecting the

---

Lough Nafooey (*overleaf*) lies in a tuck of mountain within the district known as Joyce's Country, with the slopes of Benbeg rising from its southern shore, and the vaster, steeper sides of Maumstrasna (left) to the north.

73

blue or grey of the sky, heavy rain among the lakes making it seem that the world was made of water. It seems timeless, even now that the new tourism, the new bungalows, the new Brussels budget have made their mark. People still speak Irish, for this is one of the Gaeltacht heartlands, where those who have given up almost everything else traditional hold on to their language and are, of course, encouraged to do so by the prospect of government carrots. Another Irish ghost haunts the area. Patrick Pearse, the poet and schoolteacher who led the Easter Rising of 1916 and was shot after it, had a cottage beside Lough Aroolagh, near the head of Kilkieran Bay. He built a little house here and spent holidays learning Irish and writing. The house, now a memorial to him and open to visitors, is vested by many Irish with a kind of holiness, for they see Pearse as the country's latter-day Messiah.

The fishing which does go on successfully is for lobster and scallops, and there are oyster beds and salmon-farming in Kilkieran Bay. Inland there are the characteristic plants of the bog: bog myrtle, bog asphodel, purple moor grass, which in autumn dyes the landscape, along with heathers and sedges, and the bright illuminations of springtime gorse.

Of sea-birds, there are three kinds of diver and common scoter out in the bay in winter, and terns breed on the islands in summer. Bird life actually gets richer further east at this season, and the sandier, more sheltered coves and creeks of the east coast of Galway bay support abundant populations of wintering duck, geese, waders and gulls.

In the interior of Iar Connacht the vegetation is not such as to support a rich bird life. The modest, graceful meadow pipit can normally be counted on. There may well be cuckoos in evidence in early summer, for they parasitize pipits in these parts. Ravens are around. Red grouse make occasional, and fewer, appearances; they may be victims of the surfeit of sheep and overgrazing of the heather

on which they depend. Nobody is going to come here to see rarities, even though they may occur. No, the rarity here is the character of the landscape. Climbing the higher of the hills – Cashel Hill or Errisbeg further over to the west – shows it well, set in a sensational frame of inner Connemara mountains, Atlantic, Aran Islands, and the varied silhouettes of Galway Bay. But of course their dazzle obscures it. Better to walk its roughness and take the reward of a bathe from one of its scatter of sandy beaches.

Before you go *Maps:* OS Discovery Series maps Nos 37, 38, 44 and 45; OS half-inch maps for Ireland maps Nos 10, 11 and 14.

Guidebooks: The Mountains of Connemara, A Hill Walker's Guide by Tim Robinson, Joss Lynam and J. May (Roundstone, 1988).

Getting there *By car:* from Galway follow the N59 (west) to Clifden. The R341 travels down to Roundstone and back to Clifden. The R336 (west) from Galway travels right along the coast to just past Kinvarra; from there coastal routes follow the R340 and R341 past Kilkieran Bay, then the R342 and finally the R341.

By rail: the nearest station is Galway; services run out of Dublin Heuston four times a day.

By bus: Bus Eireann Expressway and local services run from Galway to Clifden six times a day all year round.

Where to stay *Hotels:* there are quite a lot of small hotels and bed and breakfasts in Clifden, and all round the coast to Galway, including Roundstone House Hotel, T:(095) 35864, and Mrs V. Feeney, outside Spiddal, T:(091) 83145.

Outdoor living: sites include Carrow Caravan and Camping

Only plants adapted to acidic peat, which is frequently waterlogged and leached thereby of nitrogen and phosphorus, can survive in Ireland's bog-lands. Characteristic varieties include (from left): the bogbean, which thrives in pools; the sundew, augmenting thin rations with insects it traps; sphagnum moss, forming hummocks a few inches high on raised bogs; bog asphodel which can conserve water in its fleshy leaves; and St Dabeoc's heath, a rarity, found only in Galway and Mayo.

Park, T:(091) 95266, and Gorteen Caravan and Camping Park, T:(095) 35882.
Activities *Walking:* there are plenty of good walks and good views around all of this wild coastline. Most of the accessible routes around the coast follow the R roads mentioned above. The Twelve Bens and Maumturk mountains have some strenuous ascents, while the 130-mile (200-km) Western Way, a way-marked route, runs between the foothills of both ranges.
Fishing: Oughterard, on Lough Corrib, is one of Ireland's principal angling centres. There are also good salmon rivers in this area such as the Owenglin river, just north of Clifden. For further details contact the Manager, Western Regional Fisheries Board, The Weir Lodge, Earl's Island, Galway, T:(091) 65548/68452.
Further information: there is a tourist-information point in Monahans on Main Street, Oughterard, T:(091) 82224. There is also a Bord Failte tourist office in Clifden, T:(095) 21163.

Inishbofin

An inhabited island off the north-west coast of County Galway, a haven of historic remains but wild, windswept and precipitous on its westward side, and host to breeding sea-birds and peregrines

A haircut and the date of Easter put Inishbofin on the map. It was 664 AD. A synod was called at Whitby in Yorkshire to sort out differences in practice between the Roman branch and the Irish or Celtic branch of the British Church. The issues were the style of monks' tonsures and the method of deciding the date of Easter, but it was really two opposing attitudes and dispositions that were being judged. Wilfrid of Canterbury's Rome-trained delegates were cool and dispassionate and had lawyers' skills. Colman of Lindisfarne's Irish, who were certainly wayward in observing Vatican rules, had more fire and feeling. They were both harsher to themselves and more sentimental, not least in their attitude to animals. The Roman case predictably prevailed, and the Irish, who had successfully brought Christianity to Scotland and Northumbria, had to pack up or conform. They chose to go. Thirty English monks accompanied them to Ireland, preferring their way to Wilfrid's. Unfortunately this sad but dignified departure was not the end of the story. Colman brought his monks to Inishbofin and they started to build a monastery, but the English soon complained they were the only ones doing real work. Quarrelling set in, and the English were moved to Mayo on the mainland to build a new establishment. Nothing but ruins remain today, except, in the opinion of some, an eternal polarity between Irish and English. Ireland, of course, has for centuries been obedient (more or less) to Rome, and it is the English who are now the heretics, but underlying attitudes may remain close to what they were.

Ruins are there to see: of Grania O'Malley's fortifications, perhaps of Cromwell's concentration camp for priests, and the pirate Bosco's castle. Like most of the west, Inishbofin had more happening in the past than the present. Unlike most islands (including Inishark next door) it remains inhabited – by about 250 souls – and a regular ferry service is maintained from mainland Cleggan, famous for its lobsters. Earlier this century the lobster industry was more important than it is today. A French agent lived at Cleggan and boats took off for St Malo with 3,000 Paris-bound lobsters in tanks. In those days, while most lobsters were caught in pots or kreels, baited with lugworms, some were taken by hand – or with an iron hook – from their rock-holes.

With a deeply serrated coastline the island is at most nearly four miles (six kilometres) long. The few hills are low. Cultivation is kept mainly to the south, leaving the rest mainly as stony moorland, from which most of the old peat has been cut away. There is a wonderful broad sandy bay on the east side. It is a good area for walking in, along the coast which is dramatic in parts or on the superfluous abundance of lanes inland. Getting on for 350 plant species grow on the island. Spotted rock-rose (*Tuberaria guttata*) occurs here and in very few other

77

parts of Britain or Ireland; a low, pretty cistus with a red dot on each of its five yellow petals. The island is also rich in lichens, of which about 200 kinds have been noted. Hardly any trees or sizeable shrubs grow, but this does not unduly deter birds, which are present in surprising numbers. Among them is the corn bunting (*Emberiza calandra*), an undistinguished little brown bird getting rarer in Ireland. There are fulmars on the rocks, a few choughs and plenty of common terns in summer. Irregular rarities are recorded, but Inishbofin is not a bird-watcher's Mecca. Inishark, over the water, is more so, with its variety of sea-birds and breeding peregrines. To cross to it you have to make your own arrangements. Grey seal breed around both islands. Last time I was there a school of dolphins had appeared close to the harbour on the previous day.

BEFORE YOU GO
Maps : OS Discovery Series map No. 37.

GETTING THERE
By car: from Westport follow the N59 (south-west) to Moyard. Then follow the tracks out to Cleggan, where the ferry crosses to the island. From Galway follow the N59 (north-west) to Moyard.
By rail: the nearest railway station is in Westport, where services run to and from Dublin Heuston about three times a day.

By bus: a summer-only Bus Eireann Expressway service between Westport and Clifden stops once a day on Mon and Thurs in Moyard. Another summer-only local Bus Eireann service between Galway and Clifden stops in Moyard once a day, Mon–Sat.
By boat: boats leave Cleggan on the mainland. For details ring the Sundancer, T:(095) 44649/44690/44761, or the Dun Aengus, T:(095) 45806/44642.

WHERE TO STAY
Hotels: there are two hotels on the island, Days Hotel, T:(095) 45827, which also hires out bikes, and the Doonmore Hotel, T:(095) 45804. There is one hostel, the Inishbofin Hostel, T:(095) 45855, but no camp-site. Campers can pitch their tents on any unfenced ground or by the beaches.

A geometry of stone walls, each stone extracted by hand from the soil that now appears so green and bountiful, recalls an age of want, when too many sought their livelihood from a miserly terrain.

ACTIVITIES
Bird-watching: there are several species of bird on Inishbofin island including choughs, corn buntings, fulmars and common terns..
Walking: many of the beaches around the island provide good walks.

FURTHER INFORMATION
Tourist offices: the nearest Bord Failte tourist office is in Clifden, T:(095) 21163, which is open all summer.

The common seal is seen all round Ireland – often keeping its head above water to observe human life on the shore. It keeps mainly to sandbanks and mud-flats while the grey seal frequents the rockier coastline.

Lough Corrib

Ireland's second largest lake, dotted with drumlin islands and magnetic to anglers, Lough Corrib divides the flat, fertile limestone-based east of County Galway from the barren, romantic west

The neck of land dividing Corrib from Mask was for a long time Guinness territory. The Guinness family occupies a unique place in the Irish social system: native brewers who made good in the eighteenth century, acquired titles and English (as well as Irish) estates and went to Eton and married into the aristocracy in the nineteenth and twentieth, and yet remain blessedly immune to the taint of landlordism that has seen off so many rich English in the last hundred years. Their product, of course, spreads feelings of well-being and goodwill. So does the record of their benefactions to Ireland, in housing and sport and education and restoring cathedrals and a hundred other fields. My own favourite charity is the Irish Georgian Society which struggles to preserve the best of old architecture all over the country and shamelessly cajoles the wealthy of all nations to make donations for this purpose. A Guinness, Desmond, founded it, made it his life's work and with his own money bought Castletown House in County Kildare, which is its pride and joy. Such things make the glugging of a cream-capped pint of porter an even greater pleasure.

Guinnesses used to own much of the land hereabouts, and a glimpse of the massive mock-Gothic walls and battlements of Ashford Castle, outside Cong, suggests the scale and grandeur of their lives. It is a luxury hotel now with lands running handsomely to the lake's edge. Guinnesses no longer (I imagine) take picnics hence to Lough Coolin on the side of Benlevy, trailed by maids and footmen ready to spread plates holding nine kinds of meat and game on the freshly laundered linen that covered the trestle tables. With fewer encumbrances, perhaps, we can. It is certainly worth making the small effort to reach the top (700 feet/200 metres from the south-east approach) because the views over Lough Corrib – not to mention Lough Mask, Galway Bay, an Aran island and much else besides – are sensational. Framed by the eastern uplands of Joyce's Country and the granite hills of Iar Connacht on the west bank and the flat green billiard table of inner Galway on the east, the lough – second biggest in Ireland after Lough Neagh – is spangled with rocks and islands and long thin headlands as it bends one way and another on its 30-mile (50-kilometre) course to Galway city and the sea.

The flatness, granite hills apart, extends for some miles beyond the west bank of the lake, for the underlying rock here, and on and on continuously through the midlands to Dublin, is limestone of the Carboniferous period, formed from shells and corals of the equatorial sea that covered Ireland 300

79

million years ago. The ease with which water erodes limestone and the rock's porosity have endowed the lake with widely varying depths and submarine cave systems and reefs and other irregularities. The porosity was oddly neglected by nineteenth-century engineers who came during the great famines of the 1840s, with the aim of providing work for men desperate to earn, to join Mask and Corrib by a navigable canal. The excavation was completed and a date set for opening. The upper sluice gates were opened and water poured through. But it did not stay. It quickly drained through the stone and was gone. The four miles of the canal are there – west of Cong – to this day, still perfectly useless.

If the lake is famous for its brown trout, it is not the monopoly of anglers. You can explore it by hired boat and see its more obvious charms from steamers that ply from Cong and Oughterard in season. The shore can be reached by any number of roads and lanes. At Annaghdown, on the south-eastern edge of the lake, are various abbey remains on the site of a monastery founded, it is said, by St Brendan the Navigator, whose claimed discovery of America is discussed on page 99. He died here, full of years, in the arms of his abbess sister. A few miles to the south, at Angliham marble quarries, and a few miles north, at Mount Ross, winter duck populations are easily seen. All year round the lake supports varied if not unusual species of ducks, waders and others, including over 8,000 pochard in early winter, the second biggest flock in Ireland (Lough Neagh has the biggest).

BEFORE YOU GO
Maps: OS Discovery Series map No. 45; OS half-inch maps of Ireland Nos 11 and 14.

GETTING THERE
By car: Galway sits at the southern end of Lough Corrib and by taking the N84 (north) to Headford, passing small roads to Annaghdown, then the R345 to Neale, you travel up the east side of the lough. The N59 past Oughterard goes up the west side.
By rail: the nearest station is in Galway; services run from Dublin Heuston four times a day.
By bus: many Bus Eireann services serve Galway. There is a Bus Eireann Expressway service that runs from Ballina to Galway, travelling down the east side of the lough, and a few local services that go up and down both sides of the lough. Private companies that operate from Galway include P. Nestor Coaches, T:(091) 97144, and Burke Brothers, T:(093) 55416.
By sea: the *Corrib Queen* plies the lake every day from Ashford Castle Quay in Cong

to Oughterard, T:(092) 46029.

WHERE TO STAY
Hotels: the five-star Ashford Castle, once a Guinness family country house, is situated outside Cong, near the lough, T:(092) 46003. There is a bed and breakfast in Clonbur, Fairhill, T:(092) 46176, and Cong, Rising of the Waters Inn, T:(092) 46316, at the northern end of Lough Corrib, and a vast selection of accommodation, from four-star hotels to bed and breakfasts, in Galway.
Outdoor living: the Barna House Caravan and Camping Park is open Apr–Sept, T:(091) 92964. Hunters Silver Strand Caravan and Camping Park is open Easter–Sept, T (091) 92452, and Cong Caravan and Camping Park is open all year, T:(092) 46089.
Youth hostels: An Oige runs the Connamona Hostel, T:(091) 48002. Independent hostels in Galway include the Galway City Hostel, T:(091) 66367, and the Grand Holiday Hostel, T:(091) 21150. There is also the Lough Corrib Hostel at Oughterard, T:(091) 82634.

ACTIVITIES
Caving: there are caves near Cong at the top of Lough Corrib and maps are available from the hostel in Cong.
Fishing: Oughterard is the fishing base for Lough Corrib; local boatmen offer trips. The Irish Wet-fly Masters Open Competition is held every year. Contact Michael Walsh, Headford and Corrib Anglers Association, Ower House, Greenfield, Ower PO, Co. Galway, T:(093) 35446. Boats for fishing can be hired from M. Healy in Oughterard, T:(091) 82736.
Cycling: bikes can be hired from Lough Corrib Bike Hire, T:(091) 82634/80194, in Oughterard.
Walking: the Western Way starts in Oughterard. For more information contact Mayo County Council, The Mall, Castlebar, Co. Mayo, T:(094) 24444.

FURTHER INFORMATION
Tourist Offices: there is a private tourist office in Cong, T:(091) 46542, open in summer, and a Bord Failte office in Galway, T:(091) 63081.

Aran Islands

An oblique line of three big, inhabited islands of solid rock and a few tiny, unpeopled ones, forming a broken continuation of the limestone pavements of the Burren and guarding the entrance to Galway Bay

There was a time when these islands would have been the wildest of all: three massive chunks of limestone obstinacy thrown at the Atlantic, fallen at a distance that takes a boat, depending on weather, one hour or as many as eight; brazening out winds, storms and waves that will eventually, if nothing intervenes, wear, rub, grind and batter them to extinction. Nature made few locations wilder.

Yet they have been inhabited and built on since time beyond knowing. The concentric stone half-rings of Dun Aenghus, hanging over 250-foot (75-metre) cliffs on the seaward side of Inishmore, are one of the most impressive, as well as puzzling, survivals in Europe. There are innumerable remains of monasteries, churches, castles and fortifications on each of the three islands. The modern population, about 1,500, have most of the technology to be found on the mainland. Each island is parcelled into little fields by solid stone walls. The people speak Irish, but English too. They know how to profit from tourists. Unless you arrive on a dark and windy winter's evening, thoughts of wildness are unlikely to enter your head.

The Aran Islands must be mentioned, though, because of their shape and position and composition, because only a hundred years ago the wildness of the elements here dictated life, and often enough, death. The formidable, centuries-old struggle to tame them makes an astonishing story. In the distant past, the islands were bare rock, protruding from a submerged line of limestone that ran from the Burren in County Clare far out into the Atlantic. Myths make the line continuous above water, and describe Galway Bay as a contained lake; this

may actually have been the case for a time. Nature provided no soil. The soil that makes crops and pasture possible has been created by islanders over the centuries using sand and seaweed from the north-eastern shores, which they spread about after stopping up the deep fissures in the limestone with pebbles and splinters. Field walls and buildings were built mostly from countless loose stones of all sizes churned up and deposited by glaciers. Last time I was there Inishmaan was getting itself a football field. In most places this would mean at most ploughing and rolling a suitable area. Here, though, certain preliminaries were necessary. Six hundred tons of soil had to be imported from the mainland and unloaded within an hour of high tide; at other times the boat could not moor. All the island's fit and young assembled for the task twice a day – about 4 am to start. It still took about a week.

The islands are still among the natural wonders of Ireland. But, like the Giant's Causeway in County Antrim, they have had the wildness combed out of them. Irish is spoken and taught, certainly. Canvas curraghs are still used for conveyance, true. Memory carries glimpses of times when fish were caught and all peat for burning carried from the Galway coast in canvas boats, in all weathers. A rich literature – including plays of John Millington Synge and novels of Liam O'Flaherty – tells of the transition, the battles between tradition and advance, between the old Celtic ways and the new mainland ways – especially those of England and America.

There are plants that like the abundant calcium of limestone, but nothing like as many as in the Burren. There is the fascinating chessboard of field walls and other human constructs. The views are sumptuous: the Atlantic to the west, the Burren and the Moher cliffs to the east, the Twelve Bens north and the hills of Kerry south. But wild? No. The 600 tons of soil imported for the football pitch made a fitting climax to one hundred years of domestication.

A grassy sloping ledge (*overleaf*) provides secluded nesting for a group of puffins, protected on one side by a mighty drop to the sea and on the other by a sheer wall to the cliff-top above.

BEFORE YOU GO
Maps: OS Discovery Series map No. 51; OS half-inch map of Ireland No. 14.
Guidebooks: *Islands of Ireland*, a Bord Failte leaflet.

GETTING THERE
By sea: several ferry companies run to the Aran Islands. From Rossaveel the crossing time is short and the service frequent. Contact Aran Ferries, T:(091) 68903/92447, and Island Ferries, T:(091) 61767. Bikes usually travel free. There are also ferry routes from Galway and Dublin. Ferry services between the islands are less frequent and quite unreliable.
By air: nine-seater private planes can be hired from Aer Aran, T:(091) 93034. Flights operate to all three islands. The

mainland departure point is at Minna, near Inveran, 19 miles (31 km) west of Galway. A connecting bus goes from outside the Galway tourist office.

WHERE TO STAY
There is a good selection of bed and breakfasts on all three islands. Camping is available at Inishmore camp-site, T:(099) 61185, and free camping next to the Kilmurvey Hostel, T:(099) 61318. There is an independent hostel at Kilronan, the Aran Islands Hostel, T:(099) 61255/61248.

ACCESS
This is easy because of frequent ferry services. The best way of getting round the islands is by bike. Walking can be

treacherous, as can cycling, because of the heavy fog that sometimes appears.

ACTIVITIES
Cycling: bikes can be rented from Aran Bicycle Hire, T:(099) 61132 and Costelloe's, T:(099) 61241.
Walking: a way-marked, circular walk on each island - known collectively as the Aran Way - takes the visitor by easy stages to the most important sites and dramatic views.

FURTHER INFORMATION
There is a small seasonal tourist office on the waterfront in Kilronan on Inishmore, T:(099) 61263, and a small tourist information desk at Inisheer harbour during the summer.

The Burren

A large, uneven region in the north-west of County Clare, bordering sea on two sides, consisting over much of its surface of huge limestone slabs, and supporting in every available crack and hollow a rich and unusual flora

Between the scenic prima donnas of Connemara and Kerry lies the quieter, flatter, altogether less dramatic terrain of County Clare. It too has features that attract immediate attention, and coaches regularly pull up for delighted tourists to inspect the jutting headlands of the Cliffs of Moher, the crescent beaches of Kilkee and Liscannor and a wealth of ruined abbeys and castles inland. The Burren is a different matter. It has its coaches disgorging tourists but, on close inspection, many of these are seen to bear an expression of courteous bemusement. A hundred square miles – about ten by ten – of bare rock, relieved only by patches of scrub, a handful of small towns, some ill-drained

fields and a scattering of stone formations evidently constructed by humans at a clumsy stage in their development – all this clearly seems to them a queer taste.

Bernard Shaw in *Back to Methuselah* called this apparent lunar void 'a region of stone-capped hills and granite fields' (wrongly, as it happened, for the Burren is all limestone). Thackeray wondered 'how the deuce' Lord Gort's nearby mansion 'got into the midst of such a desolate country'; the house 'seemed to bore itself there considerably'. Two centuries before, Cromwell's agents found the Burren wanting for different reasons: 'neither water enough to drown a man, nor a tree to hang him, nor soil enough to bury'. Between Neolithic man, who was present in some force, and relatively recent times, hardly anyone has left a good word about it.

The growth of the Burren's popularity is mainly due to the fact that certain Victorian geologists and botanists began to look carefully and closely, and marvelled at what at first they had missed. To understand the Burren's appeal to them it is necessary to go back about 360 million years, when the Burren rock was little more than a collective glint in the eyes – if they had them – of untold millions of brachiopods, corals, molluscs, echinoderms and other creatures formed mainly of calcium carbonate, floating luxuriantly in the warm sea which then covered this part of Ireland. These little animals mated and reproduced, mated and reproduced, and at the end of their mortal span sank to the bottom. Their offspring did the same, and theirs, and theirs, until the strata of their chalky skeletons grew thick on the sea-bed and, along with sand and mud, was compressed by the sea's weight into the limestone rock we see today. Every now and again the earth heaved, the climate changed or a volcano spewed, causing a crack in the accumulation. Each horizontal stratum became clearly marked off from that beneath, and vertical irregularities appeared.

These divisions and faults were compounded in subsequent eras by exposure to the air when the sea flowed away, by the pressure of ice in successive Ice Ages and by erosion caused by tons of running water when the ice melted. The water had effects similar to those produced by lactic acids in the making of some cheeses. The Burren is shot through with holes and cave systems that sometimes stretch for miles. Unlike cheese, however, limestone is porous. Water percolates not only the channels and caverns, but the fabric of the rock, too. Acids in the water continually dissolve particles of rock and imperceptibly reduce the Burren's body.

As the last Ice Age drew to its close, ten or more thousand years ago, plants that were adapted to extreme cold and a very short flowering season – wintergreens, alpine bearberry, the ethereally blue spring gentians, mountain avens and many more – moved into the high areas formerly covered by glaciers. There they were slowly hemmed in by pine forests. They would have remained rarities or possibly died out had not the earliest settlers cut down the forests

---

Stony seaboard, far and foreign,
*   Stony hills poured over space,*
Stony outcrop of the Burren,
*   Stones in every fertile place,*
Little fields with boulders dotted,
*   Grey-stone shoulders saffron-*
*   spotted,*
Stone-walled cabins thatched with
*   reeds,*
*   Where a Stone Age people*
*   breeds*
The last of Europe's stone age race.

*   John Betjeman, 'Sunday in Ireland'*

---

with the fecklessness of those deforesting the Amazon basin today. Where man cleared, alpine herbaceous plants and creepers extended their range. The Burren puzzle is that, as the climate grew warmer, attracting large numbers of plants from the south, the alpine flora was able to survive as well. A relatively consistent temperature, with the

---

COUNTRYSIDE HAZARDS

Snakes, poisonous or otherwise, are not established in Ireland, and reports of sightings are rare enough to be discounted. Nor should bulls met in fields be dangerous, though it may be wise to take the view that no bull – not even a happy heifer-haremed Hereford – is entirely pacific. Male deer, during their rutting seasons (around October), have been known to charge, hurt and even kill humans, but only a handful of times a century; all the same, it is wise to avoid coming between a buck and his does.

Leopard amanita (*Amanita pantherina*) is among the more poisonous fungi; common ink-cap (*Coprinus atramentarius*) may be harmful when eaten with alcohol, and the golden rule is to be positively sure the mushroom you intend to eat is a good one, rather than that it is not one of the bad ones. Shellfish caught on the west coast at a time of red tides (a phenomenon occurring once a year or so and not fully understood) may be poisonous, and no responsible caterer would supply them at such a time.

Gulf Stream modifying the extremes of winter and summer, is certainly one reason for this.

The result is an unusual, though not unique, mix of plants generally considered alpine with many more often associated with quite warm climates, like the Mediterranean. It is this unusual combination which makes the Burren botanically enticing, not the rarity of any particular plant. All the orchids to be found here occur in other parts of the British Isles; the presence of 22 separate orchid species, however, is almost unique; from May to July there is always an abundance of these intriguing and ingenious plants.

There is another oddity. The rock naturally attracts lime-loving plants. Yet the humus which develops in dips and clefts from algal spores, seeds and fruits brought in by the wind and subsequently decomposed, will contain acid constituents, too. As the rain falls (twice as much a year as in Dublin) and soaks into the rock, it dissolves, as we have seen, and leaches away much of the alkaline content. In patches, therefore, a preponderance of acid soil remains. That is why the limey Burren is spattered with ghettoes of acid-loving plants: heathers and ling, St John's wort, bracken and gorse.

When humans arrived, with their cattle

Bloody cranesbill with its crimson blooms, the free-flowing yellow froth of lady's bedstraw, white chickweed and other flowers throng the richly fertile gaps lying between limestone slabs on the side of Slieve Carran in the Burren.

and goats, the Burren suited them well. There was a most agreeable climate, caves in plenty to live in, and near the coast a plentiful diet of oysters, mussels, crabs, lobsters and other fish. Assuming aesthetic tastes were similar to our own, the views would have been delightful: Galway Bay and the Bens of Connemara, the Aran Islands daubed on the sea before a fiery ocean sunset, mountains like lashings of limestone cream poured from a celestial jug. Stock-farming could not have been easier. In the Burren there are no frosts to speak of and grass grows the year round. Water rising through the rock after heavy rain souses the soil with a fertilizing solution of lime. There was no need – there is still no need – to provide either winter shelter or winter hay. To get the best of the grass, the booley system was practised, and continues in modified form: cattle were moved to the high ground in summer and the whole farming family went along too, living in huts and burying butter in the bog to keep it fresh.

Walking or driving in this curious countryside reveals more than rock and plant. Doolin, a pretty fishing village on the west coast, has become through its 'singing pubs' a folk-music Mecca. Lisdoonvarna is famous for arranged marriages. Up to a generation ago Irish farmers married late, waiting till they inherited land. When the time came they turned up here, to take the spring-water cure, so they said; but as often as not they returned with a marriage bargain struck. Since few could write, marriage brokers proliferated. In the south-east you can see the track of a glacier's retreat: a patchwork of lakes between rock-strewn flats west and east of Corrofin. There are ancient graves and medieval abbeys and castles in a romantic state of ruin and, to the south-west, the dizzy screen of the Cliffs of Moher with its breeding sea-birds. On the eastern side of Slieve Elva is the Polnagollum complex, thought to be the longest cave system in western Europe. Ailwee cave is open for visitors. There are relatively few roads but plenty of tracks and miles of stone wall, cattle, sheep, goats.

All the same it is the plants which star here. In late spring and early summer, botanists proliferate almost as much as maidenhair fern, though nothing like as coyly. Insects, naturally, are present in huge numbers, not least the moths whose males are tricked by the patterns and smells of certain orchids into thinking that they are landing on females of their own species. Beetles – the most successful of all forms of life in the world – are proportionately active, and do their bit for plant pollination. But to experience the most familiar pleasures of the Burren, stop on some rough pavement in this limestone moonscape, peer into the surrounding grikes and hollows and marvel at the extent and variety and buoyancy of species which, against all apparent odds, make the area a paradise of flowers.

BEFORE YOU GO
Maps: OS Discovery Series maps Nos 51 and 52; OS half-inch map of Ireland map No. 14.

GETTING THERE
By car: from Galway take the road out to Oranmore and then follow the N18 (south) to Kilcolgan. Take the N67 (west) to Kinvarra and Ballyvaghan and then down to Lisdoonvarna. The R477 from Ballyvaghan follows the coast round to Lisdoonvarna. The R478 takes you to Doolin and the Cliffs of Moher.
By rail: the nearest station is in Galway, where trains run from Dublin Heuston four times a day.
By Bus: a Bus Eireann Expressway service runs from Dublin to Kilkee and stops at Lisdoonvarna. A summer-only Bus Eireann Expressway service between Killarney and Galway stops at Lisdoonvarna and Doolin. Local services from Limerick to Doolin stop at Lisdoonvarna. An independent company, the North Clare Nipper, also runs local services, T:(065) 81562.

The tiniest crack or dip in the limestone pavement north of Doolin provides a niche for bloody cranesbill and other Burren flowers to flourish, screened from the ocean winds.

The spring gentian is one of those alpine plants whose presence in the Burren still causes debate. It is found also in a small area of north England. Apart from that, its nearest occurrence is in the Jura.

Bloody cranesbill (right), a geranium with bright red flowers, hoary rockrose (centre) with its shining yellow petals, and close-packed clusters of white mountain avens (far right) are among the myriad decorations of the Burren's limestone slabs in early summer.

WHERE TO STAY

Hotels: there is a good selection of hotels, guest-houses and bed and breakfasts in Lisdoonvarna.

Youth hostels: there is an independent hostel in Lisdoonvarna, the Burren Holiday Hostel and Activity Centre, T:(065) 74300.

Outdoor living: camping is available at Nagles Doolin Camping and Caravan Park, open May-Sept, T:(065) 74458.

ACTIVITIES

Walking: there are plenty of scenic walks around the Burren. The 25-mile (40-km) Burren Way runs south from Ballyvaghan on the coast of Galway Bay across the lower slopes of Slieve Elva. Reaching the coast at Doolin, it clings to the top of the Cliffs of Moher,

then turns east with the coast to finish near Lehinch. Check the *Walking Ireland* leaflet from Bord Failte for more information.

Climbing: there are good climbing routes between severe and E5 grades on the limestone sea cliffs of the Burren.

Caving: there are several miles of caves around Lisdoonvarna, but they can be dangerous so take the usual precautions or go in an organized group if possible. Kilfenora Caving and Outdoor Centre, T:(065) 71422, organizes walking, caving, pony-trekking and climbing holidays.

Cycling: bikes can be hired from the Burren Holiday Tourist Hostel, T:(065) 74006, and Burkes Garage in Lisdoonvarna, T:(065) 74022. The Burren provides relatively easy cycling terrain and amazing sea views.

FURTHER INFORMATION

Tourist offices: the nearest Bord Failte tourist office is in Lisdoonvarna, T:(065) 51577.

Ecology: The Burren Centre at Kilfenora explains the nature of the region in a museum and video display, T:(065) 88030. The centre also has guidebooks for sale.

Coole Lough

A park, in east County Clare, of powerful literary associations, with a landscape of lakes and woods interesting for flora, fauna and limestone formations, and an imaginative interpretative centre

I cannot imagine that when families consider where to go for their annual holiday – a decision made in most cases around New Year, amid a litter of Sunday-paper travel supplements – they pass remarks like 'I've always wanted to get my teeth into the geology of Norway' or 'the plant life of Portugal', or 'Sicilian sea-birds' or whatever it might be. Some, yes; but not, surely, most.

Yet the Irish Tourist Board and the Northern Ireland Tourist Board have put a huge investment into programmes of digestible education to be enjoyed by tourists. All down the west coast and in many other parts of Ireland you can call in at regional centres and watch films, look at displays and hear lectures about local ecology, history and geography. I can almost foresee the time when tourists will appear before examiners and take away diplomas or academic robes in recognition of the knowledge they have acquired during their stay. Though standards vary from centre to centre, you can certainly acquire an awful lot.

The best centre for learning about the surrounding district is at Coole Park, a place of interest on many counts. It was the home for centuries of a family of Anglo-Irish imperial administrators, the last survivor of whom was a great literary patron and important collector of local folklore, Augusta, Lady Gregory. The poet Yeats was a close friend and stayed here often. So did almost everyone of literary eminence in the early part of the century. Yeats loved the lake, with its fifty-nine swans, and the woods where he once actually brushed against a badger. After Lady Gregory's death the house was allowed to decay and was finally pulled down in 1941 by the Forestry Department, which had bought the estate, now run as a nature reserve.

A converted stableyard occupies part of the site, and a film and a clever visual display show the unusual nature of the landscape round about and the abounding wildlife. This district is an extension of the higher limestone landscapes of the Burren, a few miles west. Here water is elusive. Rivers come and then go underground, to reappear a mile or several miles further on. Lakes are of the special kind known as turloughs (meaning dry lakes, a habitat unique to Ireland within Western Europe), scooped out of the prevailing limestone by the movements of ice or formed by solution hollows. The water in them also comes and goes.

The trees are in their autumn beauty,
  The woodland paths are dry,
Under the October twilight the water
  Mirrors a still sky;
Upon the brimming water among the stones
  Are nine-and-fifty swans.

        W. B. Yeats, 'The Wild Swans at
                                Coole'

Where it survives the summer it might be at a level 30 feet (9 metres) below the winter high. The furtive behaviour of water here is due to its action on the limestone, eating away the softer rock to make caves, swallow-holes and subterranean channels. While some water enters and runs out of the turloughs in the form of streams, a lot of it simply sinks and rises within the natural porosity of the limestone. This provides plants with an important benefit, for the rising water brings with it fresh quantities of dissolved lime, a natural fertilizer.

The variations challenge the birds and plants which have settled here. Turloughs often hold large numbers of waterfowl in winter, although in early summer breeding waders can be in trouble if water suddenly appears. Many plants have to survive submergence through the winter and prolonged dryness in the summer. Their adaptations illustrate the ingenuity of evolution. The violet family, for instance, is represented on the turlough's sides by heath dog violet (*Viola canina*) at one level, common dog violet (*V. riviniana*) higher up, and the rare fen violet (*V. persicifolia*) close to the highest attained edge. Nature, of course, is crowded with such multiple adaptations. The Centre's film shows how each member of the tit family, all of which live in the woods, has evolved a beak ideally fitted for specialist problems such as coping with conifer needles or with deep or shallow fissures in different nuts.

You can walk through the thick woods of the demesne to Coole Lough, a turlough which always retains a good deal of water. Bewick's, whooper and mute swans are present in winter, along with a number of ducks and waders and the ringed plover. There are pine martens and red squirrels in the woods.

The river which tops up Coole Lough flows through the town of Gort from Lough Cutra, which lies within a grand demesne whose ownership has ricocheted between the noble and military families of Gort and Gough – Lord Gough having defeated both Chinese and Sikhs in days when you were rewarded for doing so. Between Lough Cutra and Gort, signposted just off the Ennis road, is a deep dank tree-girt depression into which the river flows from the underground channel in which it has been confined. The scene is the very model of an eighteenth-century romantic print. The river stays visible as far as Coole. Thereafter it reappears as a turlough in Garryland, surrounded by a fine old native wood once part of the Coole estate. It then returns to its tunnel and stays mostly submerged till its passage into the sea at Kinvarra.

BEFORE YOU GO
Maps: OS half-inch map of Ireland No. 14.

THE BURREN WAY

OS half-inch map of Ireland No. 14; 1:35,200 map of The Burren by Tim Robinson (T. D. Robinson, 1977)

Half the projected Burren Way is so far marked. The other half will in due course make a circular route of it. The existing path takes in the most dramatic scenery of west Clare. It starts at Ballyvaghan and after a short coastal stretch plunges south and then south-west through the Burren heartland, mostly at a height which offers good views of the Aran Islands, the ocean and the south coast of Galway. It regains the coast at the music-rich fishing village of Doolin, and stays with it along the tops of the Cliffs of Moher, one of Ireland's more breathtaking features. The last few miles are eastward, still along the coast, which here overlooks a sometimes storm-wracked bay noted for the multitude of ships it has dragged to the bottom. Ballynalackan and Doolin are good places for a more or less central break.

GETTING THERE
By car: from Galway, take the N18 to Gort which is within a mile of Coole Lough and the Nature Forest and Wildlife Park, near the lough.
By rail: the nearest station is in Galway, where services operate from Dublin Heuston four times a day.
By bus: the Bus Eireann Expressway service from Ballina to Cork stops at Gort and Galway. A local service that runs from Limerick to Galway also stops at Gort.

WHERE TO STAY
There is one hotel, Sullivan's Royal, T:(091) 31401, and a handful of bed and breakfasts in Gort.Otherwise, the nearest youth hostels and camp-sites are in Galway.

ACTIVITIES
Cycling: *Cycling Ireland* (available from Bord Failte) suggests a route that travels past Lough Coole through Gort.
Walking: marked trails run through the National Forest and Wildlife Park, near Coole Lough.

FURTHER INFORMATION
The nearest Bord Failte tourist office is in Galway, T:(091) 63081. More information regarding the flora and fauna surrounding the lough is available in a display at Coole Park.

Getting there *By car:* From Galway follow the N18 south-east to Kilcolgan and take the N67 west to reach Ballyvaghan. For Liscannor, follow the N18 south-east from Galway to Ennis, then the N85 west to Lehinch and the R478 north-west.
By bus: Summer-only Bus Eireann Expressway services running between Killarney and Galway, and Galway and Doolin stop at Ballyvaghan, as does a local service between Galway and Doolin. The summer-only Expressway service between Killarney and Galway also stops at Liscannor, as does a local service between Limerick and Lisdoonvarna.
By rail: the closest stations are Ennis and Galway.
Where to stay *Hotels:* bed and breakfast accommodation is available at several places in Liscannor, including Sea Haven, T:(065) 81385; and in Ballyvaughan, where you could try Rusheen Lodge, T:(065) 77092, Lough Rask House, T:(065) 77026, and Oceanville, T:(065) 77051.
Outdoor living: Camping is also available at Nagles Doolin Camping Park, Doolin, T:(065) 74458.
Youth hostels: there are two hostels at Doolin: Old Doolin Hostel, T:(065) 74006, and New Doolin Hostel, T:(065) 74006, which, unlike its older counterpart, is open all year.
Activities: The 28-mile (45-km) Burren Way is split into 2 main sections: Ballyvaghan–Doolin (18 miles/29 km); and Doolin–Liscannor (10 miles/16 km).

This consists of one entire rock with here and there a little surface of Earth, which raiseth earlier Beef·and Mutton, though they allow no hay, than any land in this Kingdom, and much sweeter by reason of the sweet herbs intermixed and distributed everywhere.

Journal of Thomas Dineley, on the Burren (seventeenth century)

The Mouth of the Shannon

Key
- - - Footpath.
— Exploration zone
▲ Points of interest.

0   5   10miles
0   5   10   15Km.

-N-

Milltown Malbay
Ennis
Killaloe
O'Brienbridge
Creegh
N67
N68
R473
N18
Kilkee
Poulnasherry Bay
Clonderalaw Bay
Killadysert
Shannon Airport
CLARE
Kilrush
Labasheeda
Shannon Estuary
Loop Head
Doonaha
SCATTERY ISLAND
N67
Ferry
Shannon
Foynes
Askeaton
Limerick
N24
LIMERICK
Loop Head
Kilbaha
Mouth of the Shannon
Ballylongford Bay
Tarbert
Adare
Ballybunnion
Ballylongford
Rathkeale
Kerry Head
Listowel
Galey
N20

Loop Head

A long spearhead of land jutting out into the Atlantic, lined along part of its north coast with steep cliffs and rock stacks, summer home of thousands of sea-birds

The west coast of County Clare from Kilkee north-eastwards to Lahinch is fine and dandy but dedicated to the family holiday, evoking the bucket and spade more than the chough and lordly raven. South-west of Kilkee the scene is more cliffy, wilder, less peopled. But there are people, and there are farms and villages. At Loop Head itself there is a walled-off working lighthouse. The wildness rating could at best be middling. Worth seeing, to overquote the great doctor, but not worth going to see.

Kilkee, hugging its broad sandy bay, lives for tourists. Trading – or over-trading – on distinct scenic advantages, it has, in building all it imagines tourists may want, considerably uglified itself. All that stops at

its boundaries, however, and after a minute or two of climbing the sights are of chunks of cliff seemingly broken and floated from the mainland to make clearly striated islands, rimmed with foam: cliffs, ravines, tapering or top-heavy stacks. Back from the sea is a seemingly simple ecology of grass, thrift, buttercups, rabbits, wheatears springing from every wall and post, hooded crows, rock pipits, and a fine herd of feral goats, most white, some dark with spectacularly black faces, black beards and their elegant twin plumes of horn.

Ten miles from Kilkee the coast has become a giants' tip of mighty slabs, once piled like sheets, now bent, toppled, folded and broken by underlying settlement and the corrosive action of waves. These are the shales and flagstones which lie underneath the carboniferous limestone that forms the surface of so much of middle Ireland. Sea water has tunnelled through and gurgles into pits and swallowholes. Nevertheless nature has neatly created two broad arched bridges – the bridges of Ross – whose bent

slabs have broken to look like the slabs human builders would have used. It is a freak construct amid stormy deconstruction.

Inland, where the rock has neither been broken nor its inner strata exposed, the country is dull: a flat, treeless landscape of unadorned villages and rough pasture. A field thick with buttercups is the biggest treat. Along the coast the discordant ballet of rock shapes and movements continues to Loop Head, where electrified wire ensures that you do not stray from the cliff-side. (It is a peculiarly pugnacious thing, electric wire: the threat of physical pain imposed by some absent landowner, another lapse in conventional Irish friendliness.) Twenty or so feet from the cliff a huge, elongated vertical stack is drawn up like a petrified liner riding at anchor. Through the dividing ravine water wars and storms its way through in waves of cobalt, turquoise, aquamarine and white. Aeronaut fulmars and smart dark-booted kittiwakes nest on the stacks. Fleets of guillemot and razorbill float on the sea, and lesser black-backed gulls dive with uttered menace at intruders (but always turn aside well in time). You can lie on a bed of pink thrift, look down at this crowded world and wonder, if you are like me, at the wagtail or swallow that flies six feet above you and an instant later a hundred feet above the sea without appearing to register any difference. Eskimos are said to have twenty words for snow. I cannot imagine swallows have even one word for vertigo.

Before you go *Maps:* OS Discovery Series map No. 63; OS half-inch map of Ireland No. 17.

Getting there *By car:* from Kilkee, the R487 travels southwest to Loop Head at the end of the peninsula.

By rail: the nearest station is Ennis, on the line between Limerick and Galway. Trains from Dublin terminate at Limerick but the service is regular and frequent, with ten arrivals a day.

By bus: the Bus Eireann services to the coast are infrequent. Contact the bus station at Ennis for further information, T:(065) 24177.

Where to stay: there is a campsite at Kilkee, and the Kilkee Independent Hostel, T:(065) 56209. There is also a large number of bed and breakfasts to choose from in Kilkee and Kilrush.

Activities: bikes can be hired from Gleeson Wholesale, T:(065) 51127, and from the Korner Shop, T:(065) 51037, both in Kilrush. Bord Failte's *Cycling Ireland* suggests a route that runs right round the peninsula.

Further Information: Kilrush Bord Failte tourist office is open during the summer, T:(065) 51577. There is also a summer-only Bord Failte tourist office in Kilkee's Central Square, T:(065) 56112.

Shannon Estuary

A broad inroad of ocean, much used by man, but hiding sanctuaries of wilderness to north and south

Like the Severn, which is also the longest river in the countries it flows through, the Shannon debouches in a huge and important estuary on the west coast. The works and influence of man are never far away. Long before it begins to broaden at O'Briensbridge, ten miles above Limerick, the bulk of its water has been snatched from its channel, forced to walk the plank of a canal, and dropped 100 ft (30 m) at Ardnacrusha to furnish vast quantities of electricity. The scheme, completed in 1929, created a huge reservoir between O'Briensbridge and Killaloe, drowning villages whose steeples and gables continued to appear, at low water, for years afterwards.

Canals and river channel are reunited above Limerick, a town of some 65,000 inhabitants, whose industrial and domestic effluents can hardly enhance the nature of the water. Here and there along the estuary banks are lesser towns, docks, industries, power stations and what was once the country's principal airport. The dimensions and illuminations of some of these make them conspicuous for miles. The amazing thing is that it is all absorbed. Along the 50 miles (80 km) from Limerick to the sea there is a rich range of concealed bays, islands great and small, marshes, mud-flats, a wildlife and waterfowl population to match and every opportunity to imagine that man has not trodden here before.

The sensible means of exploration would be a motor-boat or dinghy. Half a century back this was no problem. Shannon Airport was not thought about, boats were readily available from Foynes, Tarbert and elsewhere, and steamers regularly plied between those two towns and Kilrush and Limerick. In fact, the further back we look the more important sea travel was. Roads, forests and freebooters made land travel impossible or dangerous. Trade, buoyant smuggling and war used ocean routes. Today you would be lucky to make some private arrangement. Although there is a frequent car ferry from Killimer on the Clare coast to Tarbert in Kerry, and a regular summer boat service between Kilrush and the monastic island of Scattery, the only dependable option is to go by road.

Limestone flanks both sides of the eastern half of the estuary, and the broad mouth of the River Fergus, which joins it on the Clare side. The rich pastures here have created the elegant demesnes of County Limerick, and to a lesser extent, of the opposite bank. Grand Ascendancy houses, some intact, some ruinous, most of them picturesque, recall the old landlord days. In the western sectors they thin out as the old overlay of shales, slate and coal reduces the quality of the soil. On the south side the mud-flats of Tarbert and the coast west of it support huge numbers of duck (mainly wigeon, teal and mallard) and waders. Ballylongford Bay is a good place to watch them. But the main interest and the more indented and islanded shore is on the north side – the Fergus estuary and west. Lanes and tracks lead from the

Killadysert–Labasheeda–Kilrush road to the water, sometimes across old causeways or dykes, and at Killadysert to a harbour newly spruced at Europe's expense. Two bays, each a couple of miles long, hold thousands of waders in winter. Clonderalaw Bay is also noted for its whooper swans, scamp and wader species, and Poulnasherry Bay supports brent geese, wigeon and other ducks. Both are easily accessible from the road.

The tides wash out the estuary every day, but in spite of that the water is seldom clear. The temptation to bathe is not great, not with the clear blue of Kilkee or the Dingle to right and left of the Shannon's mouth. But a boat would be good. You would probably have all the world - that you could see, at least - to yourself.

Before you go *Map:* OS Discovery Series map No. 63; OS Half-inch map of Ireland No. 17.

Getting there *By car:* take the N18 to Ennis, then follow the N68 for about 2 miles (3 km) to the R475. Take the R473 at the end of the R475. The R473 travels along the north bank of the River Shannon to Kilrush. *By train:* trains from Dublin stop at Limerick, where there is a connecting train to Ennis. *By bus:* a Bus Eireann Expressway service runs from Dublin to Kilkee via Limerick, Shannon and Ennis. A summer-only Bus Eireann Expressway service runs from Galway to Cork and stops at Kilkee and Kilrush. Local Bus Eireann services run from Limerick via Ennis, Kilrush and Kilkee to Kilbaha, and from Kilkee to Limerick. For further information contact the bus station at Ennis, T:(065) 24177. Bill O'Mahony Coaches, T:(065) 45730, runs a private service to Dublin, four buses on Friday

and three on Sunday. *By sea:* to Scattery Island, boats run in summer from Cappa pier, T:(061) 451327. A car ferry crosses the Shannon estuary from Killimer to Tarbert, Apr–Sept, T:(065) 51060.

Where to stay *Hotels:* there are plenty of hotels and bed and breakfasts in Ennis, Kilkee and Kilrush. *Outdoor living:* camp-sites in the area including Green Acres Caravan and Camping Park, Doonaha, T:(065) 57011, Cunningham Caravan and Camping Park, Kilkee, T:(061) 451009, and Aylevarroo Caravan and Camping Park, Kilrush, T:(065) 51102. *Youth hostels:* there is a hostel in Ennis, the Abbey Tourist Hostel, T:(065) 22620, and in Kilkee, the Kilkee Hostel, T:(065) 56209.

Activities *Walking:* bracing walks can be had around Loop Head, with views north to the Aran Islands and south to the Dingle Peninsula. Long hikes also run along the cliffs to Kilkee. *Riding:* hacks are available from the Smithstown Riding Centre, Ennis Road, Newmarket-on-Fergus, Co.

Clare, T:(061) 361494. *Skin-diving:* Kilkee is a well-known diving area. Shore dives are from Duggerna Rocks and boat dives from Black Rocks. A diving centre has opened on the harbour with equipment and air bottles for hire. *Cycling:* bikes can be hired from Gleeson Wholesale in Kilrush, T:(065) 51127, and the Korner Shop in Kilrush, T:(065) 51037. *Cycling Ireland*, a leaflet from Bord Failte, has a suggested route that runs right along the Shannon Estuary from Ennis. *Bird-watching:* the mud-flats of the estuary attract large numbers of waders and wildfowl, but the colonies are widely scattered. Best single area is the Fergus estuary with black-tailed godwits in spring and large winter populations of dunlin.

Further information: there is a Bord Failte tourist office in Kilrush, T:(065) 51577, and one in Kilkee, T:(065) 56112. Both are open only during the summer. The Bord Failte in Ennis, T:(065) 28366, is open all year.

The pine marten, on the decrease but still found in some central and western counties, has a sweet clean look but is a ruthless killer of small birds and insects.

CHAPTER 3

Kerry and Cork

Most easterly, landward approaches to the south-west of Ireland lead you up, over the watershed, and then pleasurably down, as if this region of long, bony red sandstone fingers pointing westward into the sea is a reward for uphill toil. Some say its attractions are fatal. Many of Killarney's beauties are defaced by an excess of tourists, and lesser-known parts are getting better known by the year. Really, it's no matter. The place is big enough to retain its wilderness and secrets. Standard tourists stick to celebrated routes and prescribed areas, many preferring an audio-visual presentation of the Skelligs on the mainland to a rough, ten-mile sea crossing and a wet strenuous climb when you get to them. These four peninsulas, and the smattering of islands round about them, have grandeur, drama, wildness and stirring beauty. Small wonder that the great and good who want escape from crowds and recognition – General de Gaulle, Benjamin Britten, Françoise Sagan, Charlie Chaplin and many more – had or have holiday homes in the area. Numbers of young Irish and English people, in search of some kind of alternative Nirvana, have settled here, too. You can still, in most of the area, imagine yourself a thousand miles from people.

Each ridge-backed promontory has its own character, and the biggest and best-known is the Iveragh ('Eve-raw' comes close to the pronunciation). The coast-road of this promontory is called for obscure reasons the Ring of Kerry.

Sunset brings a golden haze to the smoothly rounded mountains of the Iveragh Peninsula, seen here from the Beara Peninsula, across the 5-mile (8-km) width of the Kenmare River.

With Killarney at one end, the Skellig Rocks at the other and the Mac-Gillicuddy's Reeks (a mountain range of great beauty containing Ireland's highest peaks) in between, it is perhaps the most spectacular. Other peninsulas have more exotic, even alien, appeal. Indeed, the foreign character and connections of this part of Ireland are deep and legion. Spanish and French traders have come and gone for 2,000 years or more. Fleets from France and Spain, Barbary privateers, German U-boats have raided. As long ago as Neolithic times the Atlantic here was one of the great communicating waterways of Europe. From Dingle, there are plausible reasons to believe, the first Europeans to find America set off. And on the hills and mountains are long-settled plants that have arrived, by uncertain means, from more familiar quarters in Spain, Portugal and America. According to legend, the King of the World once did County Kerry the honour of invading it (he was repelled after much slaughter). From here, it was thought, a boat could take you over the water to the Land of Eternal Youth. It is a mistake to think, as many have and do, that in coming here you are approaching the limits of the civilized world.

The Dingle, north of the Ring of Kerry, is the peninsula most pervaded by the taste and feel of other countries and climates. Dark hair and Spanish looks are sometimes remarked upon, and there is talk, less dependable maybe, of an elusive monster from the Amazon in one of the mountain lakes. I think it is the people from whom the alien impression comes. On a dark wet day, I have to say, Dingle looks as darkly, wetly Irish as anywhere else, and on a fine day under a clear blue sky its sweeps of green and purple mountain, its rocky bays, broad sandy beaches and enchanting islands with their ghost-dwellings are utterly Irish too.

South of Iveragh lies the Beara peninsula. It too has bays, beaches, mountains, lagoons, bog, moorland, off-shore islands, sea-birds, rare plants – but these are no more than the local currency. The character that marks it off from Iveragh to its north and Mizen to its south is harder to name or define. A little wilder, I should call it, rather rougher textured, agreeably short on tourist amenities, though by no means without them. (There is even a ski-lift for getting over to Dursey Island, situated at its north-eastern tip.) Many resident tradespeople are trying to sharpen Beara's tourist appeal, which at its extreme means, I suppose, Killarne-fying. Before they succeed, if they ever do, I for one shall return and return.

The southernmost peninsula is double-pronged, with the mighty natural ramparts of Mizen Head at its south-western end and much rough and indeterminate landscape on the way to it. It is in the southern edge that its appeal lies, in its curlicued coastline and dazzling views over an archipelago of islands – the lone and no-longer-manned lighthouse of Fastnet solid and upright in the distance. Of the two islands served by regular ferries, Cape Clear is famous for its resident and, even more, its migratory birds. It was here thirty years or so ago that systematic scanning, with the benefit of improved optical technology, began to disclose the astonishing wealth of sea-bird life on Ireland's coasts. In comparison, Sherkin Island is not at first sight spectacular, but a recent survey shows a plant count far in excess of that previously accepted.

Baltimore is one of the ferry ports: a pleasant town, with a new restaurant added every time you turn your back (as seems to be the way in these parts), it was once a fishing depot, where agents from Britain and continental Europe waited to bid for incoming catches. The foreign link here is a bloody one. In 1631 Algerian pirates, who often prowled this coastline, landed, slaughtered a large number of townspeople and took away more as slaves. The bay here is spattered with rocks and islets, and the neighbouring land not so much undulating as bumpy or choppy. Round the corner, at the beginning of the ravels of County Cork's south coast, a first pretty inlet narrows to a tidal channel which feeds Lough Ine, a rarity in that it is an inland lake made up of salt water. Its richness in marine fauna and flora – a richness which extends out to sea but is more easily studied within these confines – is only one of the natural wonders in this south-west corner of Ireland. Mile after mile of lane is edged with fuchsia and escallonia. Rarities like the strawberry tree flourish in certain locations. Only a few miles off-shore lie Ireland's largest gannetry and the largest breeding colonies of storm petrels in the world.

GETTING THERE

By air: air travellers can arrive either at Shannon or Cork Airport. Shannon is the arrival point for many transatlantic flights.

By boat: ferries arrive at Cork from Swansea in the UK and from Roscoff in northern France. The Swansea–Cork crossing takes 10 hours and is operated by Swansea Cork Ferries, T:(01792) 456116.

By rail: the Dublin to Cork service runs five times a day throughout the week. The journey takes four hours.

WHERE TO STAY

Killarney is usually very crowded in the summer; however, there are generally enough hotels, hostels and camp sites in the area. More information can be found in Bord Failte's accommodation guide. The Dingle and Iveragh peninsulas are particularly well provided with hostels and camp-sites catering for walkers and nature lovers.

ACTIVITIES

Walking: the Killarney/Ring of Kerry area is the most visited part of Ireland. The Kerry Way is a 134-mile (214-km) way-marked route round the Iveragh peninsula through Caherciveen, Waterville, Caherdaniel, Kenmare and Kilgarvan. It often follows old drovers' roads and offers an opportunity to explore the spectacular uplands and MacGillycuddy's Reeks. It is split into 9 sections: stage 1, Killarney–Black Valley (13 miles/21 km); 2, Gearhameen–Glencar (13 miles/20 km); 3, Glencar Glenbeigh (11 miles/18 km); 4, Glenbeigh–Foilmore (13 miles/20 km); 5, Foilmore–Dromod (11 miles/17 km); 6, Dromod–Castlecove (11 miles/16 km); 7, Castlecove–Tahilla (14 miles/22 km); 8, Tahilla–Kenmare (13 miles/21 km); and 9, Kenmare–Killarney (15 miles/24 km). The 95-mile (153-km) Dingle Way circles the Dingle peninsula, taking walkers past Slea Head and Dunquin, which commands views of Europe's most westerly islands, the Blaskets (see page 103); it is split into 8 sections: stage 1, Tralee–Camp (12 miles/19 km); 2, Camp–Anascaul (11 miles/17 km); 3, Anascaul–Dingle (14 miles/22 km); 4, Dingle–Dunquin (14 miles/22 km); 5, Dunquin–Ballydavid (15 miles/24 km); 6, Ballydavid–Cloghane (14 miles/ 22 km); 7, Cloghane–Castlegregory (14 miles/22 km); 8, Castlegregory–Tralee (14 miles/23 km). Maps or guides are essential for walkers wishing to follow these routes. For more information on both these walks contact Cork/Kerry Tourism, Killarney Tourist Office, Town Hall, Killarney, T:(064) 31633; the all-year tourist office at Tralee, T:(066) 21288; or the seasonal office at Dingle, T:(066) 51188.

Climbing: Kerry and west Cork make up the finest walking and climbing country in Ireland. MacGillycuddy's Reeks contain Ireland's highest peaks and provide exciting ridge walking. Carrantuohill is the main peak at 3,414 ft (1,024 m). Iveragh peninsula contains the Mullaghanattin and Knocknagantee groups, with their isolated complex of combes, corries and lakes. On the Dingle peninsula, there are challenging climbs to be experienced on Mt Brandon. There are several walking and climbing holiday agencies, including Erin Encountered, contact Clive Garrett, Shronedarragh, Headford, Killarney, Co. Kerry, T:(064) 54366; Horgen Bergwandern,

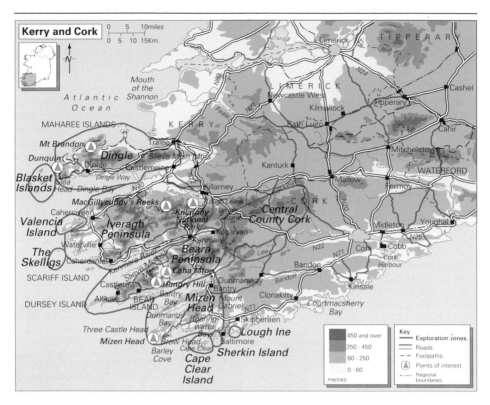

contact Michael Horgen, 2
Ballymullen, Tralee, Co..Kerry,
T:(066) 23174; Irish Wilderness
Experience, contact Terry
Carruthers, 50 Woodlawn Park,
Killarney, Co. Kerry, T:(064)
32992, and Walk-A-Way
Holidays, contact Donal Sowd,
Lower Bridge Street, Killorglin,
Co. Kerry, T:(066) 61940.
Fishing: information can be
obtained from the South
Western Fisheries Regional
Fisheries Board, 1 Neville's
Terrace, Masseytown,
Macroom, Co. Cork, T:(021)
41221. Salmon rivers in the area
include the Upper Caragh, the
Laune, the Sheen and the
Cummeragh. The River Laune
also contains brown trout.
Brown-trout lakes include
Lough Leane, Lough
Barfinnihy and Lough Guitane.
Cycling: west Cork has two

long-distance cycleways that are
described in the *Cycling Ireland*
leaflet available from all Bord
Failte offices. Cyclists with
plenty of energy for serious
climbs should experience the
lakes, rivers and coast of west
Cork. The Ring of Kerry has a
129-mile (206-km) route, while
the Dingle peninsula takes
cyclists through an area that is a
monument to Ireland's early-
Christian history. Cycle Ireland,
T:(064) 32536, and O'Callahan
Cycles, T:(064) 31465, in
Killarney can provide bikes and
accommodation vouchers.
Sailing: the Irish Association
for Sail Training, T:(01) 779801,
can provide details of sailing
clubs. The International Sailing
Centre, T:(021) 811237, in Cork
offers tuition for all levels.
Baltimore Sailing School,
T:(028) 20141, offers wind-

surfing and sailing tuition and
equipment.
Riding: trail rides around the
Dingle peninsula are organized
by W. O'Conner, El Rancho
Farmhouse, Ballyard, Tralee,
Co. Kerry, T:(066) 21840. This
centre also offers residential
horse-riding packages.
Rocklands Stables, T:(064)
34003, in Killarney offers riding
hacks and treks.

FURTHER INFORMATION
Killarney's tourist office,
T:(064) 31633, is in the town
hall in the town centre. There is
a year-round tourist office at
Tralee, T:(066) 21288, and a
seasonal office at Dingle,
T:(066) 51188. Tracks and
Trails provide information on
mountaineering, fishing and
other outdoor pursuits in the
area, T:(064) 35277.

Dingle

*Northernmost of the long mountain-spined
promontories of Kerry and Cork, stretching
into the Atlantic*

Early Christian monks chose wonderful
wild places in which to live and pray:
Delphi, Iona, Sinai, Mount Athos, the
Grande Chartreuse. Mount Brandon,
Ireland's second-highest mountain, and the
six-mile (ten-kilometre) range that almost
blocks off the western quarter of the Dingle
peninsula equal any of these sites. The
mountains' spiny ridge, hanging above a
series of ice-carved cirques and ice-cold
corries, commands Olympian views of
Connemara to the north, MacGillicuddy's
Reeks to the south-east, and the Atlantic to
north, south and west. But the view that
makes magic of this place is the blazing
golden turmoil far out over the water when a
bright sun sinks below the horizon.

I saw Mount Brandon first when, as a stu-
dent, I spent a holiday month at Anascaul,
on the south side of the peninsula. Here, for
the first time I read about my namesake St
Brendan and climbed the mountain to see
the spot where, in the early sixth century AD,
he built an oratory and gazed on perhaps a
hundred such sunsets. Brendan saw within
that golden submersion visions of blessed
and immortal lands, and resolved to go in
search of them. Back in my lodgings, eating
Mrs Kennedy's beefsteak (whose excellence
owed something to her being the butcher's
sister), I quickly forgot the climb and that
inspiring view as my landlady told me of a
walk she had arranged for me with two
village girls and a visit the following week in
other company to Puck Fair at Killorglin.
Both occasions were delicious, as were most
encounters with the courteous, subtle,
weathered residents of the Dingle, with their
lilting tones and sweet assentings. But that
mountain-top vision returned. In time I read
virtually all that had been written about the
sailor saint; about his preparations, his setting off with a crew of monks in a coracle of
cowhide, and the many miracles he encoun-

tered on the sea – at Easter an obliging
whale docked beside the coracle so that
mass could be held on its broad back – before discovering a land that many since have
identified as America. (Though a nineteenth-century sceptic recognized in all the
saint's landfalls features distributed around
Galway Bay.) In due course I fell in love with
Celtic Ireland and wrote a book about
Brendan and his contemporaries.

The Dingle peninsula is 30 miles (48 kilometres) long and varies from five miles
(eight kilometres) to 12 miles (19 kilometres)
across. It is the northernmost of the long
bony fingers which Kerry and Cork point
into the Atlantic. It is the most westerly land
in Europe, a spit of old red sandstone raised,
like the other promontories, from its archaic
sea-bed by the east–west folding and faulting,

Black-headed gulls – a small, noisy, boisterous,
scavenging species with a distinguishing dark brown
hood – fish and play above Inch Strand, a long
sandy spit protruding from the southern coast of the
Dingle peninsula.

squeezing and cracking that took place during the so-called Armorican orogeny nearly 300 million years ago – long before the Himalayas were formed. For most of its length the central (and broken) mountain chain rises – from flat, sand-fringed coastlands – steeply, cut by threads of falling water on the north side, but with more gentle gradients in the south. Three-quarters of the way along, the ridge turns sharply northward, to rise in turn to the Dingle's most spectacular pinnacles, Brandon Peak and Mount Brandon, this latter being (at 3,127 feet/938 metres) the second-highest mountain in Ireland.

The peninsula thrusts on westward for ten miles or so to the curved and foamy ceramics of Slea Head, pounded by waves blown in from America, with views of the humpy Blasket Islands (see p.103) and their abandoned habitations. The cliffs at this extreme of the promontory and along its northern flank are among Ireland's most dramatic: Sybil Head, the Three Sisters, Ballydavid Head and Brandon Head. Up to 1,000 ft (304 metres) high, they are the haunts of chough, raven and the elusive Manx shearwater, and more often than not assaulted by sheets of spume. Yet alongside such gothic pandemonium the Dingle offers mile upon mile of uninterrupted, flat and tranquil sand. Stradbally, within Brandon Bay on the north side, is Ireland's longest beach. It runs a full 12 miles (19 kilometres). There are long strands (the Irish word) at Smerwick and Ventry. And far from the Atlantic thunderings of the west lies the three-mile (five-

The shoveler duck is mainly a winter visitor to the lakes, rivers and estuaries of Ireland, though it does breed in the midlands and at various coastal points.

kilometre) sandspit of Inch, protecting the extensive mud-flats of Castlemaine harbour.

This area, tucked between the Dingle and Iveragh promontories, contains a rare colony of Kerry toads (*Bufo calamitas*, known in its few British sites as the natterjack), distinguished from the common variety by its smaller size, a yellow line running down its back, and a much moister skin. Here and nowhere outside the county, it wallows, swims, spawns, hunts. Occasionally seen at night on the sands, it spends most of its days cooling damply underneath.

There are other natural rarities. The dull but well-camouflaged Sandhill rustic moth (*Luperina nickerlii* ssp. *knilli*) occurs among Dingle dunes, on the Aran Islands, and nowhere else. The feral goat is sometimes, not quite reliably, reported in the west, though it has the talents of the abominable snowman for eluding humans. In recent years a bottle-nosed dolphin has commonly turned up to play with all comers in Dingle harbour.

The great wealth of the area is its birds. On either side of the base of the peninsula, Castlemaine harbour and Tralee Bay afford the brent goose one of its main winter homes in Ireland. Several thousand are present on each site, along with strong populations of sea-ducks. Some winters, Inch accommodates the red-throated diver (loon); more often seen is the great northern diver, whose call, rising from a coordinated babble and then falling sadly away, is to my mind one of the most poignant sounds in nature. Lough Gill, on the Maharees promontory, and Akeragh Lough, a series of duney lagoons eight miles (13 kilometres) north, receive large winter populations with a rich record of rarities.

Dingle has changed since my stay at Mrs Kennedy's. Then the vehicles parked outside the church at mass were almost all pony and trap. Cottages were thatched and traditional – no such thing as a Spanish bungalow. Bank-notes were deposited more under mattresses than in banks. The old talked Gaelic until on the approach of an Englishman they courteously switched to English; the young forgot Irish the moment they could and emigrated for work. There were scarcely any tourists, hotels or restaurants to keep them even seasonally busy. Nobody wasted effort climbing mountains or rocks and the only thing people went to sea for was fish. Smiling Killarney, to the south, was left to net all the tourists. The Dingle was magnificently private, gruff and magical, as it must have seemed to St Brendan and those hardy anchorites who sheltered in the cramped helmet-shaped stone huts which survive in relict townships along the way.

The tourist is accommodated now. Bungalows sprout, signs shout, caffs and B and Bs and souvenir emporia proliferate. Dingle has a new pier. Daily ferries run to the Blaskets. Paths and mountain ascents are way-marked, and the tarmacked roads, financed by Euro-money, grow broader and smoother by the year. During the holiday season, walkers following the official way-marked Dingle Way, a round trip starting and finishing at Tralee, will find that others have been funnelled into the same routes, particularly the easier stretches.

Yet they will frequently lose the world of this century as they climb to the heights of the Slieve Mish and later, on the return leg (and if weather allows), ascend and explore the Brandon complex and its purlieus. These include the west coast of Brandon Bay and the broad and daunting blanket bog that stretches westward from it, the cluster of corrie lakes below Slievanea, the raven-priested isolation of the pass of Mul-lachveal, and the valley of the Owenmore, falling away from Brandon Peak. A way-mark sign does not mean there is anybody up there. Brandon's ascent offers a continuous disclosure of new hills and valleys, slits of sea and distant blue mountain ranges, besides the powerful views close-to, of lakes suspended under towering bays of rock, and the tweedy colour-subtleties of the pervasive blanket bog. It used to be a common pilgrimage, second in status only to Croagh Patrick in County Mayo. Less difficult from Tiduff on the west than from Cloghane on the precipitous east, it always calls for the usual precautions for dangerous ascents.

BEFORE YOU GO
Maps: OS Discovery Series maps Nos 70 and 71. **Guidebooks**: *The New Irish Walk Guides: Southwest* by Sean O'Suilleabhain (Gill and Macmillan, 1991), *The Hills of Cork and Kerry* by Richard Mersey (Alan Sutton and Gill and Macmillan, 1987), and *Walk Cork and Kerry* by David Perrott and Joss Lynam all include walks on Dingle. *A Visitor's Guide to the Dingle Peninsula* by Steve MacDonogh (Brandon Book Publishers) is highly informative about place, history, nature, climbs, culture, language and archaeology.

GETTING THERE
By car: from Tralee follow the N86 towards Dingle. This is the main town on the Dingle

The Dingle Peninsula

peninsula. The R559 travels from Dingle to Slea Head, up the west coast and back. Tralee can be by-passed by those arriving on the N22 from Cork and Killarney by turning left on to the R561 at Farranfore.

By rail: the nearest station is Tralee, where trains run to and from Mallow, with connections to Cork, Limerick Junction, Shannon, Dublin and Rosslare.

By bus: several buses a day reach both Tralee and Dingle from Dublin, Cork and Limerick Junction, with links to Waterford, Galway and Shannon Airport. There is a local Bus Eireann service that runs about three times a day between Killarney and Dingle, and another that runs between Dingle and Tralee. The service from Dingle to Slea Head takes you around the coast of the peninsula. Contact the Travel Centre, Casement Station, Tralee, T:(066) 23566.

WHERE TO STAY

Hotels: there are lots of bed and breakfasts and hotels to choose from in Dingle and many more scattered round the peninsula.

Youth hostels: there are plenty of independent hostels in the area, including Ballingart House Hostel and Equestrian Centre, T:(066) 51454, in Dingle; Bog View Hostel, T:(066) 58125, halfway between Dingle and Tralee; Seacrest, T:(066) 51390; Inch Hostel, T:(066) 58181, 10 miles (16 km) from Castlemaine; and Lovett's, T:(066) 51903, in Dingle.

Outdoor living: there are lots of camp-sites around the peninsula, including the Seaside Caravan and Camping Park at Camp Village near Tralee, T:(066) 30161; Anchor Caravan and Camping Park, Castlegregory, T:(066) 39157; and Oratory House Caravan and Camping Park, Dingle, T:(066) 55143.

ACCESS

The Dingle is kind to car-drivers. Decent roads, the R561 and the N86, loop the Slieve Mish and Beenoskee mountains in the centre; and though no road could climb to the precipitate sea-facing side of the Brandon range, there is a staggering view to be had of the corrie-pocked east of the mountain – and much else besides – from the Conor Pass, north-east of Dingle.

ACTIVITIES

Walking: the Dingle Way is a 95-mile (153-km) circular way-marked route that goes right round the edge of the Dingle peninsula. It takes around five to six days to walk, takes in towns, villages and tarmacked roads, but also offers unrivalled views, Celtic remains, Gaelic speakers and colourful myths. Contact tourist offices at Tralee, Dingle or Killarney for further information. While the standard of way-marking is generally high, a Dingle Way map or guide is essential.

Riding: four- and seven-day treks are available at El Rancho Horse Holidays near Castlegregory, T:(066) 21840.

Climbing: the best climbing is on Mt Brandon and Brandon Peak. The cliffs to the north are fine for the specialist. A large-scale map and compass are essential if the weather is not perfectly clear. R. Mersey's book (see above) is very helpful. For more information contact the Mountaineering Council of Ireland, c/o Rory Boyd, 25 Cranford Court, Stillorgan Road, Dublin 4.

Fishing: good sea-trout fishing is available off the north coast of the peninsula in Tralee Bay, near Castlegregory, and near Dingle. Contact the local boatman, T:(066) 51163, to arrange sea-fishing trips.

Cycling: bikes can be hired from

Moriarty, T:(066) 51316, in Dingle.

Sailing: dinghy sailors and wind-surfers will find good sailing conditions off the north coast of the peninsula, in Tralee Bay.

Bird-watching: Kerry is the favoured first landfall of more than half the birds that migrate to or through Europe from America. In spite of the relative shortage of nature reserves in Ireland, there are three on and about the Dingle peninsula, and more within a few miles. At Castlemaine harbour, *Zostera marina*, a plant whose seeds can be ground into good flour, grows in abundance and, along with natural shelter and spacious mud-flats and salt-marsh, induces thousands of wildfowl to winter here. Brent goose, wigeon and pintail occur by the thousand, shoveler and common scoter by the hundred. There is good viewing from various points along and below the road from Castlemaine to Anascaul. With similar inducements to those of Castlemaine harbour, Tralee Bay attracts huge winter colonies of brent goose, wigeon and common scoter. Lough Gill, on the promontory leading to the Magharee Islands, attracts, along with three species of swan, many kinds of duck, including gadwall, teal and shoveler. Further up the coast, among the lagoons of Akeragh Lough, migrating waders, flocking in from northern Europe and Greenland, add substantially to the bird count.

FURTHER INFORMATION

Tourist offices: the tourist office in Dingle is open from April to October, T:(066) 51188/51241. The one at Tralee is open year-round, T:(066) 21288, as is Cork/Kerry Tourism, Town Hall, Killarney, T:(064) 31633.

Blasket Islands

Group of islands off the west end of the Dingle peninsula, virtually uninhabited since 1953 and rich in bird life

Ireland is full of the Ozymandias effect: greatness gone by, gathering dust, its meaning forgotten. It inspires the great Celtic gloom, known from the Hebrides to Portugal, a weeping for a lost culture, a lost language, lost loves, the wild ducks and the wild geese flown away. The Blasket Islands, a stone's throw beyond the end of the Dingle peninsula, are the site of a great loss recent enough not to be quite forgotten, but slipping away through the hourglass as those old enough to remember disperse or die, and memory is formalized in remnant writings. They say that careful observation could pick out former inhabitants of the Blaskets in Dunquin and Dingle, the mainland towns to which they were finally transplanted in 1953. A lifetime of rowing curraghs in all weathers had made the men's neck sinews stand out hard and strong; walking along sheep-walks had predisposed them to proceed in single file. There is less, if any, point looking for these characteristics now.

It would scarcely matter if the Blaskets were not so beautiful, and if the several written accounts of the life lived there were not powerfully beautiful too. Geologically the islands are a continuation of the peninsula, heavily folded seams of stripped sandstone and slate on which the sea has encroached and, in doing so, changed everything. The humps of the Great Blasket, the biggest of the islands, rising to 1,000 feet (300 metres) on the north edge, begin hardly more than a mile from Dunmore Head. It is three and a half miles (six kilometres) long. Beyond it, to the left, is Inishvickillaune (privately owned by Charles Haughey, former *taoiseach* or prime minister), with an erratic history of occupation, and Inis na Bro, with Tearacht hidden behind the big island. Over to the north looms the sharp-toothed silhouette of Tuaisceart, rather like a miniature Skellig Michael. Much closer in lies the flat plain of Beiginis, overlooked by the old ruined village of the Great Blasket.

From the mainland, using field-glasses, you can see the ruins of Great Blasket, and the sheep that have been left to graze by those who own or have inherited land. One or two of the houses have been restored for basic habitation. Tourists go over on day-trips and some people camp. For years after the abandonment, the islands were visited by Americans who had migrated as children when a hundred or more people still lived there. They were often shocked, quite unprepared for the desolation, the short brutish work that nature had made of their childhood world.

Nature had never been a dependable ally, and the islanders had suffered its buffets. To pay for their clothes and tobacco, they had

Guillemot, razorbill and kittiwake (anti-clockwise from left) are three common sea-birds which during the breeding season often occupy the same sheer, ledged, coastal cliffs. The first two are auks: brilliant fishers and underwater swimmers. The kittiwake is particularly attractive and very graceful in flight.

taken what they could from it: fish from the sea, lobsters, seals, birds and eggs from their nests, rabbits from their warrens. They hunted thrushes and lifted unsuspecting puffins from their roosting holes. It was not Arcadia. But there was a wholeness, a harmony, a need each for the other, poetry, music, dance, deep humour, wry irony. They knew the land like their hands and read the sea like a blind man braille, telling its mood and motions by feel and touch through the taut skins of their air-light curraghs. And for all the hardship they could still wonder at the sunsets and seas and mists and the changing colours of the mainland mountains, and celebrate it all in ancient ritual dances. More than one ambitious young man crossed the sea in search of fortune, disembarked at Dunquin, climbed the pass below Mount Eagle and seeing for the first time little Ventry and its two hundred houses ahead, turned about and returned home, deciding the world was too impossibly crowded for comfort.

It was the decline of the herring shoals that did for the islanders in the end, though Richard Mersey in his book *The Hills of Cork and Kerry* points to something else. For Maurice O'Sullivan, one of the trio of authors whose sublime books will continue to keep some memories of the islands alive,

the neon sign of the Capitol Cinema in Dublin represented civilization's peak. The lure of modernity had been draining humans off the islands for years before the final break. We who sing its praises with such facile sentiments never lived the life. The sinews in my neck are quite hidden.

That will not stop us going. The birds have not left. The outer islands in particular are home to many sea-birds: guillemots, razorbills, fulmars and various gulls, all of which are easily seen by day. Another species, which comes in and leaves by night, is more likely to be seen as shadows or heard as coos and shrieks. These are the Manx shearwaters, present in their thousands during the breeding season, and storm petrels, which appear in their tens of thousands. The female shearwaters lay one egg each, and the newly emerged chick would be vulnerable to gulls if it did not remain within a hillside burrow. Intensely security-conscious, the foraging parent birds – most of whose life is spent on the open ocean – float near the land as darkness comes and fly in only when they gauge it safe. On brightly moonlit nights they do not come at all, and the young must go hungry. This influx of birds, scarcely seen, hauntingly heard, almost touched, is one of the eeriest things in nature.

BEFORE YOU GO
Maps: OS Discovery Series map No. 70.
Books: *The Blasket Islands* by Joan and Ray Stagles (O'Brien Press, 1980), *Twenty Years A-Growing* by Maurice O'Sullivan (Oxford University Press).

GETTING THERE
By boat: there is no car ferry service to the Blasket Islands. Enquire at Dunquin June–Aug for boats going to Great Blasket, T:(066) 56188. The first boat leaves the mainland at 10 am and the last boat leaves the Blaskets at 3 pm.
By bus: there are two local Bus

Eireann summer services and one year-round Bus Eireann service between Killarney and Tralee, which stop at Dunquin.

WHERE TO STAY
Hotels: bed and breakfasts in or near Dunquin include Kruger's, T:(066) 56127, and Mrs Marie Thompson, T:(066) 56144.
Youth hostels: there is an An Oige hostel in Dunquin, T:(066) 56145. There is also a small private hostel on the Blaskets which is open only during the summer.
Outdoor living: camping is

permitted free in the hostel grounds.

ACTIVITIES
Walking: there are some good strenuous, but unmarked, walks along the mountainous length of Great Blasket.
Bird-watching: the islands are a good place to see many varieties of sea-bird in season, including guillemot, razorbill, fulmar, storm petrel and Manx shearwater.

FURTHER INFORMATION
Tourist offices: the nearest Bord Failte tourist office is in Tralee, T:(066) 21288.

Iveragh Peninsula

Largest of the great promontories and home to Ireland's highest mountain, Carrantuohill

A hundred years ago they called the railway round the Iveragh peninsula, opened in 1893, the 'Grand Atlantic Coast Route'. Roads have replaced the railway track now and people speak of the 'Ring of Kerry'. It is not, in point of fact, a ring nor does it encircle Kerry. The Dingle, part of the Beara, much of the Shannon estuary and all inland Kerry fall outside it.

The Iveragh lies between some of the finest sights in the world: the Skellig rocks ten miles (16 kilometres) out to sea to the west, and to the east, Killarney, which remains, if you can find or imagine it without tourists and the carnivorous end of the tourist trade (say on a sunny weekday morning in January), the equal of Eden. Most of the peninsula's approximately 40 by 17 miles (64 by 27 kilometres) is occupied by mountains, of which there are four main ranges: the Glenbeigh horseshoe in the north, with the outlying Knocknadobar to its west; the Dunkerrons running close to the south coast; the Mangerton range over-

lapping them and continuing eastward; and MacGillicuddy's Reeks, north of Mangerton and west of Lough Leane.

Among all these stands the highest mountain in Ireland, Carrantuohill, one of the Reeks (3,404 feet/1,038 metres). There are five more mountains over 3,000 feet (in other words, 'Munros', a tiresome distinction which has people who cannot tackle their mountain-climbing in a way more in tune with the landscape notching up peaks as others do railway-engine numbers), and a total of 63 over 2,000 feet (610 metres). Among so many peaks, rainfall is high, reaching 140 inches (350 centimetres) a year in certain parts. That and the relative warmth make mist a frequent obstacle and danger to climbers.

Not that obstacles and dangers put climbers off – for many they are among the main attractions. The real draw, however, must be the sights of that removed vertiginous world, suspended behind its excluding wall of rock, unpeopled, unbuilt, close to that cardinal rawness in which the earth's heavings and convulsions and contractions left it millions of years ago, sharing its plane of existence only with the sky. It is a world of peaks and dips, of neat sharp cones and long lolloping sprawls of mountain, shimmering wet curtains of solid stone, lake cavities ladled out of the rock by retreating ice, water as lake, water as stream, water as thin white

Along with fuchsia and estallonia, gorse – seen here beside a weed-cracked road west of Kenmare on the Iveragh peninsula – is one of the pervading glories of the early Irish summer.

cataract, bouncing off rock stairs in a precipitous plummet, water – rarefied – as the air you breathe and the mist that blinds you, as the cloud coiling up the valley below you, water as the contents of the corrie that offers the hot and sticky climber the shock and bliss of cold immersion. There are cols and aiguilles and saddlebacks and steps and chimneys and nunataks and sugar loaves and soggy bogs.

Each of these ranges provide fine climbs. Richard Mersey, author of *The Hills of Cork and Kerry*, who has been up them all, says the 2,539-foot (774-metre) Mullaghanattin is 'Kerry's finest peak ... the Matterhorn of Ireland'. It rises towards the eastern end of the Dunkerrons, above the lower valley of the River Caragh, being only a few miles from the Reeks, the Mangerton range and the Glenbeigh horseshoe. Taken from its northern side it presents you with toils and thrills and wonderful views, unlike the long steep and steady slope of the southern

access: 'monotonous and ghastly', according to Mersey. The advice of the experienced is clearly essential to make the best of any time here. Not far from Mullaghanattin's summit is a memorial to a climber of world class and experience who died on a stretch many might treat too lightly. Indeed most writers emphasize the treachery of apparently easy climbs. The large numbers of people climbing Carrantuohill, often in guided groups, becoming for an instant the highest people on Irish soil, give an impression that the enterprise is simple. It is, in truth, not very difficult, but there are real dangers. There are more accidents on this one mountain than on all the others in the county put together. Most arise from the over-confidence of the inexperienced.

The blessing for cyclist and driver is that roads cross these ranges of mountains, and tracks take you to an impressive array of views. There is a wonderful picture of Mullaghanattin from the pass called Ballaghisheen, on the westward road to

A dramatic cloudscape heralds the dusk near Sneem on the Kenmare river.

CHAPTER 3: KERRY AND CORK

Waterville between the lesser peaks of Knocknacusha and Knocknagapple. Ballaghisheen means the road of Oisin, poet, warrior, one of the great figures of Irish myth, son of the hero Finn. Oisin was here on this pass, when the goddess Niamh of the golden hair carried him off to the land of promise (beyond the sea to the west) to live in perpetual youth and bliss provided he never touched his native land again.

Eastward, across the main body of the Reeks, the Gap of Dunloe, with its river and string of lakes, cuts through from north to south, isolating the final eastern peaks of Shehy and the Purple mountains. The Gap marks, roughly, the western end of the district of lakes, mountains, waterfalls, cliffs, islands, castles and other visual delights known collectively after the little town of Killarney. This loveliness is adulterated for much of the time by the massive presence of people and their traces. (The traces extend a few miles west to Carrantuohill's summit, which supports not only a large steel cross but a tide of sweet and cigarette papers, cans and other jetsam.) Guides and boatmen and jarvies with their jaunting cars open their mouths along geological faults to produce smiles that have coaxed money out of the unwary for years and will for years more. But it is not too difficult to evade them and to enjoy the three principal lakes (Lough Leane, Muckross Lake and Upper Lake), the caves and cascades, and the rocks that thrilled Queen Victoria, drawing a poem out of Tennyson and a serenade from Britten. Ladies' View, just above the Upper Lake on the road from Kenmare, is as good a place as any from which to survey the scene with no more effort, if you are in a car, than turning the head. More dramatic panoramas are offered from the peaks of Torc mountain and Mangerton to the east, and Purple mountain, accessible from the Gap of Dunloe, to the west.

As always, you need only stir a few yards from the tourist beat to find lesser-known beauties and curiosities. There are the queer rock sculptures made by water eating away the carboniferous limestone around Lough Leane and Muckross (the district divides neatly between carboniferous rock in the north and old red sandstone in the south, which as in all these south-western peninsulas, erupted through the limestone to create the main heights). There is also the wide variety of plants, many of them unexpected in these islands, flourishing on lime or the more acid sandstone, on the rain and moisture-laden air, and normally benign temperatures. Snow, on its rare visits, stays high on the mountains, and even frost is not a common sight.

Ancient woodlands survive in Killarney National Park. From the lake-side limestone of Muckross rise sizeable stands of yew. Oak and, to a lesser extent, birch and holly and hazel make up the largest area of native woodland in the country. Among smaller, shrubby plants, the strawberry tree (*Arbutus unedo*) thrives in the wild, while thorn-apples (*Datura stramonium*), tree-ferns (family *Cyatheaceae*), numerous bamboos (genus *Bambusa*), mesembryanthemums and others proliferate in those gardens which fulfil their soil requirements. Two saxifrages, and the insect-eating greater butterwort, are among the colonists from the Iberian peninsula.

During the tourist season, the Ring of Kerry can seem crowded – in contrast to the Beara and other southern peninsulas. They will afford you a beach to yourself in June and September if not in August. The Ring of Kerry will assuredly not. The southern sections of road and coast west from Kenmare are relatively dull. At Parknasilla the prettiness is like pictures in frames: not wild, not quite real. (Shaw stayed in the Great Southern Hotel here to write parts of *Saint Joan*.) At Derrynane, however, things are much better. Derrynane Abbey, once the home of Daniel O'Connell, cleverest and most admirable of the prophets and campaigners of Irish nationalism, stands restored at the head of Derrynane Bay. There is also a superb sandy beach, with access at low tide to Abbey Island.

Scariff Island, a few miles further west, is a bigger affair, about a mile from end to end with formidable coastal cliffs. The wildlife here includes the petrels, shearwaters and puffins which frequent and nest on so many islands around these coasts. For a week or two a year, the Marquess of Waterford and his sons are dropped in without victuals but with guns in order to acquire them, in the form of seals, seagulls and rabbits. Their home is a wonderful Vanbrugh house in a beautiful demesne in east Waterford. I suppose they own this too. Somebody I know owns a small island not far from here. I think an aged relation left it to him. On his next visit to these parts he hurried down to the shore, from which he had been given to understand it would be easily seen. It was not. A local man explained: 'You'd have to be waiting for the tide to go out for the island to emerge from the water.'

This western end of the Iveragh is delectable. From the pass of Coomakesta (north of Derrynane and providing a first distant view of the pointed Skellig rocks), the Atlantic, innumerable islands, inland mountains, the grand profiles of Dingle and Beara, crescent strands and tumbling cliffs are constantly reshuffled into new panoramas. The prospects from the road along the south of Lough Currane are beautiful, and the area affords a good starting point for climbs in the western Dunkerrons. The next road right leads along the rising Inny valley

to the Reeks and the meeting point of all the Iveragh ranges. But keeping to the coast takes you round the sweep of Ballinskelligs Bay, and uphill to overlook St Finan's Bay, a wilder affair exposed to everything wind and ocean can throw at it. Puffin Island, rich in bird life but not (for that reason) open to the public, forms the north end of the bay. Down below is Valencia Island.

The northern section of the Ring is a wonderful land to explore, both on the seaward and landward sides. It boasts an abundance of walks among climbable hills, little lakes, pretty bays and rocks, with the continual presence to the north of the Dingle's bumpy silhouettes. Before Glenbeigh, a comfortable resort, the pinnacled wall of the Glenbeigh horseshoe curves round its clutch of corries. Out of town, a right turn leads for three or more miles past Lough Caragh, where a boat may be hired, to an unlikely refreshment of woods (mainly oak) and grassy glades, with streams purling under stone bridges and down gentle slopes. It was once a spot favoured for shooting, and the lake still draws fishermen. Above, the brotherhood of MacGillicuddy's Reeks continue their timeless conclave.

BEFORE YOU GO

Maps: OS Discovery Series maps Nos 78, 83, 84. OS half-inch maps of Ireland Nos 20 and 24.

Guidebooks: Bord Failte produces a map guide for the Kerry Way. See also *The New Irish Walk Guides: Southwest* by Sean O'Suilleabhain (Gill and Macmillan, 1991) and *The Hills of Cork and Kerry* by Richard Mersey (Alan Sutton and Gill and Macmillan, 1987)

GETTING THERE

By car: to reach the Iveragh peninsula and the Ring of Kerry from Tralee, follow the N7 (south-west) to Caherciveen. The N7 travels right round the edge of the peninsula.

By rail: the nearest stations to

the Iveragh peninsula and the Ring of Kerry are Tralee and Killarney. Services run to and from Dublin twice a day, Sat–Thurs, and three times a day on Fridays. For MacGillicuddy's Reeks and Killarney National Park the nearest station is Killarney.

By bus: a Bus Eireann summer-only service from Sneem to Kenmare travels along the Ring of Kerry three times a day and twice on Sundays; it also serves the southern edge of the Reeks. Bus Eireann services from Waterville to Caherciveen run once a day. Bus Eireann runs many services into Killarney from all over Ireland.

WHERE TO STAY

Hotels: there is a large selection

of hotels and bed and breakfasts throughout the Iveragh peninsula. There are innumerable hotels and bed and breakfasts to choose from in and near Killarney. There are also a few in Sneem and Kenmare.

Youth hostels: independent hostels on the Iveragh peninsula include Slieve Hostel, Caherciveen, T:(066) 51454; Laune Valley Farm Hostel, near Killorglin, T:(066) 61488; and the Hillside House Hostel, T:(066) 68228. The two An Oige hostels in Killarney are Glanmore Lake Hostel, T:(064) 83181, and Killarney International Hostel, T:(064) 31240. There are also a large number of independent hostels in Killarney, including Fossa

Holiday Hostel, T:(064) 31497; Neptune's Killarney Town Hostel, T:(064) 35255; Park Hostel, T:(064) 32119; and Peacock Farm Hostel, T:(064) 33557.

Outdoor living: there is a good choice of camp-sites on the Iveragh peninsula, including Mannix Point Caravan and Camping Park, T:(066) 72806; West Caravan and Camping Park near Killorglin, T:(066) 61240; Waterville Caravan and Camping Park, T:(066) 74191; and Kells Bay Caravan and Camping Park, T:(066) 77647. Camp-sites in Killarney include Beech Grove Caravan and Camping Park, T:(064) 31727; Flask Caravan and Camping Park, T:(064) 31704. White Villa Farm Caravan and Camping Site, T:(064) 32456, and Fossa Caravan and Camping Park, T:(064) 34459, are closest to Killarney National Park.

The strawberry tree has pretty white pendant bell-flowers and a red fruit that looks like a strawberry but is in fact quite inedible. A native of Spain that has found its way to Ireland without human agency and settled successfully, it abounds in the Killarney area.

ACTIVITIES

Walking: the Kerry Way is a 135-mile (216-km) long way-marked route, the longest in the Republic. The Way starts and ends in Killarney, and runs right round the Iveragh peninsula. For further information, contact Cork/Kerry Tourism, Tourist Office, Town Hall, Killarney, T:(064) 31633. MacGillicuddy's Reeks provide exciting ridge walking with lovely views. Carrantuohill is best approached from either the head of Black Valley (south) or from Hag's Glen (north). A traverse of the entire range from the Gap of Dunloe to Beenkeragh or Caher is a long,

strenuous but highly rewarding walk. Track and Trails, T:(064) 35277, can provide further information about walking and activities in the area and organizes walking tours.

Fishing: Lough Currane near Waterville is particularly good for trout. For information about sea angling (mackerel and shark), ask at O'Sullivans, a tackle shop in Waterville. The whole of this region offers excellent lake and river fishing. There is good brown-trout fishing in Lough Leane and some of the smaller lakes towards Kenmare, but there is no coarse fishing available in the area. Permits, licences and information are available from O Neills in Killarney, T:(064) 31970.

Watersports: there are quite a few facilities around Caherciveen and Waterville; further details are available at tourist offices.

Riding: riding trips can be organized by O'Sullivans, T:(064) 31686, in Ballydowney, and horse riding is also available at Killarney Riding Stables, T:(064) 31686, in

Ballydowney. This centre offers treks right through Killarney National Park.

Cycling: *Cycling Ireland*, a leaflet from Bord Failte, has a suggested route that runs right round the Iveragh peninsula, along the Kerry Way. Bikes can be hired from O'Sullivans, T:(064) 31282, in Killarney. O'Neill's, also in Killarney, will deliver bikes free to your accommodation and include map, panniers and a repair kit, T:(064) 319700.

FURTHER INFORMATION
There are Bord Failte tourist offices located in Caherciveen, T:(066) 21288; Kenmare, T:(064) 41233; and Killarney, T:(064) 31633. The Killarney office is open all year.

The cloud-capped line of the Slieve Miskish, on the Beara, is visible across the Kenmare river in this night-view from Caherdaniel, on the Iveragh peninsula.

Valencia Island

An island off the north-west corner of the Iveragh peninsula, with fine, bird-thronged cliffs. Terminal, from 1865, of the first transatlantic cable

A bridge at Portmagee takes traffic to Valencia, given its name by the Spanish merchants who frequented it. (There is much said and written about the dark Iberian looks encountered on these western coasts as far up as Galway.) The island's capital, Knights Town, is at its eastern end. It basks in old glories: a fine harbour, the old seat – now sold and sold again – of the Knights of Kerry, descendants of one of three brothers supposedly given uniquely hereditary knighthoods by Edward III after a hard-fought battle in Scotland. From 1866 well into this century Knights Town was the eastern terminal

of the Atlantic telegraph cable which gave it the handsome sea-facing terraces where employees once lived. Now history has abandoned it. The bridge to link Valencia to the mainland was sited, to the dismay of many, beside Portmagee. The manufacture of billiard tables from the slate quarries under Geokaun (888 ft/270 m) virtually died out a hundred years ago. Knights Town sleeps on with a smile on its lips. It has a renowned diving centre, where visitors may explore underwater life, along with boats, decent food, nice places to stay, and the rich subtropical flora of the garden of Glanleam, the Knights' old home. It is a quiet and underpopulated island, with dramatic outcrops in the Fogher cliffs west of Geokaun and at Bray Head, at its extreme west.

Before you go *Maps*: OS half-inch map of Ireland No. 20.

Getting there *By car*: from Tralee follow the N70 to Caherciveen. A mile down the road, take the R565 to Knights Town.

By rail: the nearest station is Tralee, where services run to and from Dublin twice daily, Sat–Thurs, and three times a day on Fridays.

By bus: a local Bus Eireann summer-only service stops at Caherciveen and Waterville, the two nearest towns.

Where to stay: there are bed and breakfasts to be found on Valencia Island, as well as an An Oige Hostel, T:(066) 7614, and two independent hostels: the Ring Lyne Hostel, T:(066) 76103, and the Royal Pier, T:(066) 76144.

Activities: Valencia Island is a popular scuba-diving centre. Contact Des Lavelle, T:(066) 76124, and Valencia Hyperbaric Diving Centre, T:(066) 76225, for more information. For sea-angling trips (cod, ling, conger, haddock and shark), contact Dan McCrohan, T:(066) 76142. Bikes can be hired from Curran's, T:(066) 76247.

Further information: the nearest tourist office is privately run and is located in Caherciveen, T:(066) 21288.

The Skelligs

Two steep sea rocks famous for their breeding birds, monastic remains and isolated grandeur

In the great medieval best-seller *The Voyage of St Brendan*, the intrepid and godly sailor and his crew come upon an island on which is a very large tree. Not a leaf of this tree is visible for its branches are covered with large white birds: one flies down – his wings tinkling like little bells – to explain that they are the spirits of those who fell from heaven with Lucifer, and now spend holy days and festivals singing the Creator's praises from dawn to dusk in penance.

It seems impossible that this description could have been inspired by any bird other than the gannet, which lives and breeds not in trees but on a few isolated rocks pitched in the seas round Britain and Ireland. The biggest Irish colony is settled on the Lesser Skellig rock, eight or so miles to the west of the Iveragh peninsula. There seems to be no particular reason for gannets representing the spirits of sinners, but that they should be thought of as glorifying God seems wholly appropriate.

You get to the Skelligs by boat from Portmagee, Knights Town or Ballinskelligs, weather permitting. The journey may take three-quarters of an hour each way, and a curious process takes place in its course. On the mainland, it goes without saying, humans call the tune. Birds, when you see them, are peripheral, glosses on the margin.

Slowly, as the boat chops through the waves, you move into a bird world. Increasing numbers fly near or over, carrying fish or grass for nests, or engaged in some less patent purpose. Almost from the start there are individuals afloat or diving, but as the miles go by they become groups and then whole fleets of puffin, gannet, guillemot or gull. They take no notice of you, expecting no harm. You are the gloss now, moving through their space as if invisible. They fly, cry, dive, plunge or ride the waves as indifferent to your existence as you were to that of sparrows back on land.

The lesser of the two Skellig rocks grows as you approach it, in silhouette a tableau of sharp crags. It seems to be a dull, yellowy-white colour, which does not square with your knowledge that both rocks, like so many of these south-western promontories and islands, consist of red sandstone and slate. The steady level of noise, too, comes out to meet you: an unrelieved crescendo of baying, braying, cawing and shrieking. An acrid whiff of guano hangs in the air. There are birds above and all around you, reminiscent of a beehive in alarm, except that this is routine pandemonium, not panic, and you are not regarded as either danger or voyeur. You are not regarded at all.

The yellowy-white is simply solid gannet. Their heads and necks are yellow, and their wings end in a triangle of black, and everything else is snow-white. You can infer the shape of the rock from the shape the gannets collectively make, filling every available niche, ledge and cranny, sitting, preening, standing, wing-flapping, waving their necks in display, disgorging or accepting fish, flying off or alighting, and all the time maintaining a raucous babble. There are over 20,000 nesting pairs at peak season.

The boat chugs slowly into a narrow channel, vertical black rock rising high on each side. No gannets here – they clearly prefer the open air and the panorama. This confined space is a kittiwake tenement, tier after tier of these neatly pretty gulls sitting on eggs in rock-based nests composed, like swallows' nests, of miscellaneous materials assembled and glued together.

Boat trips follow a standard route. There

The gannet's headlong dive into the sea, the closing of its wings just before entry, and its re-emergence with the fish it spotted a hundred feet up, can be seen up to fifty miles away from whichever raucous rocky colony the search for prey has brought it. There are half a dozen colonies round the Irish coast, containing up to 20,000 breeding pairs.

is no landing allowed on the Lesser Skellig, and you move on a mile or more to the Greater, where you can disembark and climb about five hundred rock-hewn steps to the restored remains of an early-Christian monastery, and a couple of hundred feet more to the peak. On the way up, you will – at the right time of year – find yourself walking feet away from nesting guillemots and razorbills and an arm's length from kittiwakes. Higher up, if you could stay till they return at the end of the day, you would have to wait for puffins to waddle out of your way on the steps. The burrows in which they nest often riddle the earth on either side of these ancient steps.

The monastery provokes thoughts of men prepared to endure a punishing wilderness for the sake of their god, a tradition imparted by the desert hermits of Sinai, received and continued with uncanny enthusiasm by the Irish. They even adopted the word desert – it survives to this day on the sites of many monasteries, however green and lush and wet their setting. No written records survive the monastic occupation of Skellig Michael, which lasted from the seventh to the tenth century perhaps. Everything we know about the monks' way of life involves guess-work, though given the climate, it is certain they

CHAPTER 3: KERRY AND CORK

The south-western corner of Ireland breaks up into innumerable splintered fragments, headlands with off-shore rocks and islands, among them Lamb's Head, last in a line of hilly promontories running west from Castlecove on the Iveragh coast.

were cut off in these narrow confines, above sheer precipices, often in dense mist or rain or violent gale, for weeks on end. They must have fished. Probably they grew vegetables (as nineteenth-century lighthouse keepers did). Perhaps they had grain to grind and bake. The water they drank must have been rain, caught in hollowed-out stone or rock basins. The rabbits that thrive here now were not brought in, it is thought, until the last century. A faith that may not be conceivable in our times must have driven them. An insecurity with which we are becoming more and more familiar finally did for them. Vikings, it seems, raided the island more than once, and in the end made continued residence impossible.

Nothing in Ireland makes more impression on me – and on many others – than these two sequestered, sea-whipped rocks. They stand as a testament to the faith of man in a world beyond this one, and to man's trust in nature, when he keeps in check his talents for killing, maiming and despoiling, and regards the wonders of the world with seemly awe.

BEFORE YOU GO
Maps: OS half-inch map of Ireland No. 20.

GETTING THERE
By boat: several people run boat services to these islands. Jo Roddy operates from Ballinskelligs, T:(066) 74268, on the mainland. He has two boats, a fast one that takes half an hour to reach the islands and a slow one that takes an hour. Sean Feehan, T:(066) 79182; J.B. Walsh, T:(066) 79147; Brendan O'Keefe, T:(066) 77103; and Murphy's, T:(066) 77156, also operate boat services that run from Portmagee.

WHERE TO STAY
There is a camp-site in Waterville, T:(066) 74191, and a good selection of bed and breakfasts. No accommodation is available on the islands themselves.

ACCESS
As the Skellig Islands are a nature reserve, permission may be required to visit. Further information from the visitor centre (see below).

ACTIVITIES
Walking: walkers will enjoy the hike up the 712-ft (217-m) jagged rock of Skellig Michael.
Bird-watching: the islands are

home to a large variety of sea-birds including storm petrels, kittiwakes, gannets and puffins.

FURTHER INFORMATION
There is a visitor centre, T:(064) 31633, just before the bridge from Portmagee to Valencia.

Beara Peninsula

*One of the great south-western
promontories, between the Kenmare river
and Bantry Bay, containing the Caha
mountain range*

WWW

West Cork and west Kerry contain between them the wildest parts of Ireland, mostly made up of rather secretive mountain groups or chains with many peaks over 2,000 feet (600 metres). Formed of red sandstone with slate fringes, raised, tipped, fissured and faulted by the Armorican upheaval of 300 million years ago, these ranges take a roughly east-to-west direction,

narrowing down to the promontories that are now (because of their appeal to outsiders) the pride and joy of the region. Each one ends with an afterthought of islands.

Mountains, precipitous coast and scattered islands are the three land-forms that are most likely to be ignored by farmers. Nevertheless, most of the islands were pastured at one time, and some still are, while the lower slopes of the mountains were covered by oak forest until the end of the sixteenth century, when it was thoroughly cropped for iron-smelting and ship-building. Despite these qualifications, wildness, in the rare but real sense of land virtually unaffected by man, is present here to a degree not found elsewhere in Ireland.

The heights of the Caha mountains, with their almost universally steep sides, narrow

115

serpentine valleys, cliffs and corries, occupy the centre of the peninsula, falling to the long inlets of sea that lie both north and south: respectively the Kenmare river and Bantry Bay. Westward, the range narrows to the caudal spine of the Slieve Miskish, its mostly steep and high cliffs deeply indented by the work of the sea. This process has created several natural harbours, including the well-protected anchorage of Bear Haven, an important Royal Naval base while Britain and Ireland were united (and for nearly twenty years afterwards). In spite of this kind of activity the Beara has kept to itself down the centuries. The clan of O'Sullivan, whose name easily outnumbers all others in these parts, has not always been quick to welcome outsiders. During the Tudor conquests their resistance had cruel and disastrous consequences, bringing English landlords, copper mines and the naval garrison.

Beara's essential isolation survived up to a generation ago when there were only 65 tourist beds in the whole peninsula. (One English town, Blackpool, to go to the other extreme, has 120,000 tourist beds.) Things have changed. The population is drastically reduced: no more than half what it was a hundred years ago. Fishing, which in 1891 kept a thousand men in work, died out earlier in the century but has since returned, and Castletownbere is a big centre for trawlers and fish-processing. There are plenty of places offering food, accommodation and a warm welcome. But nowhere in Beara has tourism developed to the same extent as in the two peninsulas to the north. Which makes it in some ways my own favourite.

A road goes round the margin of the peninsula, though often enough, keeping a straighter course than the shoreline, it leaves access to the sea to little diverging lanes. These can lead along quiet foothills to lovely bays, creeks and harbours. On the south coast, the further west, the quieter. Towards the east, frost-free Glengarriff and its neighbours are overdeveloped, too groomed and cosy, swathed in rhododendron, fuchsia, Chilean myrtle (*Clethra arborea*) and the so-called strawberry tree (*Arbutus unedo*), which, flourishing here and in south-western

France and Spain, but not in between, belongs to those several expatriates known as the Lusitanian flora.

West of Castletownbere, with one exception, the artifice has gone. There are wild cliffs, wild rocks, castle-capped headlands, broad bays, palely alluring strands – especially, these last, on the north coast. The exception is down a lane to the left a couple of miles west of Castletownbere. Almost immediately there is a bridge and a pretty inlet of the sea, hemmed by rhododendrons and other shrubs and trees. Among all this is a story-book gothic gate-lodge consisting of a compact cluster of towers, crenellations, round walls, slit windows, turrets. You pay your fee into an honesty box and walk (or drive) into a grand park, with the broadening inlet on the left and the huge shambling ruins of a nineteenth-century Anglo-Irish extravaganza on the right. Further on again come the sparse remains of the medieval O'Sullivan Beare castle, beautifully set among yews and other trees, beside the straits that divide the mainland from Bear Island.

This western end of the Beara is a place where the wild and the tamed come together, and where some of the main themes of the peninsula's story are united. The O'Sullivans sided with the Spanish in their attempts – towards the end of Queen Elizabeth's reign – to settle in Ireland with a view to ousting the English. The Battle of Kinsale, at the end of 1601, utterly dashed Spanish aspirations, but the O'Sullivans held out against the English, here at Dunboy, for a further six months. Two massacres ended their resistance: the one on Dursey Island, the other, after two more weeks, here. The Irish chief, Donal O'Sullivan Beare, who had escaped the siege, led a tragic but heroic march of survivors to sanctuary in the north of Ireland, from where many were shipped to permanent exile in Spain. The castle was destroyed by the victors.

By the eighteenth century, the demesne and much of the peninsula belonged to an Anglo-Irish family with mining interests in Cornwall, the Puxleys. They seem to have been mercenary, mean, mostly absentee and punitive, but for many years they engaged in

116

the important local industry of smuggling and got on well with others, notably the remaining O'Sullivans, doing so. But the real Puxley allegiance was to the crown in London, while the O'Sullivans preferred to serve the interests of the Spanish or Austrians and supply their armies with disgruntled Irishmen. Differences deepened. In 1757 a Puxley was murdered. In due course the responsible O'Sullivan was besieged in his house and shot dead as he emerged in a bid to escape.

When copper ore was discovered in the mountains behind Allihies, the Puxleys grew fat on the profits. Nobody else did. When mineworkers' tools were worn by use, and consequently weighed less, appropriate deductions were made from their wage packets. The grandiose pile whose substantial ruin was passed on the way to the old castle was erected in the mid-nineteenth century. Inside and out, it was a lump of gross ostentation. But copper ore ran thin, income slumped, and the Puxley family returned for the most part to Cornwall. In their absence in 1921 the old IRA, which used the grounds for manoeuvres, set fire to the house. As many have pointed out, being a ruin suits it better.

The themes of Beara thread out east and west, to mountains and coast. O'Sullivans are everywhere still. Puxleys are nowhere, but their story is told in Daphne du Maurier's novel *Hungry Hill*, which cloaks all the characters in pseudonyms. There is a Hungry Hill, a steep and imposing peak overhanging the road and good for climbs a few miles east of Castletownbere, but it is not – as the book makes it out to be – the site of the copper mines. These mines are located above Allihies facing the Atlantic at the west and of Slieve Miskish.

The gloom of Dursey Island, at the peninsula's tip, is said to have come down in part from the fearful massacres of 1602 (though there has, in truth, been much to depress it in between). Another novel, *Two Chiefs of Dunboy*, stirringly recounts the eighteenth-century feud between Puxleys and O'Sullivans. It was written by the historian J.A. Froude, while staying at Derreen, Irish home of Lord Lansdowne, overlooking

Kilmakillogue harbour on the north coast, ten miles west of Kenmare. A seventeenth-century ancestor of Lansdowne, Sir William Petty, was granted huge estates hereabouts. It was a wild territory then, no doubt, though not as wild as another historian, Macaulay, with the misunderstanding of an alien culture common among colonizers, painted it: the haunt of wolves, and 'half-naked savages, who could not speak a word of English, made themselves burrows in the mud and lived on roots and sour milk'. Petty, like his first patron Cromwell, tackled tasks thoroughly, opening ironworks (for which he felled oak forests), lead mines and sea fisheries. He also put forward a plan for solving the Irish problem: convey 20,000 marriageable Irish girls to England, and 20,000 English to Ireland. The latter's children would be brought up as Protestants loyal to England. A tough but ingenious policy, and more humane than straightforward annihilation of the natives, as practised in America north and south.

You see the beauty of this part of Beara as you come over the Healy Pass on the long hairpin haul from the south side to the north, with its vista of lakes, fields, woods, the compact symmetry of Knockatee, the sea beyond, and the patrician profile of the Iveragh peninsula beyond that: a promised-land vision. For the climber, the best of the region is to the right and left of the pass itself – the varied delights of walking in the Caha range. There is a lake far below the pass to the north-west, called Glanmore. A considerable climb starts from the horseshoe valley to its west, up the mountain called Tooth mountain on the half-inch map. In *The Hills of Cork and Kerry* Richard Mersey (a descendant of Petty and the Petty-Fitz-maurices of Derreen) brings these mountains to vivid life with detailed description, entertaining anecdote and the kind of knowledge only experience gives. He warns against collapsing walls, for instance, but insists that farmers make them purposely that way. A sheep will easily get over a firm wall, but will keep well away from one that a quick test shows might fall on it. Mersey calls that climb from Glanmore 'the crown of climbs'.

BEFORE YOU GO
Maps: OS Discovery Series map No. 84; OS half-inch map of Ireland No. 24.

GETTING THERE
By car: from Killarney take the N71 south through Kenmare to Glengarriff. To travel round the Beara peninsula, follow the R572 to Cahermore, then the R575 and the R571 back to Kenmare.
By rail: the nearest station is in Killarney, about 3 miles (5 km) north of the peninsula, to which services run from Dublin twice daily, Sat–Thurs, and three times on Fridays.
By bus: Berehaven Buses run services making local stops from Bantry to Glengarriff and Castletownbere, and direct services from Cork, T:(027) 70007. There are no Bus Eireann services on the peninsula.

WHERE TO STAY
Hotels: there are a few bed and breakfasts and one hotel, Craige's, T:(027) 70379, in Castletownbere; a few more hotels and bed and breakfasts in Glengarriff; and a good selection of accommodation in Kenmare.
Youth hostels: there are a few hostels around the peninsula, including Bonnie Braes Independent Holiday Hostel, T:(027) 73107, in Allihies village; Tooreen Hostel, T:(027) 63075, near Kenmare; Beare Hostel, T:(027) 70184, in Castletownbere; and Adrigole, T:(027) 60132, between Adrigole and Castletownbere.
Outdoor living: there are several camp-sites on the peninsula. O'Sheas Caravan and Camping Park, T:(027) 63140, Dowlings Caravan and Camping Park, T:(027) 63154, a small camp-site near Laragh, just off the

R574, and another near Ardee Bridge on the R571.

ACTIVITIES
Walking: the Caha mountains form the backbone of the entire peninsula. The Sugar Loaf and Hungry Hill peaks offer nice short walks, and the long valleys are worth exploring. A traverse of the range, starting at Glengarriff, offers a good two-day trek, the night spent at or near the Healy Pass. The 133-mile (213-km) Beara Way is a way-marked route, linking Glengarriff to Kenmare. It is split up into nine stages: stage 1, Glengarriff to Adrigole (10 miles/16 km); 2, Adrigole to Castletownbere (14 miles/22 km); 3, Castletownbere to Allihies (8 miles/13 km); 4, Allihies to Dursey Sound (12 miles/19 km) with an additional 9-mile (15-km) section on Dursey Island itself; 5, Allihies

to Ardgroom (14 miles/22 km); 6, Ardgroom to Inchiquin Lough (13 miles/21 km); 7, Inchiquin Lough to Kenmare, via Dowres (6 miles/10 km); 8, Kenmare to Glengarriff (15 miles/24 km); and 9, Bere Island (13 miles/21 km). For more information about the Way, contact Cork/Kerry Tourism, Killarney Tourist Office, Town Hall, Killarney, Co. Kerry, T:(064) 31633.
Fishing: among several available waters there is a brown-trout lake just outside Glengarriff. Fishing-rights fees for the lake are payable at the Maple Leaf pub.
Cycling: bikes can be hired from Dudley Cycles, T:(027) 70293, in Castletownbere. *Cycling Ireland*, a publication available from Bord Failte, has a suggested route that travels around the coastline of the Beara peninsula.

ECOLOGY
Glengarriff woods are home to the speckled Kerry slug, which is found only on the peninsula and in other small areas of Kerry.

FURTHER INFORMATION
There are no tourist offices on the peninsula, the nearest Bord Failte offices being in Glengarriff, T:(027) 63084, open July and Aug, and Kenmare, T:(064) 41233. During the summer, tourist information is available next to the fire station in Castletownbere.

The large-flowered butterwort has been called the most beautiful of Irish flowering plants, its dainty violet flower swaying on a delicate stem over the broad rosette of green, sticky leves at its base: sticky for the purpose of trapping insects which are then digested by means of secreted chemicals.

The peaks and valleys of the Caha range on the Beara peninsula afford some of the finest mountain formations and scenery in Ireland

Dursey

Island with a handful of inhabited cottages and with imposing cliffs at the west end of the Beara peninsula

I was alone, swaying in a windowed wooden box maybe ten feet by five, which shook and rumbled high above a swirling sea and margins of sharp rock, and slowly progressed from east to west. On the wall, the text of psalm 91: 'a thousand may fall dead beside you, ten thousand all round you, but you will not be harmed'. Beside it, in a bottle modelled into a statue of the Blessed Virgin, holy water. The flow of water in the strait below was reported to be the fastest on Ireland's periphery: too often too perilous for a reliable ferry. This was why the county council, 25 years before, had approved the installation of a cable car to convey passengers from the end of the Beara peninsula to Dursey Island, and why I was now winging down to the island's landing place. The journey – say 150 yards or metres – took five minutes.

Dursey is unfriendly, treeless, lacking all facilities to sustain or help the visitor and, in spite of cattle and sheep pasturing in wired fields, wild. *Farouche* might be the better word. If you walk – you have no other option – towards the west end, the first mile may suggest to you, as it did to me, life after a holocaust. There are cottages that look blasted, their slates grouted with cement; a young mother smoking and answering my greeting with an uncharming, unmusical note; a car the weather has vandalized;

a tractor that might have been reclaimed from the sea. Hardly more than seven or eight houses seem inhabited.

Others have commented on the surliness, the aloof independence of a population reduced from hundreds, cut off (till the cable car came) for weeks at a time by a treacherous flood, a people who have lost even their language in a couple of generations – perhaps, it occurs to me, for want of talking. It may have to do with the only recorded drama of their history, when in 1602 the English piked, impaled, shot and drowned three hundred men, women and children, and left the castle and church the ruins they remain, down by the harbour.

Beauty and interest are found here and there: grassy banks sliding away to sheer, 300-foot (91-m) drops into the liquid blue, hemmed by staves of yellow-lichened rock. Further west, approaching the terminal cliffs, are carpets of orchids, and the continual cautionary barrage in summer of meadow pipit, robin, stonechat and wheatear. It is a good place to see migrating sea-birds, but what have caused most surprise in recent years are sightings of smaller perching birds: warblers or finches blown wildly off course by Atlantic gales.

Naturally, the views are beautiful on fine days: long peninsulas to the north and south, bony headlands resting their chins on the sea, a scattering of islands. There are three islands of jutting rock out in the Atlantic beyond Dursey's tip: the Bull Rock three miles off, The Cow two, and The Calf one. The names refer to their relative sizes rather than their shapes. Gannets breed on the Bull Rock, taking the overflow,

perhaps, from the Skelligs to the north. The inimitable gannet, diving, plunging and emerging moustached by a large fish, is one of the most entrancing sights in this whole region.

There is nowhere to stay on Dursey, but permission to camp would be readily given. I myself preferred to run again the gauntlet of the cheerless straggle of houses known in some quarters as a village, and churn across the swirling strait without further delay.

Before you go: OS Discovery Series map No. 84; OS half-inch map of Ireland No. 24.

Getting there: from Kenmare take the R571 west along to Cahermore, then the R578 to its end beside the cable car terminus. The only cable car in Ireland connects the island to the mainland. Services run 9–11 am, 2.30–5 pm, and sometimes 7–8 pm, although cattle may get precedence over humans, T:(027) 73017.

Where to stay: there is no accommodation on the island, but it is easy to find somewhere to camp although it would be wise to seek permission before you do so.

Activities *Walking:* although there are no marked trails on the island, it is small enough for the average walker to make short work. The treeless landscape offers decent walking terrain along the coast.
Bird-watching: a visit to Dursey presents the opportunity to witness the sometimes spectacular migration of sea-birds. Bird-watchers may also be interested in the surprising recent sightings of smaller birds blown off course.

Further information: the nearest Bord Failte tourist offices are in Kenmare, T: (064) 41233, open from April to October and in Bantry, T:(027) 50229, open from June to September.

Mizen Head

Southernmost of the great south-western promontories, between Dunmanus Bay and Roaringwater Bay, with a south coast known for its coves and harbours

In some ways the south-west of Ireland has always kept up to the minute. In the nineteenth century passengers on ships from America would toss messages into boats bound for Clear Island, where they could be telegraphed all over Europe. In this way the islanders learned the news of the American Civil War long before anybody in Britain or on the Continent. For the best part of a century transatlantic telegraph cables ran from Valencia Island, off the Iveragh peninsula. Here on the Mizen promontory an aircraft-tracking station is marked by two gleaming futuristic domes atop Mount Gabriel, making it seem from a distance that Martians have landed. But beside and under and around, older ways persist. This ancient, gnarled finger of old red sandstone pointing out to the Atlantic carries a bounty of natural delights, many having nothing at all to do with human agency.

The sand of the sandstone was washed away, reddened by rich quantities of oxidized iron, by rivers and tides to be dried, toasted, compacted and folded in the Armorican and Hercynide upheavals, caused by tectonic collision some 300 million years ago. In the previous geological era limestone had drifted down through the warm sea which then covered the country. After the ruptures much of it remained on the surface, sandwiched between strata of sandstone, but in time, being of weaker consistency, the limestone eroded faster than the sandstone, and the result is the row of high, west-directed, old red sandstone peninsulas along the coasts of Cork and Kerry, divided by deep inlets, loughs or rias. You might think these long lines of land would be difficult to distinguish the one from the other, but nothing could be further from the truth. Dingle and the Iveragh (or Ring of Kerry) get most of the limelight, but I am not sure that Mizen and the Beara are not my favourites.

The sea, of course, is what makes them: the stretched coastline with its bays and estuaries, islands near and far, distant views of isolated rocks, the natural fortress of Fastnet, like a formidable square keep, supporting its lighthouse. Schull, halfway along the south coast, has a pretty, rock-strewn harbour with a daily ferry to Cape Clear (also reached from Baltimore). You can fill a basket here with your dinner of mussels. The town is attractive, its houses painted many colours (as they tend to be from Macroom westward) and with the sort of shops not common in many parts of Ireland: antique shops, second-hand bookshops, pastry shops, delicatessens and a range of restaurants.

There is no need to be specific. You can turn off the road at a dozen points to enter a little world of steamily burgeoning plants beside sand, rock or rock-pool. You look around at the ingredients of one particular brew of Irish magic: the bay, the headlands, ruined castle, cove, beach, aquamarine sea. Treasure Island has to be somewhere beyond. Thrush, robin, wren, and blackbird

The stonechat is encountered on rough grassland and heath all over Ireland: a bold and conspicuous bird whose male is a dandy with black head, buff to orange chest and white collar (which does not go round the bird's back).

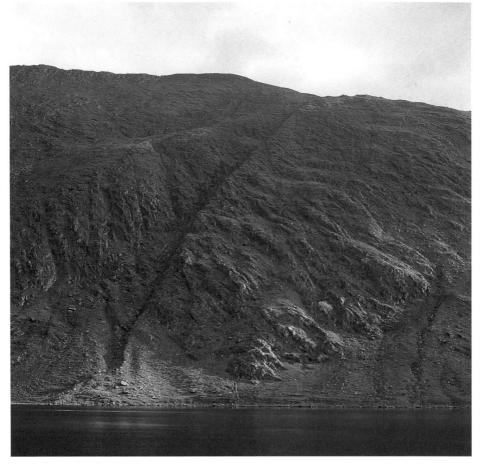

Glenbeg Lough, easily reached from Ardgroom, on the north coast of the Beara peninsula, is a 2-mile by ½-mile valley of water edged north and south by sheer walls of cliff. Unmoved by this grandeur, sheep graze on the lake's edge.

repeatedly announce their presence; when they flag, the tuneful willow warbler – possibly the rarer garden warbler – takes over the midday watch.

Richest of all is the rocky sward on which you are standing: a pattern of flowers which for some reason – light, clarity of air, freedom from pollutants – are more brightly coloured than their counterparts elsewhere in Europe. Out of a bed of mosses and grey or orange lichens or white-flowered stonecrop (*Sedum anglicum*) rise taller

flowers in placements and confluences never achieved by any gardener in the world's history, though they are mainly common cranesbill, bird's foot trefoil, melilot, oxeye daisy, plantain and dandelion, thrift, sea campion. How dainty and delicate the wild can be. And always in these parts there are orchids: mainly the common spotted orchid (*Dactylorhiza fuchsii*) and the early marsh orchid (*Dactylorhiza incarnata*). If I were to advise someone beginning to learn the identification of plants where to start, I might say come to one of these unpeopled backwaters on a sunny day, bring book, strong and middling lenses, and notebook; and be prepared to work hard and with concentration. But I should be wrong, of course. The

122

attention of all but the toughest would stray.

Further west come crescendos of scenery (whose only significant drawback is that people know about them). There are three high headlands at the end: Three Castle Head, Mizen Head and Brow Head, the last two divided by the broad expanse of Barley Cove, where gannets plunge into the clear blue waters and skim the large expanses of sand. Inland is a large, sandy shallow lake, Lissagriffin, where a few whooper and Bewick's swans, along with some teal and wigeon, pass the winter, while mute swan and mallard may be present at any time of the year. You might if you are lucky see a peregrine or a chough hereabouts.

Mizen Head dramatically shows off its angular cliffs of clearly striated sandstone, the lines going along and down, curving like race-tracks or stacked like shelves of deckle-edged paper. Guillemots and fulmars nest on any available niche in the cliff faces, the latter displaying their customary mastery of the air in incredibly long glides without benefit of wing-beat, or by hovering motionless on air-currents like ping-pong balls on invisible jets of water. In the spring and autumn many of the untold thousands of seabirds which cross Cape Clear, a few miles just south of east across Roaringwater Bay, cross here too: the various species of shearwater, auks, kittiwakes, skuas and others. Rarities occur here, but I have no wish to encourage the twitchers who transport their huge and expensive lenses by car, rail or plane when some enfeebled creature, blown off course and possibly starving, is reported to them. The rarer the bird, the more certain it is that, when they have had their way of it, patted themselves on their backs and added its name proudly to their 'life-lists', it will do the only thing left for it – die.

BEFORE YOU GO
Maps: OS half-inch map of Ireland No. 24.

GETTING THERE
By car: from Skibbereen follow the N71 to Ballydehob, on the coast of Roaringwater Bay. The R592 and R591 (west) lead to Crookhaven, near the end of the peninsula.
By rail: the nearest station serving the area is Killarney, where services run to/from Dublin twice daily, Thurs–Sat, and three times on Fridays.
By bus: Bus Eireann Expressway and local services operating between Cork and Goleen stop at Ballydehob.

WHERE TO STAY
Hotels: bed and breakfasts in Ballydehob include Mrs Coughlan's, T:(028) 37272; Mrs Morris's, T:(028) 37139, and Mrs Vaughan's, T:(028) 37124; there is a hotel in Goleen, the Barley Cove Beach, T:(028) 35234, and a few bed and breakfasts in Schull, including Mrs Holt, T:(028) 28528.
Youth hostels: there is an An Oige hostel in Allihies, Allihies Hostel, T:(027) 73014, as well as an independent hostel, the Bantry Hostel, T:(027) 51050, at Bantry.
Outdoor living: there is a campsite near Crookhaven, Barleycove Caravan and Camping Park, T:(028) 35302.

ACTIVITIES
Watersports: there is a watersports centre in Schull that rents out dinghies, windsurfing and snorkelling equipment and wetsuits,

Orchids still survive in Ireland, sometimes abundantly and mostly in the west; these are not the large and exotic tropical species, but smaller, daintier blooms, including (from left): marsh orchids, which flower in early summer and are sometimes prolific in wet grasslands; the bee orchid, which attracts certain male bees for pollination purposes by looking and smelling like a female bee, and keeps to dry sites; the pink-flowered pyramidal orchid, a lover of sand-dunes; and the lesser butterfly orchid, happy in damp heathland and pastures.

T:(028) 28554.

Cycling: bikes can be hired at Freewheelin in Schull, T:(028) 28165; *Cycling Ireland*, a leaflet from Bord Failte, has a suggested route along the coast, through Ballydehob, and past Roaringwater Bay.

Bird-watching: Roaringwater Bay provides a home to many sea-birds, including shearwaters, auks, kittiwakes and skuas. Inland there are many breeds of duck to be seen, including teal and mallard. The lucky few could see a peregrine or a chough.

FURTHER INFORMATION
Tourist information is available during the summer from a small private office in Schull, opposite the Spar supermarket, Main Street.

Cape Clear Island

Inhabited island with enterprising fish-farm and wind-power. Site of an important bird observatory

If you are a native of Clear Island and your name is not O'Driscoll it will probably be Cadogan. But it is much more likely to be O'Driscoll. That sort of thing is often the way with islands. The last time I was there I stayed at Mary O'Driscoll's guest-house, though I could equally have stayed at Eleanor O'Driscoll's. I had no cause to regret the choice.

I spent the day tramping the island, and came near to being, and but for idleness would have been, the most southerly person on Irish soil, for Fastnet is the only Irish territory more southerly than Cape Clear, and it is no longer manned. I talked, looked at birds on the western and southern cliffs, and watched fishing boats hauling in lobster pots out at sea. Without success I scanned the blue for a sight of the minke whales which are quite often seen, or the turtles which had been seen a week or so before. I watched children who had come to learn Irish – for O'Driscolls and their fellow islanders are resilient Irish-speakers, and people of all ages come from the corners of Ireland to learn from them. The children were taking their afternoon exercise of canoeing, swimming and sailing in the warm blue southern harbour of the cape.

I had some surprises. There is a lake in the west from which a narrow stream leads towards the cliffs and, as I walked along it, I saw the laws of gravity confounded by a perpetual upward spray of water ahead of me,

as if when it reached the end of its channel the water ascended into the air instead of dropping into the sea below. Well, it did, for the reason I now saw: a powerful and consistent current of air, rising beside the cliff – the same which birds delighted to use as elevator and support – was catching the water and transporting it several yards in a powerful upward shower. The other surprise was the spotting of a rare bird. It was big and heavy and a field or two away. I peered through binoculars. It was something like a guinea fowl. And here was another, its mate. They were indeed guinea fowls, but there was no call for excitement. An islander, it turned out, had brought them in to breed.

Mary and Ciaran O'Driscoll have a large room for the use of their guests. Along two sides there are tables at which to eat (or write or talk). The rest is a couple of feet lower with a fireplace and sofas, books and magazines. The differing levels of the floor make it easy for people to see each other and talk if they so wish. There is a nice unforced intimacy, and Mary O'Driscoll, a native of Schull over the water – she was born a Molloy – is a good and bright conductor of conversation. A young Swiss couple – she an air hostess – were staying, and two women and a boy from the mainland. An older islander called and stayed an hour, and young Alan Dalton of the bird observatory with his huge knowledge and not so easy nasal Dublin accent came in for a while. An awful lot was talked of, a great deal told.

No, said Mary to the Swiss girl, no, she did not feel out of touch on Cape Clear. So much went on here, it was a good place to live, and it was sometimes said that Cape Clear was the hub, and Ireland the off-shore island. Not that things were ideal. Some of the vanished past was to be regretted. Vegetables and most other provisions came over from the mainland now; few if any grew their own. With 25 island boats and 8 men to each, fishing had once provided 200 men with jobs: more than the present total population. The fishery now is part of a mainland co-operative – far the best arrangement for the times, but at a cost of enterprise and control over decisions. The efficient and graceful wind-propellers set up by a German company to generate energy some years ago would lose pride of place when electricity was piped in off the national grid for the first time. Worst, Mary's two sons, now at the island's excellent primary school, would have to proceed to school on the mainland (where they would board except at weekends), there to be educated beyond any job the island could offer. There was no other option. A kind of progress nobody much wanted would prevent an island, which all hoped to prosper, from prospering.

Some people, said the old man, claimed the Capers were pure descendants of the Milesians, a prehistoric race from whom the Irish have always been prone to trace their descent. He thought there was little truth to it, and remembered hearing as a child that soldiers landed and stayed during Napoleonic times, took local wives and bred families. That kind of dilution, he thought, had gone on all down history. Indeed it was said that many Aran islanders had the blood of Cromwell's soldiers running in their veins.

What was beyond dispute was the hardness of the lives islanders used to lead. There were no mills on the island, and all grain was ground with a hand quern. Selling fish never presented a problem: both Irish and English dealers in Baltimore were ready to buy every last mackerel, but there had been times when the fish went away and hauls were count for years on end. Now, of course, the state took care of everything and the young did not know what it was to be without food or money. Nor had they any idea about sailing, or the skills, hazards and salty joys of their forefathers. I asked Alan about the island's bird life. It had occurred to me that keeping a check on birds was a little like taking the world's ecological temperature. Birds are international, deeply sensitive to changes in farming methods and patterns, desperately

vulnerable to pollution from the Arctic to the Antarctic. Being considerate of arctic terns in Ireland or nightingales in England – not that we necessarily are – did not ensure their well-being. Obligations do not stop with national boundaries. They must, nevertheless, start in our own gardens. We berate farmers whose silage-making slowly wipes out the corncrake, or the French or Italians who shoot larks and thrushes so as to clear the whole firmament of birds; but do we not seal our own attic and neatly net our thatch-roofs and lofts against bats and swallows? Do we not cut weeds in which warblers may nest, or poison slugs and snails a thrush might catch and eat?

On Cape Clear pollution is minimal. What the records reveal is the astonishing legacy and responsibility that the Irish and the rest of us inherit. Cape Clear well illustrates the global significance of Ireland's sea-birds. An acid-soil island, dowsed with salt water on up to 200 days in the year can host a very limited number of plant species. Desperately short of trees, Cape Clear is little use for nest building birds unless, like some thrushes (song and mistle), blackbirds, wrens and robins, they have learned to build in holes in rock walls. For sea-birds, of course, island status and surpluses of rain are no handicap. Sea presents no barrier. On the contrary, it is the source of densely packed fish. Hence the rich turn-out and variety on, beside and above the Cape Clear cliffs. There are times when the air of Cape Clear is alive with the beat of wings. Over a small part of these 741 acres (300 hectares) of rock and heath and marsh there fly, during periods of migration, thousand upon thousand of various species of sea-bird. Counting birds in flight takes skill and experience. Alan has both, and can affirm that at certain times in late July and August up to 30,000 Manx shearwaters are passing overhead every hour. Other shearwaters – sooty and great – along with great and arctic skuas, guillemots, razorbills and kitti-wakes, swell their ranks. All sorts of other birds occur in lesser numbers, and over 280 species common and rare – two-thirds of the number for all Ireland – have been recorded here.

BEFORE YOU GO

Maps: OS half-inch map of Ireland No. 24.

Guidebooks: *The Walkers' Guide* (from the tourist office on the island) and Sharrock's *The Natural History of Cape Clear Island* (London, 1973), only from libraries.

GETTING THERE

By boat: boats leave Baltimore, at the end of the R595, from Skibbereen. They take 45 minutes to reach the island. The tourist office in Baltimore has more information or you could telephone the boat office direct, T:(028) 39119. There is also a passenger ferry service available from Schull.

WHERE TO STAY

Hotels: bed and breakfast is available on the island from both Mrs C. O'Driscoll, T:(028) 39153, and Mrs E. O'Driscoll, T:(028) 39135.

Youth hostels: there is an An Oige hostel on the island, T:(028) 39144; the bird observatory provides limited accommodation that can be booked through Kiren Grace, T:(01) 785444.

Outdoor living: a small campsite is open on the island from June to September, T:(028) 31149.

ACTIVITIES

Walking: there is a marked walk that runs right round the

coast of the island and takes around three hours.

Bird-watching: the bird observatory (no 'phone) is in a white-fronted building by the harbour. Bird-watching trips are run from here. Blananartagaun, on the south-west coast, is a good place to view the sea-birds.

FURTHER INFORMATION

There is a private tourist office in Baltimore, T:(028) 20441, which can provide information on boats to Clear Island and will book accommodation. Information is also available from an office on the island that is open during July and August.

Lough Ine

A lake-like sea inlet with a nature reserve and marine biology station

I should like to own Lough Ine and its surrounds, live in the big white house that sits on a grassy bank at its north-east corner, close the roads that now give me and the rest of the public access to its northern and western shores, and enjoy in selfish seclusion this rough rectangle of salt-water lake. I should relish its curious and abundant natural life, its islands, the castle ruin, the thin rocky channel which the tide in its motions turns into rapids, the curlicued coast beyond – a labyrinth of inlets and islands – and the hills furred with forest trees that rise on all sides. Last time I was there I even envied the cows that lay chewing and mooning below the house and the rhododendrons, for not · having to leave.

An inland lough consisting

of salt water is a rarity in itself, but the slow comings and goings of the tides and the great depth of the lake – up to 164 feet (50 metres) in parts – mean a slow rate of change, allowing time for the fresh water coming down from the hills to dilute it to a weaker salinity than the sea itself. Its consistency is thus unusual. So are its inhabitants, for it contains a wide variety of habitats.

A small building beside the rapids is used as a research base by the Cork University team, who keep an eye on life on and under the surface. The rest of us have to take things on trust. There is fishing. Swimmers must take the greatest care not to put their feet on the lough bed for fear of stepping on a common sea urchin or its very bristly cousin the purple sea urchin. A walk along the side will present arm's-length dogfish to view. Others of the 60 species of fish recorded may be more elusive. It is a remarkable tally, which includes goldsinny wrasse, tompot blenny, pipe-fish,

butter-fish, sometimes the subtropical trigger fish, and the red-mouthed goby, seldom found anywhere else in north-west Europe.

Reading the lists of the lough's inhabitants made me pine for an aqualung or a glass-bottomed boat, for the sea-gooseberry or comb jellyfish, the variegated scallop, snakelocks anemone, sea hare (a marine slug), common and spiny starfish, sea scorpion, sea cucumber, sea butterfly, fifteen-spined stickleback, mussel, prawn, brittlestar, velvet fiddler-crab or bristleworm *Sabella*, which brought the young Julian Huxley here early in the century for thesis research, will be seen, if at all, only through luck during a walk along the accessible parts of the rim. Plankton – the sea soup of embryonic life, an infinity of minute plants and the eggs and larvae of fish, shellfish, starfish, worms and thousands of other creatures – require a microscope to be seen at all. The nearest we can come to awareness of them is by means of some helpful illustrations, diagrams and texts placed on boards beside one of the parking places. But a visit is not wasted. You can drive or walk to watch the four-times daily passage of the tide, or visit Bullock Island Bay, from which fishermen carry their lobster pots out to sea. This is one of those many places on the Irish coast where I wish my car would, in good weather anyway, turn into a sailing dinghy.

Before you go: OS half-inch map of Ireland No. 24.

Getting there *By car:* from Cork follow the N71 (south-west) to Skibbereen, then the R595 to Baltimore. Signposted lanes off the R595 lead south to Lough Ine. *By bus:* A Bus Eireann Expressway summer-only service between Cork and Killarney stops at Skibbereen, as do a similar Bus Eireann

service between Cork and Bandon and a frequent local Bus Eireann service between Goleen and Cork. **Where to stay:** there are several bed and breakfasts and one hotel, the Beacon Park, T:(028) 20143, in Baltimore, and quite a few more in Skibbereen. There is also a hostel in Baltimore, Rolf's Hostel, T:(028) 20289.

Activities: Baltimore is a popular sailing centre, and there is a small nature reserve just above Lough Ine that has a few walks running through it. Bikes can be hired from Roycroft Stores, T:(028) 21235, in Baltimore. Pony trekking is available at the Limbo Trekking and Riding Centre, T:(028) 21683. **Further information:** There is a Bord Failte tourist office open all year in North Street, Skibbereen, near the town hall, T:(028) 21766.

The purple sea urchin, whose greenish globular shell, or test, is about 2 in (4 cm) across and covered with a dense nap of purple spines, is essentially a Mediterranean animal, but is commonly found off the south and west coasts of Ireland and the south-west coast of England.

Sherkin Island

Inhabited island with rich flora close to Baltimore in south-west Cork. Site of an important private marine-research station

Sherkin is easily reached from the pretty little harbour town of Baltimore. The ferry comes and goes all day. On the island there is nothing you could call a town or village. Near the quay is an old abbey, built by fifteenth-century O Driscolls and sacked fifty years later, recently much restored. Nearby there are ruins of a castle and a large Becher family house, and off to the north, overlooking Hare Island, the ghost of a settlement where boats were built a hundred years ago. For the rest, habitations are spaced well apart, in the Irish manner.

The most dynamic enterprise on the island is the marine-research centre started and run by Matt Murphy. It is not open to

the public, but used to be. There was an aquarium and an informative exhibition. People crossed from the mainland and began the mile and a half walk but almost all succumbed to the lure of warm blue sea or to fatigue and the wish to go home long before they reached their destination. So it closed to the public. Its work continues, based on Matt Murphy's desire to expose the hidden life of the sea about him: something nobody – not even, to their shame, coastal universities like Galway – had thought of doing before he and his late wife settled here 25 years ago. Young scientists drawn here by love, not money – carry out continuous marine-research programmes. They have good facilities and an excellent library. The world they explore, though not the complexities of their work, is disclosed in a wonderful book of underwater photographs published by the centre, suggestive far more of life in tropical or subtropical waters than in these northerly latitudes. Yet a multiplicity of colourful and exquisitely intricate starfish and jellyfish and sea urchins and squirts and scorpions and bristleworts and polymorphous plankton are resident hereabouts, all valid denizens of Ireland's wilderness.

Matt Murphy says he knows no science, only how to push those who do in the right directions. His primary concern is practicable conservation. He wants better awareness, use and protection of Ireland's natural resources, and to further these ends produces an authoritative, deeply interesting, often rather cross, slightly impatient quarterly review called *Sherkin Comment*. In this he is as likely to sound off at airy ecologists – Greenpeace and others have been carpeted – as at greedy farmers or totalitarian civil servants. What seems to me of most value about him and his paper is his constant attempt to focus on truth, the simpler the better, without regard to received or lazy opinion or widespread prejudice. He clearly approves of fish-farming. It does not improve the look of coastal bays and it has introduced new problems related to fish disease. Matt Murphy swipes equally at those who sentimentally deplore the whole business and those who try to gloss over the complications. His paper made it suddenly plain to me that fish-farming has only just started to do for fishing what agriculture did for hunting five or six thousand years ago; that it is here to stay and that, in spite of detractors, it can bring enormous benefits. It could turn out to be the most effective way of allowing ravaged ocean stocks to heal and revive.

Sherkin offers more than theory. The north coast is a succession of bays and rocky or sandy coves, generous reward for the walk needed to get to them. Off-season, in migration times, waves of duck and wader settle along the shore, either for a respite of a few days, or to stay for the winter while ice and snow put their northerly haunts out of bounds. Advancing summer sees a dense, rich and varied growth in vegetation. Trees and shrubs burgeon with blossom in the lanes and hedges. Like the other islands which crowd Roaringwater Bay, Sherkin has a dense mosaic of plant habitats: marsh, rock, sand-dune, pebbles, heath and caves. There is not, as in many parts of Ireland, an altogether excessive sheep population (subsidized by a grant from Europe) to hoover the variety of plants into a bland uniformity. But nobody had given much thought to Sherkin's flora until, a few years ago, Matt Murphy brought in Dr John Akeroyd to supervise a detailed survey. It took five years' work by resident botanists and has resulted in a book; what this tells us is that no equivalent area in the whole of Ireland has such a rich variety of plants. Sherkin supports some 540 species, vastly more than anyone previously suspected.

Apart from native species there are species introduced by settlers – including seventeenth-century Algerian pirates, and also the Normans, whose castle precincts are always likely to yield rare species. A new spotlight has been turned on the flora of this part of Ireland by the survey, and it would be rash for anyone interested to go to Sherkin without identification book and lens.

BEFORE YOU GO
Maps: OS half-inch map of Ireland No. 24.

GETTING THERE
By car: from Skibbereen follow the R595 to Baltimore, which is the nearest mainland village to the island.
By bus: a summer-only Bus Eireann Expressway service runs from Tralee to Baltimore, and another summer-only service runs from Drimoleague to Baltimore on Mondays,

Fridays and Saturdays.
By boat: there is a regular and frequent boat service to Sherkin island leaving from Baltimore, T:(028) 20125.

WHERE TO STAY
There are a few bed and breakfasts on the island, including Garrison House, T:(028) 20185, and Cuina, T:(028) 20384. Also you can camp in many parts of the island, providing you have sought permission.

ACTIVITIES
There are sandy beaches at many points around the island.

FURTHER INFORMATION
Tourist information is available from the post office on Sherkin Island, T:(028) 20181. The private tourist office in Baltimore can provide information on boat trips to the island and can arrange accommodation for you, T:(028) 20441.

Central County Cork

Mountain country lying between the scenic valleys of the lake-rich Lee and the Blackwater, offering quiet surprises

Measure for measure, this country is not the equal of that ravishing region to its west, comprising Killarney, Iveragh and the other promontories of Cork and Kerry. Between the Rivers Lee and Blackwater, with Mangerton mountain and Lough Guitane as a western boundary, rise two ranges of old red sandstone mountains, the Derrynasaggart and the Boggeragh. They are largely cultivated, in part grazed, in part drearily afforested. Though the action of ice is evident in their forms, they lack for the most part the lake-filled corries that bejewel so many other Irish ranges. Why, then, mention them?

Three reasons. Firstly, they possess a few stunning features. There is Gouganebarra Lough, with the forest park rising westward and the lovely River Coomhola just over the hill, descending to Bantry Bay beside the good walking country around Lough Nambrackderg, Knockboy and Priest's Leap. At Gouganebarra Lough itself the island is sacred to St Finbarr (from whom the place-name derives), a sixth-century evangelist with some nice Celtic attributes: he founded an oratory here, overcame a murderous monster, drowned it and crossed the sea to Scotland, for missionary work, on horseback. When he died, the sun shone continuously for a fortnight. He is the sort of saint I for one

find it delightful to summon as company on local walks and climbs. Nothing would have got him down.

The withdrawn and commanding ridge of Sheehy mountain a few miles south of the Lee is another site which appeals. Still more impressive are the Paps, twin bosoms of the goddess Anu, according to legend, consisting of sandstone and rising to 2,273 ft (693 m) and 2,283 ft (696 m). They break the local rule and hide two deep and steeply flanked lakes among their upper reaches. The valley of the Lee from Gouganebarra to Macroom is another star of this region, winding broad (the best part of a mile in some stretches) and narrow, among picturesque bluffs of rock, many topped or propped by castle ruins with dramas to relate. Carrignacurra and Carrignamurk can be seen on one cliff, and Carrigrohane on another, while Carrigadrohid, where the English hanged a stubborn bishop three centuries ago, protrudes into the river three miles or so below Macroom. Another castle, Carrigaphouca, five miles west of Macroom on the Killarney road, is built on one of those rotund relics of the Ice Ages, a *roche moutonnée*, or rock carved by ice action into the shape, very roughly, of a sheep. The castle's name is cognate with that of Puck the fairy, and is said to mark the presence of little people, or leprechauns, in the area.

Just above Macroom the river widens, as a result of damming for hydro-electric purposes, into a three-mile stretch of marsh, water and riverine woodland known as the Gearagh. In the winter this becomes a great centre for whooper and Bewick's swans, and various geese and ducks, most commonly wigeon and teal.

The second reason for staying hereabouts rather than further west is that the region derives some benefits from being second best. It is with certain exceptions less known, less crowded in season, less exploitative; it prepares you for the climax of the west. Or – and this is the third reason – it acts as an alternative to the west, offering here and there serendipitous discoveries of lush glen, mountain stream and remote valley, meetings with the kind of amiable country people whom, further west, too much tourism has made prone to turn on their rustic charm to order, and off again if it seems to be going nowhere.

Before you go: OS half-inch maps of Ireland Nos 20 and 24.
Getting there *By car:* from Killarney, the N22 passes through the Derrynasaggart mountains to Macroom. From Macroom the R584 goes west along the River Lee, passing Gouganebarra before reaching Bantry.
By rail: the nearest station to the western part of this area is Killarney.
By bus: a summer-only Bus Eireann Expressway service operates from Killarney to Cork, stopping at Macroom and travelling through the Derrynasaggart mountains. Local Bus Eireann services operate between Macroom and Bantry, passing Gouganebarra, and between Cork and Ballvourney, in the middle of the Derrynasaggart mountains.
Where to stay: there is a good selection of bed and breakfasts and a few hotels in Macroom.
Activities: a walk to the summit of Bealick mountain behind Gouganebarra affords good views, and there are signposted trails through the Gouganebarra Forest Park.
Further information: there is a private tourist office on the main street in Macroom.

CHAPTER 4

Lakeland and the Central Plain

Wild Ireland – wilderness, wildlife, landscape left by humans to itself – exists inland as well as along the coast. It is quieter, more discreet, less extensive, but in its way just as beautiful and fascinating as seaboard wildness. It is rich in bird life, plants, animals and insects, rich in diversity of greens and variety of landforms.

The sea is absent; water decidedly not. Chains of linked lakes make large parts of Counties Cavan, Monaghan, Fermanagh, Leitrim, Roscommon and Longford more water than land. By many the region is known as Lakeland. Among these counties and on to the south, the River Shannon runs its eventful course. It takes in the tributaries that vein the 4,553 square miles (7,285 square kilometres) of its catchment area, and here and there opens out into lakes which are among the largest in the country and look at times very much like inland seas. For almost all its length the river is navigable. So too are the lake link-waters. In fact, Lough Gowna, down in County Longford, is the source of the River Erne and from it you can take a small boat through both Upper and Lower Lough Erne to Belleek – one of Ireland's longest navigable stretches.

The Shannon is Ireland's central artery, draining in the course of its 230 miles (370 kilometres) almost every sort of terrain the country possesses. It

Deep blue trout-rich waters, densely wooded islands and forest and parkland hems give Lough Key its pretty, pampered look.

starts among high mountains close to the national border, implying disdain for the Six Counties by turning immediately to the south. Its official source, in County Cavan, is a bubbling spring known as the Shannon Pot on the lower slopes of Cuilcagh mountain. Other early supplies come from the mountains Slieve Anieran and Arigna, and from the hills of south Sligo and north Roscommon. The infant river drops into Lough Allen, a fall of 300 feet (90 metres) in ten miles (16 kilometres). The next hundred miles or so will lower it only 40 feet (12 metres) more. From Lough Allen the river emerges to wind through bog-lands and overgrown, intriguing little towns – Drumshanbo, Leitrim, Jamestown, Drumsna (second syllable stressed: Drumsnah), Roosky – that a generation ago seemed to be dying of neglect and that owe their survival to the recovery of holiday river traffic.

Below Carrick-on-Shannon, dusted by willow and ash, the Shannon sidetracks into reed-beds like Carnadoe water and the western parts of Lough Boderg. These are much patronized by water-birds. Broad Lough Ree opens out beyond, rich in fish, islands, history and sanctity, and not many miles later there will be Lough Derg, equally well stocked with fauna and associations. Between the two, south of Athlone, where the Shannon meets the Grand Canal and passes some mighty buildings associated with the short-lived flowering of waterborne transport, it coils through a quietly charmed area of flat pasture, ancient monasteries and the callows. These are low-lying riverside pastures which are flooded regularly and for long periods in winter and so afford dependable sanctuary to thousands of geese, swans, ducks and waders, well out of the reach of predators. The callows occur beside the Little

Brosna, which joins the Shannon at Meelick, and beside various stretches of the Shannon itself between Meelick and Clonmacnoise. In summer some of these latter fields still sustain the corncrake, a bird so common and well-known (from its grating, nocturnal call) a generation ago and so rare and precarious now that it stands as a symbol of our age's ecological calamities.

Underwater, naturally, Lakeland seethes with fish. To angling people, the region is famous. The Cavan, Westmeath and Longford lakes are known for their coarse fish; Loughs Ree and Derg for trout. Salmon come to breed in streams running into Lough Derg. Along stretches of water popular with game fishermen, much attention is paid at the appropriate time of the year to a fly with a knobbly head, outstretched wings and a long, gracefully curved three-strand tail. The iridescence of its wing panels resembles some stained-glass ornament of subtle colours made by Tiffany's in the 1920s. The mayfly's main hatch is likely to take place long after Easter, in late May or early June. It is of the order *Ephemeroptera*, and its existence is indeed ephemeral. The two sexes mate and the female lays its eggs into the water within hours of emerging. Many fail even in this respect and simply breast the air, exert themselves in a mighty bid for height, slip, fall and moments later struggle for their lives on the water's surface. Many are blown together and rotate in eddies, flapping wildly and ineffectually as if the surface were of syrup. A fish – likely as not a trout – sees the disturbance, checks the colour-code, and snaps. Or a swallow or sand-martin scoops up the flies in a surface skim. The brief life of the mayfly, the culmination of up to three years spent as egg and nymph among the mud and stones, is generally over in an hour.

The luckier among them will survive a day or two. During that time they eat nothing. The most they can achieve is that others will come after them and repeat a seemingly joyless curriculum.

The first mayflies are noticed by locals with practised eyes. Some varieties do, in fact, appear earlier than May, such as the March Brown, which rises out of fast-flowing rivers. Observers pass on the news. People hear for miles around. Messages are sent on the telephone to Dublin. Once upon a time the lines hummed with telegrams to London. Straight away, or the weekend following, city-weary anglers begin their migration. The mayfly is arrived, trout are biting, and local hotels and guest-houses rapidly filling.

Lough Derg is deeply indented with bays and coves of great variety, gnawed into the bordering limestone. They may be wooded, built round, or lapping pasture or rougher patchworks of heather, gorse and bracken. Like Ree, Lough Derg is seasonal home to wildfowl which, when danger threatens in one bay, like to be able to fly to another nearby. In the south the lough narrows between highlands of rumpled sedimentary rock, and at Killaloe returns to river dimensions for its final windings, through Limerick, to the estuary.

A few miles east of Lough Derg, as the Shannon approaches the end of its journey, three famous Irish rivers begin theirs, the River Nore and the River Barrow on the slopes of Slieve Bloom and the River Suir a few miles south, continuing south or south-east until they reunite and enter the sea as one at Waterford harbour. The Slieve Bloom is the most substantial protrusion from Ireland's limestone heartland. Not mountain-high (it is well below 2,000 feet/600 metres at its highest), it is all the same a world apart from the hurly-burly of people and houses below: a land of smoothly rolling carpet bog, huge baize spreads of conifer, good farmland on its lower levels, cracked at intervals by the deep glens where, because they are not susceptible to human exploitation, plants and animals of interest survive. None of these features, alone or collectively, quite conveys the air of abstraction, of antiquity, of remoteness that shrouds you as you wander among old trees and old paths and boisterous young head-waters which in their maturity, far below, will irrigate the farmlands of the South-East.

Slieve Bloom mountains. It is an area of Ireland that is unfamiliar to many Irish people and the 31-mile (50-km) circular route to the east of Birr displays some of the best scenery in the area. Elsewhere, Forest Park trails in Killykeen, Co. Cavan and by Lough Key, Co. Roscommon, combined with underused country lanes, offer good walking. There is plenty of parking space. The area around Kildare has a selection of trails, mainly on canal tow-paths. They are ideal for those who do not fancy hill-walking, and access by rail and bus is good.

Climbing: the Slieve Bloom mountains have moorland tops, but these drop away into a series of radiating wooded valleys. Arderin is the main peak at 1,734 ft (529 m).

Fishing: the River Shannon and the abundant lakes attract anglers from all over the world. The lakes of Monaghan, Cavan and Roscommon provide excellent coarse fishing. Pike,

roach, rudd and tench are all to be found in the area. Note, however, that there are restrictions when fishing for pike; contact the Shannon Regional Fisheries Board for details, T:(061) 455171. Brown-trout lakes include Sheelin, Ree, Derg and Ennell.

Cycling: this is one of the best ways to explore the Lakeland region. The routes are less strenuous than in the more hilly coastal regions. Athlone is a good base for the 160-mile (258-km) Lough Ree and Shannon route. To the north of Mullingar, it is possible to follow a Bord Fáilte 200-mile (320-km) approved route which twists and winds around the lakes and little hills of Counties Cavan, Longford and Monaghan. There is also a Slieve Bloom mountain route which climbs to a height of 1,476 ft (450 m). Bikes can be rented from Mr Hardiman, Athlone, T:(0902) 78669; Brendan Sheerin, Boyle, T:(079) 62010; E. Clerkin,

Monaghan, T:(047) 81434; and Leo Hunt, Roscommon, T:(0903) 26299.

Riding: in Co. Kildare, Kilkea Lodge Farm and Riding Centre, T:(0503) 45112, can provide a variety of instructional and recreational holidays. Co. Laois's Glebe House Equestrian Centre, T:(0502) 33368, is open all year for trekking, hacking and trail riding. Co. Cavan's Equestrian Centre at Shalom Stables, T:(049) 32017, has a cross-country course and offers basic instruction at its indoor facility.

FURTHER INFORMATION
Tourist offices: there are offices in Mullingar, T:(044) 48650, Athlone, T:(0902) 94630, Birr, T:(0509) 20110, Roscommon, T:(0903) 26342, Boyle, T:(079) 62145, Cavan, T:(049) 31942, and Monaghan, T:(047) 81122.

Lough Allen and the Iron Mountain

Bleak, forbidding iron country and source of the River Shannon

There was a time when I used to drive quite often between Dublin and Sligo. Sometimes I took a turn round pretty Lough Key and got a look at the battery of mountains to the north-east: Arigna, and beyond it the solid and intractable furniture of Slieve Anieran, the Iron Mountain, with Cuilcagh backing it up. I knew perfectly well what was on the other side of Anieran – the top tip of County Cavan and then the national border and Fermanagh with its lakes – but something in the disposition of the mountains made me forget that. Anieran,

rising above Lough Allen, looked like a climactic and terminal barrier, world-ending, impenetrable, mysterious. I dare say Mount Everest, with out-of-bounds Tibet beyond, gives out similar signals. It is not the only time that I've had such feelings. There is a valley across the water in Somerset which I always think of as the approach to Castle Perilous, it so well matches the inner picture inspired by Malory's *Morte d'Arthur*. What it leads to has nothing Arthurian about it, but the expectation never fails.

There is, in fact, something final about Anieran. It brings the flat lakeland of southern County Leitrim to a grand, majestic end and ushers in the northern highlands. Crossing the border to Northern Ireland is, in fact, just as easy a matter here as anywhere else. Indeed, reconditioning of the old Erne–Shannon canal through Ballinamore and Ballyconnell now makes the transit possible in a boat. No, much of Anierin's end-of-the-world quality is a figment of its shape and lie. It does, however, add zest to climbs and explorations.

There used to be a lot of coal near the surface of the mountains round Lough Allen but it has been worn away to thin and local patches. In most places extraction is hardly economic, though Arigna's coal was until recently used to fuel a power station. The coal dates back to the time when a warm sea flooded much of northern Europe 375 million years ago. Coral and other calcareous matter floated to the bottom and gradually created the carboniferous limestone bed which underlies much of inland Ireland. In time, rivers brought down sands and clays from the highlands still jutting above the sea; millions more years of pressure changed these into sandstone and shale. As the sea subsided, plants, both herbaceous and woody, grew, died, rotted and were pressed by layers of later debris into what became coal.

Slieve Anieran means 'mountain of iron'. Iron was worked here and at various places southward as far as Lough Ree, and the woods of oak and ash which covered large parts of the country were felled for the work of smelting. There are furnaces and remains of other ironworks on the mountain, but Anieran now is mainly a mass of heather-covered turf. Its 1,927-foot (587-metre) peak offers wonderful views over Lough Allen, Arigna, the Curlews and Bricklieve mountains to the west, and the lake-studded peneplain to the south, but there are better walks and climbs to be had along its edges and in the smaller mountains to the north.

Low on Cuilcagh's west side is the Shannon Pot, officially but not in technical fact the river's source (since a source – for what it matters – is taken to be the waterway of highest origin, and the Owenmore is higher). This spring, billowing out from an underground river flowing through buried strata of limestone, is overhung with willows and has been favoured with Tourist Board treatment, preluded by a gravel path, car park and picnic area. Cuilcagh and the mountain known for obscure reasons as the Playground, show to advantage the drumlins of the Owenmore valley between them. The smooth oval shapes, densely packed in parts, make me think of this as buttocky country.

The fox, attracting by its intelligent face and cunning survival methods, and repelling by its pointless massacres of captive poultry, is found all over Ireland. It has fearlessly expanded its range from country to town to live off dumps, rubbish heaps and dustbins.

BEFORE YOU GO
Maps: OS half-inch map of Ireland No. 7.
Guidebooks: there is a Co. Cavan leaflet available from Bord Failte that covers these areas.

GETTING THERE
By car: Carrick-on-Shannon can be reached by the main trunk-road N4 from Dublin. From Carrick take the R280 north, and turn right after 8 miles (13 km) on to the R207, which runs along the east side of Lough Allen while giving access to Slieve Anieran to the right.
By rail: the nearest station is Carrick-on-Shannon; services to Sligo and Dublin run three times a day, Saturday to Thursday, and four times a day on Friday.

By bus: the Bus Eireann Expressway Service from Dublin to Sligo stops at Carrick-on-Shannon. The Athlone to Sligo Bus Eireann/Ulster Bus Interlink Expressway also stops at Carrick-on-Shannon as does a local Bus Eireann service. A few local Bus Eireann services stop at Drumshanbo, at the north end of Lough Allen.

WHERE TO STAY

Hotels: there is a good choice of hotels and bed and breakfasts in Carrick-on-Shannon and a handful of bed and breakfasts in Drumshanbo. Ballinamore, near the Iron Mountain, has a small selection of bed and breakfasts and one hotel, McAllister's, T:(078) 44068.

Outdoor living: free camping is available on the banks of the Shannon in Carrick-on-Shannon. To reach the site, cross the bridge near the tourist office. Otherwise find an agreeable spot and ask the farmer's permission to camp there.

Youth hostels: there is an independent hostel in Carrick-on-Shannon, the Town Clock Hostel, T:(078) 20068.

ACTIVITIES

Fishing: there is good fishing to be had in the clean lakes of Co. Leitrim, including Lough Allen. For further information and tackle, contact Geraghty's, T.(078) 21316, in Carrick-on-Shannon, or the Angling Information Centre, T:(078) 20694.

Cycling: bikes can be hired at Geraghty's, T:(078) 21316, in Carrick-on-Shannon.

Walking: the Leitrim Way, a 30-mile/48-km way-marked route, starts in Drumshanbo and runs along the east coast of Lough Allen. There are two stages to the route: 1, Drumshanbo to Dowra (10 miles/16 km); 2, Dowra to Manorhamilton (20 miles/32 km). For more information contact Leitrim County Council, Court House, Carrick-on-Shannon, Co. Leitrim, T:(078) 20005.

FURTHER INFORMATION

Tourist offices: there are two tourist information centres in Carrick-on-Shannon. The main Bord Failte tourist office, T:(078) 20170, is open only during the summer; during the rest of the year information is available from an office in the old town hall, T:(078) 20857.

Bricklieve Mountains

Mountains with megalithic tombs and rewarding views over Lough Arrow

In Boyle, a small town sloping down on both sides to the river of the same name, I had been directed to the shoe shop; not to buy stout shoes for walking, though that would certainly have been possible, but to get advice from the proprietor Maurice Corrigan, who has walked everywhere worth walking hereabouts. His colleagues Adrian and Patsy joined in the discussion. Adrian drew a map of the Bricklieve mountains, beyond the Curlews to the north of the town, in order to show me what he believed to be 'the best walk in Ireland'.

'I'd do anything to be going with you, but I've work ...' Maurice said to me. 'Now, see, I'll tell him to put in north. He can't tell his north from his back door. Put in north and south, Adrian.'

Adrian, to Maurice's chagrin, got it right. Later they wrote their names down for me. 'Go on Maurice,' said Adrian, 'M-A-U-R.' The twitting was still going on when I left. A day or two later my car, having sprung an oil leak, was lastingly repaired by a fitter, his son and grandson who happened to live close by. After the hour it took, I had the sight of three generations vehemently refusing any payment. 'Sure it wasn't your fault it broke down.' These are scenes which it is easy but wrong to imagine do not occur in the new Ireland. By the new Ireland I mean a country at pains, much of the time at least, to show itself different from other countries (above all England) and at the same time modern, progressive, European and viable. It has been very successful in its efforts. Sadly, and too often, a high price is paid: the reduction of some agreeable customs and attitudes – among them talk and kindness to strangers – that take up too much time for today's hectic pace. Other countries threw them away years ago. This makes it doubly nice to find them in pockets here and there, surviving and even thriving.

137

From different points in the distance the Bricklieves take on protean forms: various kinds of hat, upturned pudding basins, earthbound ships, but most of all those cakes from whose sides, in my childhood, you peeled strips of fringed paper, and whose summits swelled with icing. Walls of grey limestone are what the removed paper discloses, and the icing is green and brown or purple, the colours of grass and heather. The decoration consists of massive cairns of rough, sharp stones, piled between four and five thousand years ago on Stone-Age passage graves which have been excavated and are in some cases kept open to view. This is the sprawling megalithic graveyard of Carrowkeel. I was told that, to excavate some of the cairns, archaeologists early this century cleared the stones away with dynamite: not recommended.

Otherwise the summits are tussocky, dell-strewn, cave-pricked sheep-land plateaux: grass, heather, reed and crowberry (*Empetrum nigrum*) with little corners of richer vegetation. Here and there a dwarf hawthorn has almost grafted itself into a rock to take cover from winds of Atlantic or Arctic provenance; in small sheltered cuts and corners you can find golden saxifrage (*Chrysosplenium oppositifolium*), appealingly small primroses (*Primula vulgaris*), wood-sorrel (*Oxalis acetosella*), white stonecrop (*Sedum album*) and several different ferns and mosses. Not far from the summit are patches of orchid. Ravens wheel, dive and croak overhead. At irregular intervals there are old peat workings, jigsaw pieces of turf five or six feet (up to a couple of metres) high where village diggers have come to a resistant seam – of bog oak or pine maybe, hardened by three or four thousand years of soaking – and swerved.

We know little of those who made and inhabited the Stone-Age tombs of these summits save that they liked to be buried with bone pins, pottery and stone bric-à-brac, and to face the north. It seems a reasonable aspiration, for the world offers few better views. Below are the short limestone ravines, with

Lough Derravaragh, its waters and banks teeming with life, sees the sun sink beyond the boggy plain to its west.

ivy drapes and precariously sprouting ash and birch. Down to the right Lough Arrow sparkles with emerald islands. In the foreground is a playground of wavy green, cut by hedges and stone walls, dappled with yellow gorse, bright white houses and little occasional lakes. Toy country, fairy country, Yeats country: Sligo – a county quite unlike any other in its land-forms and emporium of folklore. Far ahead lies Ben Bulben (see page 36), as evocative a figure as any in Ireland, the long slant of the Ox mountains, Sligo Bay and the great hunched Slieve League headland beyond. The ascent of the Bricklieve presents little challenge, except perhaps in keeping to the correct route, and the rewards for the climb are quite out of proportion to the effort involved.

BEFORE YOU GO
Maps: OS half-inch map of Ireland No. 7.

GETTING THERE
By car: from Carrick-on-Shannon follow the N4 (west) to Boyle, continuing on it after it turns northward to Sligo. Eight miles beyond Boyle it passes to the east of the Bricklieve mountains.
By rail: The nearest station is in Boyle, where services run to/from Dublin Connolly.
By bus: A Saturday-only Bus Eireann local service from Sligo to Castlerea stops at Ballymote, and another local Bus Eireann service between Sligo and Athlone stops at Ballymote and Boyle.

WHERE TO STAY
Hotels; there is a good choice of bed and breakfasts in and around Boyle and a couple of hotels, the Forest Park, T:(079) 62229, and the Royal, T:(079) 62016. There is a handful of bed and breakfasts in Ballymote.

ACTIVITIES
Walking: there are fine walks to Carrowkeel Tomb Cemetery, on a hilltop in the Bricklieve mountains.
Fishing: boating and fishing are available at Coopeshill House, T:(071) 65108, close to Carrowkeel. Fishing is also available at Lough Arrow.
Cycling: bikes can be hired at Brendan Sheerin's in Boyle, T:(079) 62010. *Cycling Ireland*, a Bord Failte leaflet, has a suggested route that runs between the Bricklieve mountains and past Lough Arrow.

FURTHER INFORMATION
Tourist offices: the Bord Failte tourist office at Lough Allen is open during July and Aug, T:(079) 66232. The Bord Failte tourist office in Boyle is open from late May to late Sept, T:(079) 62145.

REMAINS IN THE WILD

Ireland is full of discarded ruins, some of them dating back 4,000 and even 5,000 years. They occur everywhere and anywhere. Certain of them fit into categories.

Dolmen. Neolithic tomb dating from 2000–3000 BC, consisting of vertical flagstones on which rests an often huge capstone, the whole formerly covered with earth. May be rectangular or wedge-shaped. Mainly found in the northern half of Ireland.

Court cairn. An open courtyard surrounded by one or more covered burial chambers. Mainly found in the northern half of Ireland, many in Mayo and Leitrim.

Passage graves. Neolithic burial chambers approached by stone-walled passages and covered in circular mounds of earth; constructed about 4,500 years ago. The finest examples in Europe are beside the Boyne. Others can be found in Carrowmore and Carrowkeel (in north and south County Sligo respectively), and elsewhere in the northern half of Ireland.

Stone circles. Circles of free-standing megaliths dating back about 4,000 years, probably used for religious rituals, mainly found in Cork and Kerry.

Standing stones. Also around 4,000 years old (late Stone Age, early Bronze Age), these can be of enormous size, reaching up to 20 ft (6 m) in height. Probably constructed for ritual use, they occur all over Ireland. From the Iron Age, a century or two BC, there survive huge shaped stones carved with Celtic patterns. Pillarstones of rectangular section, found in south-west Ireland, date from about AD 300–600 and often have a series of notches cut down one corner. These notches are ogham script, used generally for commemorative purposes, and recording personal names.

Iron Age forts. Comprising rings of concentric stone walls, these date from about 2,000 years ago. The most impressive is Dun Aengus, built on a perilous cliff-top on the largest of the Aran Islands.

Clochain. Beehive huts of rough stones, built by corbelling. Often round outside and square in, they were in many cases used by religious hermits. Situated mainly on the Dingle peninsula, they date back to about AD 450-700.

Round towers. Tall, thin stone towers which are in some cases over 100 ft (30 m) in height and capped by stone cones. Numbering 120, they date from between the mid-tenth and mid-thirteenth centuries. Built within monasteries, they were almost certainly bell-towers that doubled as defensive sanctuaries.

High crosses. Constructed between the ninth and twelfth centuries, these massive stone Celtic crosses (with the uprights and cross-pieces joined by a circle of stone) were usually deeply carved with abstract patterns and representations of religious scenes.

Ring-forts, or raths. A series of alternating circular earthen ramparts and ditches, these were no doubt the defences surrounding individual homes or settlements. They may be anything from 1,000 to 3,000 years old. There are said to be 30,000 extant.

Crannog. Artificial island in a lake or marsh, hemmed by stakes or stones and connected to the mainland by a (submerged) causeway. Used for defensive purposes between 1000 BC and AD 1000.

Modern structures. Crosses, with or without a figure of Christ, shrines to the Blessed Virgin Mary, cairns – piles of stones – and other artefacts have often been placed on mountain tops in recent years.

Lough Gara

Popular angling lake 6 miles (10 km) west of Boyle, surrounded by moist, warm, peaty mire

It is a small-time site, a lake that came to prominence in the 1950s when draining exposed numbers of lake dwellings, or crannogs, dating from two to three thousand years ago. The Lung river and other streams feed it, and the Boyle river takes its waters on through Lough Key to the Shannon.

Greenland white-fronted geese, whooper swans and various duck spend the winter on it. It is crossed east to west by a causeway carrying a road from which at various points you can walk down on to a peaty mire. You may sink in up to your knees, unless you keep to stones or reedy tussocks which are likely to have some firmness underneath. Like most lakes, it is popular with anglers.

I like Lough Gara. I like the certain ordinariness it has about it. I like to sit in the heat, when there is some, and insinuate myself into the pleasures of concentration and empathy. From woods of willow and blackthorn comes a commotion of bird-song: warblers, chaffinch, wren, thrush and that incompetent tenor the blackbird, while snipe sometimes burble or bubble from ground level, and swallows flit, too busy for static recitals. Kingcup, buttercup, yellow flag, bog asphodel, orchids and cotton grass burgeon in the moist warmth. It is this protean natural ferment, this glory of colour, hum and buzz for which I have always treasured this part of Ireland.

The lane along the north-east side of the lough allows you closer to the water. Swans, terns and gulls pattern the view with ballets of white. From here you can walk, or better canoe, into the town of Boyle. Church ruins, a mixed Catholic and Church of Ireland graveyard, crumpled stone walls and empty windows along the way would toll endless death and decay were it not for the irrepressible tangle of vegetation that uses them as life-support. It all comprises a recurring summer festival.

Before you go *Maps:* OS half-inch maps of Ireland Nos 7 and 12.

Getting there *By car:* from Carrick-on-Shannon follow the N4 (west) to Boyle. The R294 from Boyle (west) passes close to the north end of Lough Gara.

By rail: the nearest station is Boyle, where services from Dublin Connolly stop about four times a day.

By bus: a Bus Eireann Expressway service between Dublin and Sligo stops at Boyle. A local Bus Eireann service between Athlone and Sligo also stops there.

Where to stay: there is a good choice of bed and breakfasts in and around Boyle and a couple of hotels: the Forest Park, T:(079) 62229, and the Royal, T:(079) 62016.

Outdoor living: the closest camp-site to the lough is the Lough Key Caravan and Camping Park near Boyle, T:(079) 62212.

Activities *Cycling:* bikes can be hired from Brendan Sheerin's in Boyle, T:(079) 62010.

Fishing: the Angling Information Centre in Drumsna, T:(078) 20694, can supply information, tackle and bait. Fishing tackle is also available from Crul, T:(078) 20166, or Holts, T:(078) 20184, both in Carrick-on-Shannon. Lough Key is a particularly good pike and brown-trout lake.

Watersports: wind-surfing and sailing equipment are available for hire on Lough Key.

Further information *Tourist offices:* the Bord Failte tourist office in Boyle is open late May–late Sept, T:(079) 62145.

Lakeland

Mass of lakes on a bed of slate; an angler's paradise

A woman I love long ago banned the word 'boring' from her vocabulary. I think she adopted the principle from her mother. She certainly tries – with mixed success – to pass it on to her own children. Everything is interesting, she says, provided you look at it in the right way. What bores is in the eye of the beholder.

On much the same grounds I try to avoid the cliché 'See one and you've seen them all'. It is glib and it demeans the subjects. But the lakes of Counties Cavan, Longford and Westmeath test my resolution. They would not try an angler in the same way. He would distinguish the lakes like the books in a library: different larvae, different flies, different currents and pools and temperatures, different shades from different trees, different shores and access, different – amazingly different – fish. They list them on local signposts, white on brown: Rudd this way,

---

LAW OF THE COUNTRYSIDE

Fox-hunting, which takes place all over Ireland, is restricted to the months November to March.

Fishing regulations are subject to local variation and should always be checked. Salmon fishing opens at the beginning of January and ends in September. Brown-trout fishing opens in February and ends in October. The sea-trout season runs from May, June or July to September or October, depending on the fishery. Coarse fishing has no closed season. Sea-fishing takes place throughout the year.

Shooting seasons, and the species which may be taken, are regulated by the National Parks and Wildlife Service (address on page 216).

Perch that, Bream, Pike the other. It often strikes me as a strange alliance of sportsman and bureaucrat, this matching of location and species. But I am not, it may seem superfluous to add, a fisherman. To me one lake is much like another. But they are not dull, not as long as the wild processes on which fishermen depend continue.

To those of us not dedicated to the condition of suspended animation known as fishing, the mayfly, the staple bait of the fly-fisherman, and its companions offer interest too. On warm afternoons they rise in swarms for the mating flight. The females drop their eggs when the sun has set. Other forms may gather for a while in warm, sunny or sheltered corners of the lake: stoneflies, including the angler's favoured yellow sally (*Isoperia grammatica*); needleflies (*Leuctra* spp.), gathering their wings tightly about them; the water boatman (*Notonecta* spp.), buoyed by a bubble of air, game to attack tadpoles, small fish and the occasional human finger; whirligig beetles (*Gyrinus natator*), using their legs as oars to dart towards ditched flies or floating corpses, half an eye (literally) above and half below the water's surface, receding from severed wings or hollow head-cases, turning curves and circles on the glistening rink, or congregating in huge herds. Such scenes wait at the end of every lake path leading from the road.

As to the sameness of the lakes, it is half inevitable and half untrue. Inevitable because a mass of lakes distributed across a bed of slate that dips and lifts within narrow limits are likely to have much in common; untrue in that the greater waters of this central lakeland are palpably distinct.

Lough Oughter is a huge watery labyrinth, a baffling area of lake sliced and broken by countless insertions of land and islands. It follows on, after a break, from the similar maze of Upper Lough Erne. Lough Sheelin, on the River Inny, a tributary of the Shannon, is a large lake (4 by 2 miles/7 by 3 kilometres maximum) nicely fringed with woods, some of them of a stately demesne elegance. Lough Ramor, on the Boyne, lying in the pretty country of south-east Cavan, sparkles with islands and trees. Lough Derravaragh is set in a heartland of history and myth, its eastern side well bounded with commanding hills.

Running through this vast expanse of lakes, Ireland's longest river, the Shannon, creates yet more lakes of great variety – Boderg, Bofin, Forbes, Ree – by its expansions and contractions.

Before you go

Maps: OS half-inch map of Ireland No. 12.

Getting there *By car:* from Mullingar the N4 towards Edgeworthstown runs past Lough Owel. The R394 (north) runs past Lough Derravaragh to Castlepollard, and after 10 miles (16 km) past Lough Sheelin. The R395 (east) from Castlepollard passes Lough Lene. The R394 eventually joins the N55. A few miles west of the junction lies Lough Gowna. Continue north on the N55 to Cavan. Lough Oughter and Killykeen National Park lie north-west of the town.

By rail: the nearest stations are Mullingar, Edgeworthstown and Longford, on the Dublin–Sligo line, but the area is huge and not well served by train.

By bus: Bus Eireann services that stop in Mullingar include the Athlone–Dublin and Longford–Dublin local services, and also the Dublin–

Ballina, Dublin–Sligo and Galway–Dundalk Expressway services. The local Bus Eireann Dublin–Granard service stops at Castlepollard. Bus Eireann services from all over Ireland stop or terminate in Cavan.

Where to stay *Hotels:* there is a good selection of bed and breakfasts and hotels in and around Mullingar and Cavan. There are bed and breakfasts in Granard, Longford and Edgeworthstown. In Castlepollard, contact Eithne Healy, T:(044) 61144, or Mrs Abigail Smythe, T:(044) 61140.

At any given time particles of domesticated Ireland are returning to a wild state: here a cottage, bodily discarded in favour of a bungalow.

Activities *Cycling:* bikes can be hired from Abbey Set Printers in Cavan, T:(049) 31932, and Declan and Bernadette Fagan, T:(0506) 35118, near Mullingar.
Riding: hacks are available at Cavan Equestrian Centre, Latt, which is open June–Oct, T:(049) 32017.
Fishing: the lakeland area around Cavan is known throughout the world for its excellent coarse fishing, primarily for pike, bream, perch and roach; game angling for trout is available in Lough Sheelin. Trout fishing takes place on Lough Owel, Lough Lene and Lough Derravaragh and the season usually runs from March or May to mid-October, depending on the lake. All these lakes, apart from Lough Lene, are controlled by the Shannon Regional Fisheries Board, T:(0612) 551712 or (044) 48769. For tackle contact Sam's Tackle (who can also provide boats and permits for Lough Owel), O'Callaghs or O'Malleys, all in Mullingar. For information on Lough Derravaragh, contact Mr Newman, T:(044) 71111, and for Lough Owel, Mrs Doolan, T:(044) 42085.
Killykeen National Park: this has fine walks and nature trails. Canoes can be rented on Lough Oughter, T:(049) 32842.
Further information *Tourist offices:* the office in Cavan, T:(049) 31942, is open all year, that in Mullingar June–Sept, T:(044) 48761.

The Central Lakes

Lough Ree

Fourth largest lake in Ireland; breeding ground of the endangered common scoter

On the Ordnance Survey map many more place-names are shown around the southern borders of Lough Ree than the northern. John O'Donovan, whose admirable survey of the country is still the basis of these maps, is said to have been courting at the time of this work a farmer's daughter whose home was close to the southernmost tip of the lake. He spun out his time to remain close to her, and the effect on the survey reappears with each new edition.

Whatever their romantic charms, the purlieus of Lough Ree are very flat. The tremolo undulations of Counties Longford, Westmeath and Roscommon hardly figure in the view from the lake. It has none of the picturesque appeal of Lough Derg. The Athlone–Galway railway, which runs up the west side, and an extensive acreage of reed and mud at the edges, make it difficult, often, to get to the water. The best way to see Lough Ree is from a boat.

Fifteen miles (24 km) long and at most seven (11 km) wide, it occupies 39 square miles (62 square km) and is the fourth largest lake in Ireland. Many of its innumerable islands possess remains of great interest, including castles and monastic buildings. On one of them, Inchcleraun or Quaker Island, are a number of ruined churches, one of which was pulled down by a nineteenth-century Quaker in order to build a home. The sacrilege led to a curse and his removal from the island. Rather less fortunate was Queen Maeve, whose desire to possess the Brown Bull of Cooley led her to ravage the kingdom of Ulster. While bathing from this island, the legend goes, she was killed by an Ulster prince with a stone from his sling.

Birds are present in modest numbers, possibly more than have been recorded given the difficulty of seeing them. In winter, there are diving and dabbling ducks – over a thousand tufted ducks in the north-east sector. Common terns and black-headed gulls come in spring to breed, along with a small number of common scoters, now an endangered species in Ireland. You can see them from lanes that bring you to the water's edge, but it is extraordinary how much is obscured by nearby vegetation and headlands. Again a boat is the best viewpoint, but if I were in a boat I should be off to Lough Derg or the entrancing coils of the Shannon that lie between the two lakes.

Before you go *Maps:* OS half-inch map of Ireland No. 12.
Getting there *By car:* the N6 runs between Dublin and Athlone. From Athlone, take the N61 (north) to Roscommon up the west side of Lough Ree. *By rail:* services from Dublin Heuston to Galway, Westport or Ballina stop at Athlone. *By bus:* plenty of local and Expressway Bus Eireann services stop at Athlone, Roscommon and Lanesborough.
Where to stay: there are plenty of hotels and bed and breakfasts in and around Athlone and a few more in Roscommon. Camping is available at Gailey Bay on the west shore of Lough Ree, T:(0903) 61058/61059. Also at

Hodson Bay on the west shore near Athlone, T:(0902) 92448.
Activities: boats are available for hire on the lough which is well stocked with trout. Bikes can be hired from Hardimans in Athlone, T:(0902) 72651.

This is a good area for bird-watching as there are common terns, black-headed gulls and a few common scoter..
Further information: the tourist office in Athlone is open Apr–Oct, T:(0902) 95630.

THE CAVAN WAY

OS half-inch map of Ireland No. 12

The 16-mile (26-km) Cavan Way is a fairly straight-forward walk across the extreme west of the county. Dowra, at the south-western end, stands on the border of Cavan and Leitrim, at the head of Lough Allen, and the first half of the Way is along the final ascent of the Shannon valley. The river ends at the Shannon Pot, fenced, spruced and footpathed for the delectation of tourists. The second half of the walk, north-east to Blacklion on the Northern Ireland border, goes through hilly country very rich in megalithic remains: ring-forts, chamber-tombs, gallery graves and so on. There are also several sweat-house ruins, where once a draining heat-session was followed by a plunge into the nearest water. Some walkers regret the demise of this institution. From Blacklion, at the end of the walk, the Ulster Way takes over, leading north towards Donegal and south-east to Upper Lough Erne.

Before you go *Guidebooks:* Bord Failte Information Sheet 26I.
Getting there *By car:* to reach Blacklion follow the N4 (west) from Enniskillen. To reach Dowra, follow the A4 (west) past Blacklion, then the R207 (south) towards Lough Allen. *By bus:* a Bus Eireann Expressway service operating between Belfast and Galway stops at Blacklion once a day as does another Bus Eireann Expressway service operating between Dooagh and Belfast. A local Bus Eireann service between Sligo and Enniskillen stops at Blacklion a couple of times a day. The Friday- and Saturday-only service between

Carrigallen and Sligo stops at Dowra.
Where to stay: there are a couple of bed and breakfasts in Blacklion including Lough Macnean House, T:(072) 53022, and Pinegrove, T:(072) 53061, but there is more choice in Enniskillen. There is one hostel in the area, the Sandville House Hostel, T:(049) 26297, just south of Ballyconnell.
Further information: contact Cavan County Council, Courthouse, Cavan, T:(049) 31799. The nearest tourist office to Blacklion is the Fermanagh Tourist Information Centre, Enniskillen, which is open all year, T:(01365) 323110/325050.

CHAPTER 4: LAKELAND AND THE CENTRAL PLAIN

Little Brosna River

Flooded meadows on the river are home to Ireland's last surviving corncrake population

Some places are wild in season. The flat-lands bordering the central Shannon between Loughs Ree and Derg are a magical area of peat bog, containing the remnants of human enterprises from the Stone Age to the boom-time of canals, from the pagan to the Christian. The landscape is punctuated by those serpentine sweepings of the glaciers known as eskers, curved ridges of grass-topped gravel and sand brought down by melt-waters from the mountains and deposited in deep escape channels in the glacial ice. Along the rivers there are rich pastures on alluvial soils, and footpaths for fishermen. No summer visitor could call any of this wild.

The rains come in autumn, in quantities to flood the meadows. By November these are underwater. The river is an inland sea. Then the birds arrive from the north for the worst of the winter. There are wigeon, mallard, teal, pintail, shoveler, Greenland white-fronted goose, three kinds of swan, black-tailed godwit, dunlin, greenshank and also breeding populations of curlew, lapwing, redshank and snipe. Wigeon can be numbered in thousands, as can the black-tailed godwits and other waders; swans, geese and various ducks come in hundreds. Numbers peak in February and March. In a normal year the waters recede soon after. The birds depart for Iceland and the Arctic. The callows, as these floodable meadows are called, are tame again.

In spring and summer the callows are home to most of the remaining population of Ireland's corncrakes. They survive here because grass grows more slowly on the callows and because hay or, increasingly, big-bale silage is cut later here than elsewhere in the country. The corncrake is an odd bird, with a gawky flight – it wisely prefers to run for cover – and a rather dumpy figure. At most times round the clock, but particularly for an hour or two after midnight, the males make a curious noise variously represented as a 'crake', from which comes the bird's English name, or as *Crex crex*, which is its Latin name, or as an electronic purr, or as the sound of a comb being grated. A generation or so ago everybody in rural Ireland (and a great many in rural Britain) was familiar with these characteristic nightly crakes or crexes during the breeding season. They took them for granted and never bothered to mention them. Then farmers adopted the practice of making silage. This happens earlier in the season than hay-making, at a time when the female corncrake and her chicks are in among the grass. Whereas scything in times gone by gave the birds plenty of time to get out of the way, the modern mechanical cutter is difficult to escape; more so as it tends to be steered round the field from the outside to the middle, enclosing its victims in a diminishing space until it hacks them to bits at the centre.

Another disturbing ritual is carried out by some farmers on the rich farmlands of the midlands and the East at about the same time. This is the shearing of hedges by mechanical cutter. Nests are sliced or toppled and bird populations fall further. Though rather an eccentric bird, with its shy habits and curious night-calls, the corncrake has come to be a symbol of persecuted wildlife. Every year it is reported to be losing numbers or to have disappeared from places – such as Inishbofin off the Galway coast – where it has hitherto managed to hold out. It remains on the flood plains of the Shannon, but there are experts who think it cannot last for long.

Before you go *Maps:* OS half-inch map of Ireland No. 15.

Getting there *By car:* from Athlone follow the N62 to Cloghan, then the R456 to Banagher, then lanes south-westward to the Little Brosna river between Birr and the Shannon opposite Meelick. *By rail:* the nearest station is Roscrea on a branch line from Ballybrophy, where there are connecting services to Dublin Heuston and Limerick Junction. *By bus:* the Bus Eireann Expressway services between Dublin and Portumna and Cork and Athlone stop at Birr. A local independent bus company, Kern's Coaches, T:(0509) 20776, operates a weekend and evening service from Tullamore to Galway which stops at Birr.

Where to stay: there are several bed and breakfasts in Birr and more in Banagher. Consult the Bord Failte *Accommodation Guide.*

Activities: bikes can be hired from P.L. Dolan and Sons in Birr, T:(0509) 20006. Winter bird-watchers will find a large selection of waterfowl in the area.

Further information: the Bord Failte tourist office in Birr is open May–Sept, T:(0509) 20110.

Lough Derg and the Lower Shannon

This geologically puzzling section of river and lake provides good boating and isolated walks

Lough Derg is like an inland sea: a miniature Mediterranean with counties for countries, and rather less climatic and cultural variation. County Clare to the west is the O'Brien fief: rough and rocky, poor and mountainous. To the south, County Limerick takes the outflow of the Shannon (of which the lough is really a mightily swollen section) and, at a place called Ardnacrusha, in a huge man-made hydro-electric water-

Twenty years ago and more the corncrake was well-known all over Ireland; not by sight, for it is shy, but for its sound: an absurd grating noise uttered in the middle of the night. It is scarce now, reduced to half a dozen or so localities in the whole country where the hay is cut late.

Reeds are blown aslant under a scowling sky on Lough Oughter, in the watery forest park of Killykeen.

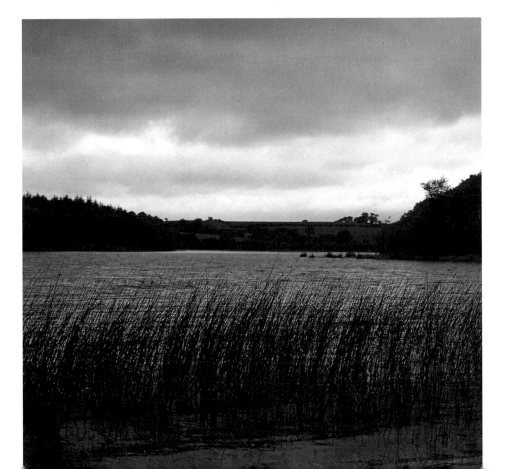

fall, drops much of it a hundred feet. County Tipperary to the east, traditional Butler territory, is a place of rich pasture and small towns and modest mountain ranges, of which the Arra comes close to the lough shore. Flat, green, damp and stony on the north-western bank, County Galway here gives no indication of the highland dramas it packs into its Atlantic half. Each county, through its soil, contours and climate, has worked its will on the porous and erodible limestone of the lake's bed to produce the variant shapes and sizes of bays, headlands and islands, the changing nature of coastal vegetation, the orientation of fields and woods. There are occasional unique features: the Irish fleabane (*Inula salicina*), which is not unlike a small sunflower, is found nowhere else in these islands. It is by no means common here. Far more than bland Lough Ree to the north, Lough Derg is busy, lively and a pretty filigree of detail.

The course taken by the lake's outflow at its southern end presents geologists with a puzzle. The mountains which edge its southern flanks are of old red sandstone with an inner core of quartzite. They are much harder than the limestone that makes up the rest of the lake's bed and, since the eruptions that threw them up 300 million years ago, they have formed three huge islands in the limestone. Instead of leaving the lake by one of the channels between these mountains, the water seems to have carved a way through the southernmost of them, giving itself a great deal of unnecessary trouble. Of course there must be an explanation, and Frank Mitchell, doyen of Irish geologists, finds it in the movement of ice from the north. Coming against the mountain wall, it divided and flowed east and west, except for a central thrust of ice which, finding a valley, forged ahead, deepened it, and eventually gouged out the gorge which now conveys the outflow.

From end to end of Lough Derg, the points at which the River Shannon respectively expands from and retracts into sensible river dimensions are 22 miles (35 kilometres) apart. Its width is not so easily given because so many deep bays have been bitten out of its edge. At its widest, from the west end of Scarriff Bay to the east of Youghal

Bay (the name denotes yew woods, no longer there), it reaches eight miles (13 kilometres), though for most of its length it is less than three (five kilometres). Border lands are rich in woods and copses and stately lone trees, and there is an uneven spattering of islands, from a mile (1.5 kilometres) to a few feet across. Many have shrubs and trees, a few of them cottages or castles, and one, Holy Island, a mile or so south of Mountshannon, preserves among its lazy sprawl of grass and bushes the remains of a seventh-century abbey with a tenth-century round tower 70 feet (21 metres) high. Some islands have a pretty green symmetry, like upturned powder puffs of tree foliage. There are grand lake-side demesnes, their mature parklands handed down from the days of the Ascendancy to an age which is doing nothing to maintain their beauty and grandeur.

Twenty years ago the tourist authorities, touting for custom, could truly claim that the density of boats on the Shannon was one one-hundred-and-eightieth of the density on England's Norfolk Broads. Today, the disparity is still dramatic but distinctly, reduced. Killaloe, Mountshannon, Garrykennedy, Dromineer and other towns and villages with quays buzz with activity in season. Ancillary shops – chandlers, provision stores and restaurants – have burgeoned, along with places to stay.

In the early 1970s I cruised down the river. There was a night at Garrykennedy, a little harbour village as wily about water and its ways as can be and, while not used to tourists, consummate in hospitality towards them. We were brought to the pub. As I remember, it was a grim succession of cells whose low ceilings and walls were stained dull yellow from decades of cigarette and pipe smoke. We sat on metal barrels and talked of twenty-pound salmon, of the pike that fought like Attila, of rough waters and the storm that years before sank a Guinness tanker, from the wreck of which barrels of stout were being hauled ashore for months afterwards. We bought each other pint after pint, we sang, and there were strong men exhibiting that strange, tense, sweaty resolve to hit the right note, or something near it, and continue it to its end, despite the attempts of alcohol and gravity to reduce them to snoring piles on the floor. I zigzagged back to the cruiser well after two and, under the spindly ruins of the old castle, contrived to lower my feet on to the boat rather than the water, and got to bed.

I do not want such Viking sessions now, and I am not sure that they are to be had. A new class of nautical amateurs has replaced the gnarled old crewmen. They wear protective clothes of many colours, talk gung-ho among themselves and never greet strangers; they comport themselves on their motor cruisers as if they were skippering schooners; their pubs are clean and bright and comfortable. No matter. The lough is big enough to absorb them (I have wished it would). It is big enough for the fishermen who sit in motionless, miserable threes in rowing boats for six hours at a stretch. It is big enough for you or me to walk without a human in sight among the lake-side grasses and occasional orchids, watch the circular ripples set in motion by a trout snapping at a mayfly, or climb to the prehistoric graves of the Leinster Men on the slopes of Tountinna, to survey the entire scene.

BEFORE YOU GO
Maps: OS half-inch maps of Ireland Nos 15, 17 and 18.

GETTING THERE
By car: from Galway follow the N6 (east) to Loughrea, then the R351 (south) and the R353 to Portumna. This takes you to the north end of Lough Derg. The R493 to Nenagh and the R494 to Killaloe run close to the east side of Lough Derg. There is a good road system right round the lake.
By rail: the nearest stations are Nenagh and Birdhill (4 miles/7 km south of Killaloe) on the Dublin–Limerick line.
By bus: Bus Eireann has a Monday to Saturday service that runs from Dublin to Portumna and a summer-only Expressway service from Galway to Rosslare that stops at Portumna and Nenagh. A Dublin–Limerick Bus Eireann service also stops at Nenagh, and local Bus Eireann services from Limerick to Nenagh and from Galway to Eyrecourt stop at Portumna.

WHERE TO STAY
Hotels: there are bed and breakfasts in Nenagh and a few in Killaloe, at the southern end of Lough Derg. There are some in Portumna, and in Scarriff on the west shore.
Outdoor living: the Lough Derg Caravan and Camping Holiday Park at Killaloe is open from May–Sept, T:(061) 376329. The Lakeside Caravan and Camping Park at Mountshannon is open Apr–Nov, T:(061) 927225.

ACTIVITIES
Walking: a good hiking route is marked out from Nenagh to Limerick in the *Walking Ireland* leaflet from Bord Failte.
Riding: trekking and hacking are available at Shannonside Carrowtaun Farm Trekking Centre, Killaloe, Co. Clare, T:(061) 376622.
Fishing: plenty of coarse fishing in the area and Lough Derg has brown-trout, salmon, pike and rudd fishing.
Sailing and wind-surfing: both available at the Shannonside Activity Centre, Killaloe, Co. Clare, T:(061) 376622. Dromineer, on the east shore, is home to the Lough Derg Yacht Club.

FURTHER INFORMATION
Tourist offices: there is a Bord Failte tourist office in Killaloe, open June to mid-Sept. Tourist information is also available at the Boat House Bar and Lounge in Portumna, T:(050) 941130.

Mayflies are common on and near lakes and rivers where water quality is good, the females laying their eggs during the few days of their adult existence. Fishermen use artificial flies as bait for trout and other fish.

Slieve Bloom

A scenic bulge in the central plain; unspoilt mountain bog and glens

Ireland's protuberant navel, a big bulge above the prosperous, peaty midlands, the pride of locals, perfectly accessible from numerous towns and endowed with the largest area of mountain bog in the country (bigger even than Wicklow's) is mercifully less visited than such a central, substantial and agreeable feature might be. Wildness persists, despite the efforts of desk-bound bureaucrats, who have dubbed the Slieve Bloom (which means the mountains of Bladh – a hero of ancient myth) an Environment Park. If we were faithful to the old meanings of words, this would quite misleadingly signify a park on the outskirts of the Bloom mountains – and how inept to try to catch this massive billow of ancient rock, which could conceal all the people of Ireland within its glens, in a suburban tag: park. Thankfully, the range remains relatively unspoilt.

There is a lot to spoil. North to south the range stretches 12 miles (22 kilometres), and east to west it is 14 miles (23 kilometres) long. Almost all the overlying rock is old red sandstone, laid down as marine sediment around 400 million years ago. Underneath it lay older, Silurian rocks, which had been bunched together into tall mountains by that clash of tectonic plates known as the Caledonian orogeny and then greatly reduced by weathering. There are areas either side of the Slieve Bloom ridge-top where subsequent erosion has allowed this older rock to break through, as has happened in bigger ranges to the south-west, similarly formed. Streams and waterfalls in the many glens have also exposed earlier deposits. But for the most part no rock is visible, being covered with several feet of peat or other soil.

The Slieve Bloom is not dramatic. It gets no higher than 1,734 feet (529 metres) and the shapes that make it up are so gently curved that you can often look about you and imagine you are on the plain. The name of its highest point – Arderin, or the Height of Ireland – sounds pretentious until you see the astounding views. On the other hand, it is greatly different from what lies about it, which actually is the plain, the endless, boggy (or formerly boggy) flat-lands of central Ireland. Really the Slieve Bloom is a sort of dry-run island, as distinctive as an island in its shapes, constituent materials, growth, outlook and activity from its surroundings. The people who occupy its villages and scattered farmsteads are hill people, grazing their cattle on grassy slopes and hilltops, among copses of oak and beech and riots of bramble and thorn. They and their dogs are used to humping uphill and striding out

---

THE IRISH SKY

Someone was praising the quality of Irish air to Jonathan Swift, the mordant champion of the Irish against English greed and exploitation. 'Hold your peace, sir,' he replied, 'lest the English should tax it.' People talk of the balminess of Irish air, cleansed by its ocean journey (it usually comes from the south-west, often enough bringing rain). Then again, Irish rain is not like that of other countries. 'The rain here,' the German novelist Heinrich Böll wrote from Ireland, 'is absolute, magnificent and frightening. To call this rain bad weather is to call scorching sunshine fine weather.' It would be silly to claim that there are no miserably sodden, dark days during which nothing feels dry, indoors or out. But summer rain can be short and refreshing, its wetness soon blown away by the same light, sweet breeze that brought it.

Clouds are another ocean import, and it is worth keeping an eye on the sky just for the scenic bonus of towering cirrocumulus, infinite mackerel patterns, darkening storm-skirts or Old Testament clouds impaled on shafts of golden sunlight. It was such a vision, appearing over the western sea, that stirred St Brendan the Navigator to sail away in his curragh and discover America.

downhill. The area's history is one of ancient myth, a record rich with tales of outlaws and highwaymen and the search for sanctuary, as well as the universal Irish themes of war, confiscation, strain and struggle between landlord and tenant, famine and emigration. There are the remains of many mines and quarries, too. On the south side is what is called a famine field, made up of the ridges and ditches used for the planting of potatoes in 1848, a year of devastating famine. The succession of long mounds appropriately suggests an uncannily packed and orderly graveyard.

Some of the finest slopes are alongside the numerous waters that ripple down Slieve Bloom's glens. Here begin three of Ireland's principal rivers, the Nore, Barrow and Suir. The pity is that, early this century, most of these glens were planted with forestry trees which gradually blotted out plants that had recurred for thousands of years. (Three hundred years before, a different human activity, the smelting of iron, a process requiring oak charcoal, had caused the uprooting of thousands of acres of oak on the south and west slopes of the range.) The Silver river is the notable exception. To ensure it remains so, it has been acquired by the council and made an official reserve complete with nature trail. Its name comes from the minute particles of silver found in its upper rocks and also, from time to time, in the water, in worthless quantities. More interesting are the layered walls of old red sandstone alternating with silts which border the current in parts, forming here and there a fairly complete geological record. Oak and birch woods still survive here, as do those lesser plants which share a fondness for acid and sandstone and root themselves often enough in cracks in the vertical rock or in boulders standing up from the water: ferns, mosses, liverworts, lichens. The walk upstream from Cadamstown is wonderfully varied as the glen's character changes. Glenbarrow is another glen where rock structure is clearly visible. Some hold it to be the most beautiful glen, too – it is one of the best known. Also popular is Glendine, its east divided from its west by the Glendine Gap, which rises close to Arderin, offering wonderful views.

The broad sweeps of blanket bog-land – distinct in character and origin from the raised bogs of the central plain – are probably Slieve Bloom's most natural and authentic terrain. They are there to walk, and it is a good experience (some say particularly good for joints) to feel the spring offered by the dominant heather (*Calluna vulgaris*) and the underlying peat. The botanist Robert Lloyd Praeger, without initially intending to, once walked from Mountrath to Kinnitty and back by a different route 'in mists and sheets of rain', a total of 37 miles (59 kilometres). 'It was nothing much', he wrote. But then 'a modest twenty to twenty-five miles per day, spread over twelve hours to allow plenty of time for botanizing, and continued for as many days as necessary' – 'done', he added, 'on a toothbrush and a collar' – was probably so routine for him that he sometimes did it in his sleep. The region is not known for its plant rarities. However, Praeger on his walk was pleased to find the Welsh poppy (*Meconopsis cambrica*)

The path down to any of the Lakeland waters – in this case Lough Derravaragh – is, in season at least, most often trod by anglers.

and filmy fern (*Hymenophyllum tunbridgense*) in a gully by the Glendine Gap. There are also bog cotton (*Eriophorum spp.*) and deer sedge (*Trichophorum caespitosum*), both of which thrive after fire, and most other standard bog plants. What may be the rarest, as well as the most beautiful, of the plants of the area, according to the polymath geologist John Feehan, is the mountain pansy (*Viola lutea*). Usually yellow, as its Latin name implies, it is here, in the one occurrence known to Feehan, 'a most marvellous blue violet'. It grows on a grassy bank of stone facing south-west.

Animals abound in the area. Fallow deer, badgers and foxes are sometimes seen, pine martens and otters only very occasionally. They have all been here since time immemorial. Others used to be. In the fifth century, according to monastic texts, St Ciaran made a friend of a wild boar in this vicinity. When the good man wanted materials for building a cell, the boar severed the necessary branches and reeds with his teeth. Soon a fox, badger, wolf and stag were added to his coterie. But such liaisons were familiar stuff in those magical times. For want of a yet-to-be-invented alarm clock, St Mochua's mouse licked his ear each morning to wake him. And when he paused from the reciting of psalms, a devoted fly stood at the point of the text he had reached, to keep his place.

AN IRISH VOCABULARY

Irish and English are jointly the official languages of Ireland. For the most part they are the same but different histories have given rise to variant stresses, inflexions and, in some cases, distinct meanings

avenue, *drive*

barney, *fight or fuss*

booley, *transhumance; farming system in which cattle are moved to the highlands each summer*

callows, *river-banks flooded widely and regularly*

cess, *evil (literally, a tax)*

cod, *cheat*

crack, *enjoyment*

crane, *heron*

crow, *rook, crow, jackdaw*

Dail, *lower house of Irish parliament*

demesne, *estate attached to a large house*

destroyed, *appalled or hurt*

ditch, *bank*

evening, *afternoon or evening*

fadge (in Ulster), *potato bread*

fir, *men*

gard, *policeman*

gas, *fun*

gentry, *fairies*

gombeen, *extortionate money-lender*

haggard, *stack yard*

he did *not, (form of agreement)*

hunting, *shooting*

jarvey, *driver of a jaunting car*

johneen, *Irishman who has assumed smart English ways*

lawn, *park*

moin, mona, *peat*

mna, *women*

pampooties, *leather sandals*

pan (of bread), *loaf*

pioneer, *member of a temperance society*

porter, *dark beer, stout*

powerful, *extraordinary*

press, *linen cupboard*

rere, *rear*

roach, *rudd*

Saherda, *Saturday*

shebeen, *unlicensed pub selling poteen*

sib, *sibling*

soft, *rainy*

stocious, *drunk*

strand, *beach*

strong, *possessing a large farm (of farmer, usually English or Protestant)*

Taoiseach, *prime minister*

this day week, *a week ago today, or a week from today*

town, *small settlement (as few as 20 houses)*

turf, *peat*

whisht, *shhh, be quiet*

will I?, *would you like me to?*

would you be able for?, *can you?*

your man, *the man in question*

youse (in Dublin), *you*

BEFORE YOU GO

Maps: OS half-inch maps of Ireland Nos 15 and 16.

Guidebooks: *The Slieve Bloom Way* from Bord Failte contains information for hikers, as do *Irish Long Distance Walks – A Guide to the Way-Marked Trails* by Michael Fewer (Moorland Publishing Co., 1993) and the Slieve Bloom Environment Park brochure (Offaly County Council). Also consult *Landscape of the Slieve Bloom* by John Feehan (Blackwater Press, 1979).

GETTING THERE

By car: from Portlaoise follow the N7 (west) to Mountrath, then follow the R440 (north) to Birr. This road travels right through the Slieve Bloom mountain range.

By rail: the nearest station is Portlaoise on the line from Portarlington, where there are connecting services to Galway and Dublin Heuston.

By bus: there are several Bus Eireann local and Expressway services that stop at Birr and Portlaoise. A Bus Eireann Expressway service between Limerick and Dublin stops at Portlaoise and Mountrath three times a day. J.J. Kavanagh's private bus company also runs local services in the area, T:(056) 31106.

WHERE TO STAY

There are bed and breakfasts in Portlaoise, Roscrea, Mountrath, Birr and several of the peripheral villages.

Outdoor living: there are two camp-sites near Portlaoise: the Cappakeel Caravan and Camping Park, T:(05032) 26460, open May–Sept, and Kirwans Caravan and Camping Park, T:(0502) 21688, open Apr–Oct.

ACTIVITIES

Walking: there are some good walks to the summit of Arderin mountain. On a clear day it is possible to see the highest points of all four of the ancient provinces of Ireland. The Slieve Bloom Way is a 31-mile (50-km) signposted way-marked trail which does a complete circle of the mountains, taking in most of the major points of interest.

It is split into five stages: stage 1, Glenbarrow–Monickew (7 miles/12 km); 2, Monickew–Glendine East (8 miles/13 Km); 3, Glendine East–Forelacka (11 miles/17 km); 4, Forelacka–Glenkeen (12 miles/19 km); and 5, Glenkeen–Glenbarrow (10 miles/16 km). For more information contact Laois County Council, County Hall, Portlaoise, Co. Laois, T:(0502) 22044 or Offaly County Council, Courthouse, Tullamore, Co Offaly, T: (0506) 21419. Dooley's Hotel in Birr, T:(059) 20052, organizes walking tours around the mountains.

Cycling: *Cycling Ireland*, a Bord Failte leaflet, has a suggested circular route that runs from Mountrath through the Slieve Bloom mountains.

FURTHER INFORMATION

Tourist offices: there is a Bord Failte tourist office in Portlaoise, T:(0502) 21178.

Ecology: there are some unusual plants in the area, including orchids, butterwort and the blue fleabane.

The Irish hare is a sub-species of the blue or Arctic hare. It occurs all over the country, wherever the lie of the land provides cover and shelter. The brown or common hare is found only in lowlands in the north-west of Ireland.

CHAPTER 5

The South-East

Wexford has a world-famous opera festival but most foreigners arriving in Ireland think of Rosslare, New Ross, Wexford, Waterford and Clonmel as towns to get through or by as rapidly as possible on their way to the West. The local coast hardly gets a thought, and the nearby mountains are neither required nor expected to be anything but a nice background for the drive. Considering that County Wexford is a few hours from the Welsh coast (nearer than England is), it is surprising how undiscovered it remains. People have said this for years and it makes little difference. Yet the South-East is an area of astonishing variety and attraction. Moreover, if wildness is confined to places too high, too rocky, too wet or too sandy to cultivate, the region is surprisingly rich in wildness. Especially with regard to sand. For while northwest Ireland consists of sheer, stark bastions of rock resisting the Atlantic battery, the surface rim of the South-East is for the most part a low, duney tousle, in which the works of man are slowly worn, gnawed, nibbled, felled and buried by the combined forces of tide and sand.

The most remarkable thing about this stretch of the country is its unheralded diversity. Only a few miles inland from the unending strands, gravel beds, dunes and lagoons of the coast, the country is all green hills, woods and pastures, not unlike the Kentish Weald. (When weighing east against west it is fair to remember another Kentish analogy: rain is half as much on the east as on the

A stunning view opens out from the northern ridge of the horseshoe of rock containing Lough Coumshingaun, in the Comeragh mountains.

west, and sunshine almost double. June sees an average eight hours of sunshine a day; even September manages six.)

Deep broad rivers like the Suir, Barrow, Nore and Slaney cut across the land in valleys rich in trees, broken now and again by ancient, elegant market towns, crumbling castles and monastery ruins. This is a lush, fertile, gracious national garden. Beyond – again only by a few miles – the wavy lowlands bubble up into mountains: the Blackstairs range dividing Counties Wexford and Carlow, the Comeraghs, Monavullaghs and Knockmealdowns rising in County Waterford, and the Galtees enhancing Tipperary with their bouncy east–west squiggle of a silhouette. The Comeraghs and Galtees in particular offer all kinds of walking and climbing, up and down gradual gradients or sheer rock-faces, among beguiling and evocative contours, with icy lakes, mountain birds, moorland plants and occasional broad views across endless plains or out to sea. From the Comeraghs the Saltee Islands can be visible on a clear day.

Islands on this coast are few. Indeed the north, east and south coasts of Ireland, in sharp contrast to the west and its sprinkled archipelagos, have scarcely more than half a dozen islands each, and only one or two of those possess life or landscape worthy of note. The Saltees, five miles (eight kilometres) out from the coast of Wexford, have character and to spare. Great Saltee is a crucial bird reserve, whose winged population at the end of the breeding season approaches 100,000. These consist mainly of those sea-birds familiar on inaccessible Irish cliffs and islands. There is besides, on cliffs at the south end of the island, a multiplying colony of gannets. Several hundred shags breed here, but not their similar and close cousins the cormorants. These are found on Little

Saltee, in one of their biggest breeding accumulations in the whole of Ireland.

Inhabited and farmed during the nineteenth century, the two islands, like many off the west coast, lost their populations during the first half of the twentieth. When the present owner, the self-styled Prince Michael of the Saltees, bought them for a few pounds in 1943, the wild was inexorably returning. In fact, the islands provide a tiny glimpse of the nature of wildness, its course and force and drive to repossess what has once been taken from it in one particular habitat. Embryonic wilderness in such a setting takes the form of wild flowers in hedge and pasture, slowly giving way to bramble and suffocating bracken. More noticeably, it gives way to rabbits. Such were their numbers back in the 1930s that as they moved the land itself seemed to be in motion.

There were rats too. They could be killed in their hundreds by tempting them with bait under a propped-up door and letting it drop on them. During the Second World War rabbits were trapped for meat, but afterwards their value fell away, especially when their grubbing and burrowing ended an expensive afforestation project. Destroying them proved a problem. Imported ferrets died in their first winter. Foxes settled but none of their offspring survived infancy. Forty-six cats were let loose. They killed rats, which was thought fine, and puffins, which caused outrage. The cats died, or charmed and went home with picnicking visitors, while rabbits continued to thrive. It was myxomatosis, introduced in 1962 and recurring every few years since, which has controlled rabbit numbers. There are rats, too, but some sort of balance seems to have been established.

Out beyond Carnsore Point the sometimes-visible turbulence is due to the meeting of two currents, the Gulf Stream coming in from the Atlantic and the southward flow from St George's Channel. The collision ensures a rich mix of plankton. It brings fish, birds, seals and shark to feed off it or off each other. It creates currents which can here and there make bathing dangerous. More insidiously, over decades and centuries, it has amassed long, hidden reefs of sand which have dragged down untold numbers of ships. For millions of years it has pulverized the ancient rocks of the region into sand. This destructive process has nevertheless created sand-dunes where plants thrive that thrive nowhere else, sand-hemmed lakes and lagoons where several kinds of birds breed in relative safety, and miles and miles of white strands. Where it has buried or half-buried stone keeps, churches, walls, even whole villages – places where history was made by invasion, the signing of treaties or dynastic marriages – it evokes a desolation as pungent as the pyramids, and a suggestion that the final winner in the old struggle for dominance between humans and wild nature will always, in the end, be nature.

GETTING THERE

By air: it is possible to fly from UK airports to Waterford Airport. Alternatively, travellers can take a shuttle service from Dublin to one of the regional airports. Manx Airlines, T:(01424) 824313 in the UK, flies from Stansted; Orient Air, T:(01452) 855656 in the UK, flies from Coventry and Staverton.

By boat: there are regular services from Fishguard and Pembroke in South Wales to Rosslare. For travellers from mainland Europe, Rosslare also has connections with Cherbourg and Le Havre. Companies include B&I Line, T:(0171) 734 4681 in the UK, or (053) 33311 in Rosslare; Stena Sealink, T:(01) 280844; and Irish Ferries, T:(053) 33158. The crossing takes about 4 hours.

WHERE TO STAY

For the south Tipperary and Waterford sites, either Tipperary or Waterford town will serve as a good base. Waterford tourist office, T:(051) 75788, can provide accommodation information. Tipperary tourist office is open only during the summer, T:(067) 31610. If you want to get out into the country, the region is dotted with bed and breakfasts and camp-sites. For information about the eastern part of the area, try Wexford tourist office, T:(053) 23111.

ACTIVITIES

Walking: the Wexford coast path is still under development, but completed sections offer some spectacular sea views between Arklow, round Carnsore Point to Arthurstown. Similarly, the Munster Way is far from complete. It will eventually connect with the South Leinster and Wicklow Ways, the Kerry Way and the projected Beara Way. The present 50 miles (80 km) of the Munster Way are split into 3 stages: 1, Carrick-on-Suir to Clonmel (18 miles/26 km); 2, Clonmel to Newcastle (11 miles/16 km); and 3, Newcastle to Vee (11 miles/16 km). the Suir tow-path, the Comeragh foothills, the ancient town of Clonmel, the Nier valley and the broad, boggy Knockmealdowns make for fine walking. The uplands offer magnificent views across the plains of Tipperary, or over to the swelling silhouettes of the Galtees. There is also a particularly good hike up Mount Leinster along the 62-mile (100 km) south Leinster Way, which is split into 5 stages: 1, Kildavin to Borris (13 miles/20 km); 2, Borris to Graiguenamanagh (8 miles/13 km); 3, Graiguenamanagh to Inistioge (8 miles/13 km); 4, Inistioge to Mullinavat (13 miles/20 km); and 5, Mullinavat to Carrick-on-Suir (14 miles/23 km). Much of the route is rich in rural scenery: the heathery Blackstairs mountains, a few miles of old tow-path beside the River Barrow, the rich pastoral undulations of County Kilkenny and, finally, the River Suir itself.

Fishing: Carlow town and Graiguenamanagh offer good fishing on the River Barrow. A popular angling festival is held on the river in May. Contact the Southern Regional Fisheries Board, T:(052) 23971. Waterford's sea-angling service, T:(058) 41514, can arrange deep-sea fishing. The Clonanan Angling School, Ballymacarbry, Waterford, T:(052) 36141, offers tuition and can arrange walking,

The South-East

Key

- ▲ Exploration zones.
- Roads.
- Footpaths.
- ⓐ Points of interest.
- Regional boundaries.

2000 and over
1000 - 2000
200 - 1000
0 - 200
metres

0   5   10miles
0   5   10   15Km.

cycling and equestrian holidays for non-angling companions.

Cycling: the South-East offers a relatively easy challenge for cyclists, with the exception of the Knockmealdown and Comeragh mountains. Bord Failte has four suggested routes in the region. See its *Cycling South East* information sheet.

Riding: the arable farmland of the area offers pleasant riding, and the sandy beaches exhilarating gallops. The 5-Star Trail, Tipperary, is organized by John and Rosetta Ann Paxman, T:(067) 21129. In Waterford, Melody's Stables arrange mini-trails through the Comeragh mountains, T:(052) 36147. The Horetown Equestrian Centre in Four Mills, Co. Wexford, T:(051) 63786, offers riding from a 17th-century manor house.

POTEEN

Traditionally, poteen is a potato spirit, illicitly distilled. It used to be served mixed with goat's milk in little shops called shebeens, distinguished by clods of turf hanging on their doors. The goat's milk and shebeens have gone but poteen continues to be made all over the place. One reason for its survival is that avoiding duties was a gesture of defiance against the occupying English and gained a respectability which has not entirely faded, even 80 years after the English left. The word means a little pot.

Grain of one kind or another is often used to make poteen instead of potatoes. It does not too much matter, since the motive of drinkers is more tipsifactory than epicurean. Poteen can be procured in most parts of Ireland through discreet inquiry. One strong argument against it is that the quality is sometimes very bad and even dangerous – there are tales of painful deaths. Whether this is propaganda put about by the authorities is hard to say. Some poteen is undoubtedly delicious and without bad effect. It should be. The Irish are practised distillers. They invented whiskey (as they generally spell the word), and it was an Irishman, Aeneas Coffey, who took his patent method to Scotland and started the process there.

Slievefelim and the Silvermine Mountains

Rolling highlands with isolated valleys and little lanes and waterways, dominated by Mauherslieve, the Mother Mountain

From the rich pasture of the Suir valley in County Tipperary the land rises to a spread of smooth-backed mountains contoured like a school of porpoises. This is a clutch of highlands of which the Slieve Kimalta, or Keeper Hill, in the north-west, rises to 2,278 feet (694 metres), Slievefelim to 1,411 feet (423 metres) and most of the rest – Knockastanna, Ring Hill, Knockalough and the substantial centre-piece of Mauherslieve or Mother Mountain – to altitudes in between. Around 300 million years ago, because of tectonic pressure from the south as the plate on which Africa rests slowly closed with that underlying Europe, subterranean quartzite, edged by sandstone, broke through the limestone layers laid down by an invasive sea 50 million years previously.

The resultant ranges are not grand or dramatic – more animal and interesting, with deeply incised little valleys providing routes for an abundance of lanes and waterways. Unregenerate, too, for somehow the new Europe's golden touch does not seem to have penetrated here. An old, sometimes tumbledown mellowness hangs about farm buildings and fences, and roads are more than normally pocked and cratered. Hard-skinned farmers wave in courteous astonishment in the lanes. Reeds and cuckoo flowers (*Cardamine pratensis*) and other marsh plants clog the undrained boggy pastures of the lower slopes. You could walk almost anywhere and see, at the risk of a bootful of marsh water, an old-style wealth of butterflies, birds, ichneumons, sawflies and others – except, that is, among the conifers of various ages which cover parts of Mauherslieve and elsewhere like drilling regiments on the parade ground. Higher up come friendly workaday plants found all over Ireland and Britain: gorse, primrose, violet, bedstraw, bugle, more cuckoo flower, with much bracken and moss, and hedges of thorn, elder, honeysuckle and some box, shaded at times by a benison of beech or ash. In the face of nature's variety, houses are reticent, beige painted or grey pebbled, as against the shining whiteness of the new bungalow. Every so often an enclosed vista contains stone ruins engulfed by ivy, melancholy and beautiful though beyond function, set among sympathetic trees that nod overhead. Here and there the wildness turns to a Wild West variety, exemplifying that careless human disdain for rural beauty which daubs a wood mill, its clutter and refuse, or a huge wire-fenced motor-works, its spilt oil and prowling Dobermanns, across unoffending valleys or water meadows.

There is, too, the uglier face of old Ireland. A mangy, skin-and-bone cat and a scrawny mule put me in mind of the hobbled cattle seen not so many years ago on the western peninsulas, and tinkers' horses lame and pus-ulcered by the roadside. There are the informal refuse tips – a kind of hypermarket excrement voided into Arcadia. It seems you are never far from one of these (and, oddly, a charge is made for garbage taken to the proper tip).

There is also that almost stage-Irish inconsistency which can make you smile or smoulder according to your mood. Without warning the road deteriorates to battle-site unevenness. A car limps as if two of its wheels had been mined away. The hazards are passed. The road is fine again. Looking back through your rear window you see all of three notices unfairly favouring the traveller in the opposite direction with full warnings. What matter if the words used, SLOW, ROAD WORKS AHEAD, are somewhat fictional.

The region has not been neglected by the tourist authorities. Little is. There is the 'Keeper Hill Drive' and the 'Slievefelim Way' and 'Sarsfield's Ride', commemorating a dash by the Jacobite general Patrick Sarsfield to ambush an artillery train of the invader King William III. There are many viewpoints, not to mention 'Community Alert Areas' – all of them scrupulously signposted, at times indigestibly. They all have merits. My own preference is for the Silvermine mountains and, given the energy, Keeper Hill. There are wonderful views: to the north-west the Arra mountains, with Tountinna and the southern tip of Lough Derg; to the east a mountainous playground, a succession of nature's peaks and trampoline dips stretching far away and out of sight.

BEFORE YOU GO
Maps: OS half-inch maps of Ireland Nos 17 and 18.

GETTING THERE
By car: from Nenagh follow the R497 (south) to its junction with the R503 and turn right towards Limerick. These roads take you through the middle of the Silvermine mountains and past Slievefelim.
By rail: the nearest station is Nenagh, where services from Dublin and Limerick stop about twice a day.
By bus: there are a few Bus Eireann Expressway services that stop at Nenagh. A local Bus Eireann service running from Limerick to Nenagh stops at Silvermines, just north of the Silvermine mountains. A private company, Tuohy's Coaches, runs a daily service to Dublin from Nenagh, T:(067) 312900.

WHERE TO STAY
There is quite a selection of bed and breakfasts and a couple of hotels in Nenagh, including Ormond, T:(067) 31404, O'Meara's, T:(067) 31266, and Mrs Kennedy, T:(067) 31193. More of both types of accommodation is available in Thurles, Tipperary and other local towns, villages and farms.

ACTIVITIES
Cycling: bikes can be hired from J. Moynan in Nenagh, T:(067) 31293.
Walking: for those interested in exploring the region there are trails through the forests surrounding the Silvermine mountains and Slievefelim.

FURTHER INFORMATION
Tourist offices: the nearest tourist office is in Nenagh, open May–Sept, T:(067) 31610.

The Galtees

A roller-coaster single-ridge range offering tough walks past desolate lakes and corries

There is something pampered and comfortable about the south riding of Tipperary, with the fertile greenery, bulging hedges and velvet woodlands of its broad, loamy valleys: those of the Suir river, the Glen of Aherlow and the Golden Vale. This snugness is made more obvious by the contrast of the dark bog-covered mountains hemming all sides of the lowlands: the Slievefelim, Slievenamon, the Comeraghs, Knockmealdown, Kilworth and the Galtees. Of these, the Comeraghs stand flat plateau-topped, in quiet and rarefied dignity, in the region's south-east. The Galtees are a grand but more animated affair to the north-west, easily reached from any direction, with an outline seen from north and south that suggests the course of a bouncing pingpong ball. They are made up of a single ridge, rising at intervals to conical peaks, one of which, the more or less central Galtymore, is at 3,018 ft (905 m) the third-highest mountain in the south of Ireland.

For the walker and climber the options are not so numerous as in the Comeraghs, but wonderful scenery and views reward any ascent in fine weather. Essentially you choose to walk from end to end – the Cahir end to the Mitchelstown end or vice versa – or over the top between the northern and southern valleys. In either case it is desirable to have two cars or a non-participant driver of one car who will drop you at the start and pick you up at the end. Of course, there are plenty of round walks, but a linear route from one side or end to the other shows you a good deal more of Ireland and best suits the ridge form.

Of the starting points, Cahir is a pretty and historic town, but the Cahir to Mitchelstown road along the south of the mountains is straight, fast and nasty. On the north, the leafy lane among the forestry plantations, meadows and hamlets of the Glen of Aherlow is a prettier, quieter approach, and gives good and tantalizing views of the scree-scrapes, massy buttresses, grooves and groins on the north faces. Higher up, too, the north has the advantage, with the most dramatic scenery of the Galtees – several mountain lakes – ranged along that side of Galtymore and Greenane. While all of these have character, each has an individual personality. Lough Muskry and Lough Curra are big and generous, Curra being easily got at and with a formidable 1,000-foot (300-metre) curtain of rock as backdrop. Of Lough Diheen,

The hen harrier may be seen in any part of Ireland, but in decreasing numbers, hunting low over moor, heath, marsh or estuary.

on the other hand, lying between them, Robert Lloyd Praeger, while admitting he saw it on a dull and windless day, says, 'I think I never saw a more lifeless or gloomier place in Ireland'.

A mile south of the Cahir to Mitchelstown road and not far to the west of its mid-point are the Mitchelstown caves. It was Praeger who did the original mapping of this complex underground system, which is privately owned. Regular guided tours are conducted along a large section of the system. It is worth seeing, though similar systems can be seen elsewhere and many more must exist unexplored. Rain, with carbon dioxide superadded from the air, exploits faults in the limestone beds that form so much of Ireland's foundations. They burrow through joints and excavate pipes until the water finds the prevailing water table. The process has carved out a subterranean Gruyère, with huge hollow caverns, slowly dripping stalactites and slowly rising stalagmites, as well as water coursing through the most recently carved channels. All this is shown to advantage.

Before you go *Maps:* OS Discovery Series maps Nos 66 and 74 (available in 1995); OS half-inch maps of Ireland Nos 17, 18, 21 and 22.

Getting there *By car:* to reach the Galtee mountains, take the N24 from Clonmel to Cahir and either follow the N8 (west) or the N24 (north), which both pass the mountains. To reach the Mitchelstown caves follow the N8 from Cahir towards Mitchelstown and turn left after 9 miles (14 km) following the signs to the caves.

By rail: the nearest stations are Clonmel and Cahir, where direct services run to Rosslare Harbour three times a day.

By bus: Bus Eireann Expressway services between Dublin, Kilkenny and Cork, and Limerick and Waterford all stop at Clonmel, as do local Bus Eireann services between Limerick and Waterford, and Kilkenny and Cork (this service also stops at Clogheen). A Tuesday-only Bus Eireann service runs from Clonmel to Clogheen. Quite a few Expressway services stop at Mitchelstown and local services also run through the town, There is a local Bus Eireann Limerick–Mitchelstown bus that runs about three times a day.

Where to stay: there is a good choice of bed and breakfasts and a few hotels in Clonmel and about the same number in Cahir. There is one hotel in Clogheen, the Vee Valley, T:(052) 65254. Bed and breakfast is also available in farms and houses scattered about the area.

Outdoor living: there are two camp-sites near Clonmel, the Apple Caravan and Camping Park, T:(052) 41459, which is open 1 May–30 Sept, and The Powers the Pot Caravan and Camping Park, T:(052) 23085, open 1 May–30 Sept. There is one camp-site near Clogheen, Parson's Green Caravan and Camping Park, T:(052) 65290, open all year.

Hostels: An Oige hostels in the surrounding area include the Bally David north of the Galtee mountains, T:(062) 54148, and the Mountain Lodge Youth Hostel at Burn Court, Cahir, T:(052) 41906. There are also two independent hostels: the Kilcoran Farm Hostel, T:(052) 41906, and the Lisakyle Hostel on Ardfinnan Road, Cahir, T:(052) 41963.

Activities *Walking:* the main summit of the Galtee range, Galtymore, is the third highest peak in Eire. The approach from the south is dry and grass-covered, while the north side is covered in crags and scree, though there are perfectly good tracks among them. The traverse along the main ridge from the north of Mitchelstown to Cahir is well worth the effort. For further information on walks in the area contact Galtymore Adventure Holidays in Cahir, T:(052) 41313/41047. They offer one-day guided walks of the Galtee range and can organize guided and independent walking programmes for individuals and groups. Independent walkers can contact Bord Failte offices for further information,

Heavy rain (*overleaf*) shrouds the broad, reedy, islanded expanse of the River Blackwater at Villierstown jetty, 10 miles (16 km) upstream from its estuary at Youghal.

guides and maps.

Riding: hacks and treks are available at Melody's Riding Stables, Ballymacarbry, near Clonmel, T:(052) 361467, open Mar–Nov.

Fishing: coarse and salmon fishing are available on the River Suir. Contact the Southern Regional Fisheries Board in Anglesea Street, Clonmel, for further information, T:(052) 23971.

Caving: the Mitchelstown caves are open all year 10am–6pm, T:(052) 67246. The system has about a mile (1.6 km) of passages and some spectacular chambers.

Further information *Tourist offices:* the nearest Bord Failte tourist office is in Cahir, open May–Sept, T:(052) 41453. There is another seasonal Bord Failte tourist office in Clonmel, open June–early Sept, T:(052) 22960. The nearest Bord Failte office that is open all year is in Tipperary town, T:(062) 51457.

Knockmealdowns

A graceful 15-mile (24-kilometre) old red sandstone range north of Lismore

For most who pass this way, the Knockmealdowns *are* the Vee Gap, more or less, and the Vee Gap is the Knockmealdowns. The Vee itself is a hairpin bend – V-shaped – in the main road crossing the mountains between Lismore in County Waterford and Clogheen in County Tipperary. Close to it a track leads down to a lovely, ice-cold mountain lake, Bay Lough, the result of a lens of ice, formed from compacted snow and with rocks embedded in it, scouring a cavity out of the rock. In early summer the slopes rising steeply behind the lake are splashed with the

vibrant mauve of the rhododendron – a colour people seem to have become increasingly sniffy about, though it still seems pretty to me. On the other hand, the plant's spread in many parts of Ireland, especially the West, has choked out so many other species that it is considered and treated as a pest.

From a distance the Knockmealdowns, a range of old red sandstone stretching some 15 miles (24 km) east to west, form a graceful outline of bosomy heights, mostly not as high as the Comeraghs to the east or·the roller-coaster range of the Galtees to the north, but rising to the respectable 2,608 ft (782 m) of Knockmealdown mountain itself. Much of the area, but not the peaks, is under cultivation, and besides the usual forestry plantations there are some thick concentrations of oak, beech, birch, alder (on the wetter ground), shrubby hazel, holly, yew and other natives and broadleaves in the cuts and valleys on the north and south sides. From these there is the usual progression to heathery heights, broken by shoals of anaemic grasses and splashes of bare or lichened rock.

In open competition the Knockmealdowns score somewhat lower than their mountain neighbours. Apart from Bay Lough and tiny Lake Moylan to the south-east of Sugarloaf Hill, there are no picturesque mountain corries – rather a severe aesthetic lack by Irish standards – and no great crags or precipices. But the mountains provide wonderful outward views and make the southern half of County Tipperary, which is what you see to the north, seem as broad and unending as a continent. On the south side you can see County Waterford to the east,

The Galtees and Knockmealdowns

County Cork to the west and in the distance the sea. It is not difficult to be at the summit of the Knockmealdowns and bathing in the sea with only a two-hour (or less, if you step on it) interval. Above the Vee is the stone beehive grave of a certain Samuel Grubb, one who certainly appreciated the view, and had himself buried upright to be able to see his former Tipperary estates. He may have taken his cue from the eighteenth-century local landowner Henry Eeles, to whom, long before Benjamin Franklin, the sight of lightning on these mountains suggested a connection with electricity. He, too, had himself buried, along with his horse and dog, at the summit of Knockmealdown, but all trace of the grave has since gone.

The range is not noted for natural rarities, but many of the familiar birds and plants of the blanket bog may be seen. Ravens and peregrines visit Bay Lough. Claims have been made that the last killing of an Irish wolf took place here in 1770. (Rival claims are made for

other regions.) The gap would have been a wilder spot then, with the harridan Petticoat Loose haunting Bay Lough, the ever-present hazard of highwaymen, and nothing but a mud track to carry carriages between north and south.

Before you go *Maps:* OS Discovery Series Map No. 74 (available in 1995); OS half-inch map of Ireland No. 22. *Guidebooks: New Irish Walk Guides – East and South* by David Herman and Miriam McCarthy (Gill and Macmillan, 1991).

Getting there *By car:* from Dungarvan follow the R672 (north-west) until you reach the N72, then follow this road to Cappoquin. The R669 and R668 running between Cappoquin and Clogheen to the north cut through the Knockmealdown mountains. *By bus:* the Waterford–Mallow Bus Eireann service, the Dublin–Tallow Bus Eireann service and the Waterford–Cork Bus Eireann service all stop in Cappoquin, every day. There is a Bus Eireann service between Clonmel and Clogheen

and the Dublin–Cork Expressway service stops in Clogheen every day. There is no bus service that links Clogheen to Cappoquin.

Where to stay: there are a few hotels in Cappoquin, including Flyns River View, T:(058) 54073, and the Toby Jug, T:(058) 54317, and one in Clogheen, The Vee Valley, T:(052) 65254. There is one camp-site in Clogheen, Parson's Green Caravan and Camping Park, T:(052) 65292.

Activities: the Blackwater river, near Cappoquin, provides excellent fishing for brown trout and salmon, and Glenshane Park has forest walks. There are some good walks in the mountains, the best of them taking in Knockmealdown and the Sugarloaf peaks, neither of which is hard to reach from the Vee Gap road, the R668; see *New Irish Walk Guides – East and South* for information on routes.

Further information: the nearest Bord Failte tourist office is in Clonmel, T:(052) 229560, open June–Sept.

River Blackwater

Following an unlikely course, the River Blackwater passes wooded gorges and haunted houses into a tidal estuary rich with bird life

In the early nineteenth century the Smyths of Ballynatray, a heavy, handsome, Hanoverian house on a bend of the Blackwater a few miles from the river's mouth, had the good sense to take over the captain's barge from a Napoleonic man-of-war wrecked along the nearby coast. They decked it with velvet hangings, put musicians aboard and kept it as their state barge, floating up and down the broad wooded

river with the sounds of trumpet and drum echoing off the rocky defiles. Later in the century paddle-steamers with German bands on board took tourists upstream from Youghal, advertising the river as Ireland's Rhine. Cargo craft were plentiful. Nowadays if you want to see the river by boat you paddle your own canoe, or beg or borrow a rowing boat or launch. Otherwise you come at the water wherever the road or other access allows.

It is not the likeliest target for travellers in search of the wild. This is a valley of rich land and one old Ascendancy estate after another. Castles and mansions alternate down the bank like lamp-posts in a lane. Salmon are netted in the tidal reaches and fly-fished upstream by – for the most part – persons of means, paying high prices. (One lawsuit over netting rights continued for several centuries.) At the river's mouth is a town, Youghal, with a rich past, present and future, and there are substantial towns every few miles along its 75-mile (120-kilometre) length. You might ask if there are any grounds at all for calling the Blackwater wild.

Ten miles (16 kilometres) above the estuary there stands on the east bank a handsome, haunted house called Dromana, whose supporting walls drop sheer into the river. Opposite, a tributary, the River Owbeg, debouches. Three miles (five kilometres) downstream another tributary, the Bride, flows into the Blackwater. These meetings take place amid spreading marsh, liable to flood when the rivers are in spate. They attract waders. There are autumn evenings when the curlews' falling cries make the air pregnant with Celtic melancholy. A mile or two up the Bride is one of the county's heronries. On spring evenings the air around the swaying, aerial tenements is thick with fishwife screeches, essential, it seems, for the co-existence of close-packed heron families. But the most varied bird life is seen around the tidal estuary. Various ducks and waders, including black-tailed godwit, coot and moorhen, some hen harriers and short-eared owls are to be found on the mud-flats and flooded fields occurring riverward of Kinsalebeg on the east bank and between the river-bridge and Youghal on the west. They also congregate on the reed-beds and marsh a mile or so south of the town, where the main road turns inland.

The route taken by the river in its last 15 miles (24 kilometres), from Cappoquin to the sea, has puzzled geologists. As is seen clearly by anyone travelling the south-west of Ireland, the great Armorican earth movements (sometimes known as Hercynide, after the Latin name for the Harz mountains, which were formed at the same time) squashed the surface of the land from the south and caused several sandstone ranges to rise in an east-west direction. The Atlantic promontories of Cork and Kerry are among them. Rivers, naturally, tended to follow the limestone valleys in between, flowing west to east because of the general tilt of the land. But the four principal rivers, the Bandon, Lee, Blackwater and Suir, having followed this rule almost up to the last minute, suddenly disregard it entirely, and turn wilfully southward, cutting through the raised sandstone in what seems a far more difficult course than carrying on eastward. No river illustrates this more clearly than the Blackwater, whose obvious outlet would seem from both map and land to be Dungarvan harbour. We must not, of course, attribute conscious decisions to rivers. The flowing waters followed the easiest route. The problem is why this lay in a southward direction.

The facts have been explained in different ways, based on the pattern of the land before the upheaval, in which the general orientation of contours was north–south. The main reason may be that, after the upheaval, rain was falling and rivers forming their channels on a thick covering of accumulated limestone. Routes were determined by climate and by the surface conditions of the limestone more than by the shapes of the underlying rock. When eventually the upland limestone was eroded and the rivers were thus lowered on to the newly revealed beds of sandstone, they dug channels corresponding to their previous routes. Had they started to form on the sandstone they would no doubt have followed more closely its trends and features.

What this southward cutting means today is a valley much more picturesque than it would otherwise have been, with rising bluffs and rocks, woods and rapids, for the kingfisher and anyone in possession of a rowing tub or bedizened state barge to enjoy.

BEFORE YOU GO
Maps: OS half-inch map of Ireland No. 22; OS Discovery Series map No. 74.

GETTING THERE
By car: from Cork follow the

N8 and then the N25 (east) to Youghal. Between Cappoquin and the N25 bridge a couple of miles north of Youghal the river is broad, tidal and without bridges, but lanes approach it and run alongside here and

there. Above Cappoquin – to Fermoy, Mallow and Rathmore – the road is always close though seldom contiguous.
By rail: the nearest stations are Cork and Mallow. Services for Cork depart from Dublin about

15 times a day, most of them stopping at Mallow.

By bus: plenty of Bus Eireann services run to Youghal, Tralee, Rosslare and Waterford from Cork. Expressway and local buses from Dublin, Cork, Kilkenny and Ballina stop at Fermoy and Mallow.

WHERE TO STAY

Hotels: there is plenty of accommodation in Youghal. Bed and breakfasts include Mrs P. Brooks, T:(024) 92617, and Mrs M. Goggin, T:(024) 92292. Upstream, there are a few bed and breakfasts at Cappoquin, including Flynn's River View, T:(058) 54073, and at Lismore, Fermoy and Mallow.

Outdoor living: there is a campsite to the west of Youghal, the Summerfield Caravan and Camping Park, T:(024) 93537.

Strong winds clear the clouds, revealing a glimpse of Lough Coumshingaun from the middle of the horseshoe ridge in the Comeragh mountains.

Youth hostels: there are several hostels in Cork including Isaac's, T:(021) 500011, and Campus, T:(021) 343531.

ACTIVITIES

Fishing: excellent salmon and trout fishing is available on the River Blackwater. There is a two-week fishing festival in May/June in Fermoy. Contact Jack O'Sullivan, T:(025) 31110, for details. Also pick up angling guides to Counties Cork and Waterford from tourist offices. Deep-sea angling is available in Youghal.

Cycling: bikes can be hired from Troy's in Youghal, T:(024) 92509.

Bird-watching: bird-watchers may see many varieties on the mud-flats at Youghal.

FURTHER INFORMATION

Tourist offices: there is a tourist office in Youghal, T:(024) 92390, open Apr–Oct, one in Fermoy, T:(025) 31811, open all year, and one in Mallow, T:(022) 42222, open May–Sept.

Its cap recently restored, the round tower at Ardmore, on the coast of County Waterford, is one of the country's finest. It dates probably to the tenth century.

The Comeraghs

Ghostly mountain mists often shroud this gaunt range

I had been minding a house for its absent owners. A nineteenth-century occupant, an amateur archaeologist, had brought back mummies from Egypt and, although these had later been given to the National Museum, a chill aura hung or seemed to hang around the place where they had been displayed. As a consequence, I suppose, ancient Egypt was on my mind.

One day I was driving from Dungarvan to Clonmel, along the east side of the Comeragh mountains. A gaunt, strong, dignified, timeless range, commanding the central south of Ireland, they form the zenith of the east–west protrusion of old red sandstone and carboniferous limestone squeezed up by the great convulsions of the Devonian period 300 million years ago. Much of their surface is a desolate central plateau, seen from some angles as tamely flat. But their ice-gnawed edges are anything but tame: deep, steep slopes often pivoting to precipice angles and plunging to lonely tarns held in by · palisades of moraine.

Some of these cliffs are visible from the road. In particular the site of the corrie of Coomshingaun is recognizable from the two protruding buttresses which enfold it. Probably because I had been sharing midnights with Egyptian ghosts in an ancient house, these two massive bolsters made me think of the knees of the statue of the pharaoh Rameses II at Abu Simbel. The lake would have been contained in his lap, and his body and head rising into the mists that so often crown the range. My feelings of awe for the Comeraghs intensified.

Next time I climbed to Coomshingaun this impression was very much on my mind. The climb itself is simple; I am tempted to say you follow the trail of cigarette butts and chewing-gum papers which smear so many upland Irish tracks. It was a sultry June day. The mist was thick, and the sound of traffic was soon behind me. Here and there a sheep bleated. The mist closed in to a distance of yards, but the way among the scattered rocks (another legacy of the ice) and gorse and bracken and fairy lights of honeysuckle was still not in doubt. The only thing I did not know was how far I had come – there was no question of overshooting, but I kept anticipating a cooling of air from that desolate glacial tarn.

Mountain mists are alive, I have never had any doubt of that. Not organically alive but certainly alive in having moods and the power of wilful motion. They approach and come no nearer, recede and go no further away. They are sweetly innocent, trailing their wispy pleated skirts towards you, lifting a little to show a distant line of green lowlands. Then they settle and condense, and exclude you from your world, puff cold air and spit at you with drops of moisture, encircle you and close. Ghostly? They are for sure the mother and father of all ghosts. Things I don't, of course, believe in, so that any fear I felt was self-induced. And it was not fear so much as a sensitive apprehension. Really, I was enjoying myself. And then the one thing happened that caused me to miss one heartbeat before returning to normal. Rameses shook his knee.

I shall not try to convince you that this movement took place, because you will not trust me. But the consequence is beyond doubt. The air rippled. Like a cloud of flies the mist cleared from the left knee, which now took form, rounded, firm and sheer-sided, looming above me on my right. He had shaken off an irritation, and the thinned tassels of mist remained distant enough for me to walk through the chill air down to the water's edge. I could dimly descry the vertical wall of rock that forms the opposite bank of the tarn, feeling more than ordinary respect for a handsomely horned ram that watched me from a cottage-sized erratic boulder. I returned to the knee, from where I walked back to the road, and thence drove to centres of population that could have been a million miles from the solitude, from the glacier track in a wall of mountain raised by the clash of the tectonic plates on which Europe and Africa float, from the hauntings of Celtic gods and the possibly spurious overlay of an ancient Egyptian pharaoh.

The tougher climb was out of the question that day. In clearer weather you can turn left where I stopped, cross to the other buttress, ascend, as it were, the right thigh and, having reached the plateau, cross over to complete the circuit of Coomshingaun. A small detour on this route takes in Fascoum, which at 2,597 feet (789 metres) is the highest point of the Comeraghs – though you have to look for it across the bog as it is not much higher than the surrounding levels. There are some quite tough slopes, loose scree and cliff-drops on this journey.

The Comeraghs and the Monavullaghs, which are for most purposes part of the same range, together with their various outliers, are rich in good climbs, both easy and challenging. Almost all of them offer

PRECAUTIONS FOR HILL-WALKERS

The only way to remain safe from outdoor hazards is to stay at home and risk indoor ones. Still, people die on Irish mountains and it is foolhardy to leave everything to luck when walking or climbing. Whatever the conditions before you set off, you may soon be on steep, rough ground and much colder, wetter and blown about than you were at the start. You or one of your companions may be immobilised by injury sustained in a fall. Depending on circumstances, any of the following precautions and prescriptions can help, to the point of saving life.

Before you go:
Weather can be the great enemy. It could be up to ten degrees colder 3,000 ft up, since temperature drops two or three degrees centigrade every thousand feet (300 m). The breeze down below becomes a strong wind up above. Thick mists can float in unannounced, cutting visibility to a matter of feet. Consult a local weather forecast, and assume that the weather will get colder and wetter while you are out.

Pack a map, compass, whistle, torch and first-aid kit, some chocolate or glucose and perhaps a hot drink. Wear strong clothing and boots that protect and support the ankles. Maintain a healthy suspicion of the accuracy of all maps, especially on the heights and where cliffs are concerned. The old half-inch Ordnance Survey of Ireland series has many inaccuracies. Published walk and climb descriptions can be misleadingly ambiguous, and it is worth checking map and text together to avoid confusion on the spot. Arrange to walk or climb with at least three other people in the party and be sure there is

time to go up and come down, allowing for delays and pauses, well before dark. Discounting extended stops and difficult ground, but allowing for short breaks, reckon on covering a distance of 2 miles (4 km) or an ascent of 1,300 ft (400 m) an hour. Leave a note of your planned route at your hotel or guest-house, or with a friend, or in the car if you drive to the starting point.

On the walk or climb:
Remember that in a mist, within only a few minutes, you may double back on your track when you think you have gone in a straight line. Keep consulting your map and compass. When visibility is poor keep as clear as possible of cliffs, especially in high wind.

Be aware that turning signposts and waymarks to point in the wrong direction is a national sport.

Take extra care on the way down hills and mountains when, due to tiredness, most accidents occur.

In trouble:
The official mountain distress signal is six whistle blasts over a minute followed by a pause of a minute, indefinitely repeated; or six torch flashes and a pause of similar timing, also repeated. An acknowledging response is a series of three blasts or flashes repeated with intervals.

If a companion is injured and help is needed, and if signals bring no response, make him or her as comfortable and warm as possible, and try to establish your exact location. When you come on a telephone dial 999 and ask for Mountain Rescue. If there is any difficulty consult the local garda station.

Sky and land almost converge as the sun goes down over the Comeragh mountains, but from here, at a vantage point beneath the west face of Knocknaree peak, it is still possible to see the ridge of Laghtnafrankee mountain in the distance.

Slievenamon and the Comeraghs

spectacular views over the surrounding countryside. North of Coomshingaun is the eponymous rock from which the highwayman William Crotty could survey half Ireland to his north while keeping watch for redcoats ascending the slopes immediately below. They got him at last and hanged him in Waterford in 1742. His faithful widow, to escape the law, jumped to her death from this same rock. Other bandits took his place. In the nineteenth century, lawlessness took on a political flavour, threatening the Anglo-Irish Ascendancy at home and at sport. Those who hunted over the Beresford lands to the east put about false information on the whereabouts of their meets, to avoid ambushes, and carried loaded pistols in holsters on their saddles. (Nothing would have forced them to cancel hunting. These were the days when a gentry devotee might have himself buried in a fox's lair, while a Beresford lady had a tiara, necklace and brooch made of foxes' teeth.)

Equally wild are the Mahon falls, thin white lines of plummeting water in a broad bay of a valley under the cone of Knockaunapeebra, just south of Coomshingaun. They reduce to a trickle in a dry summer. Not far south is Seefin (2,387 feet/716 metres), one of the Monavullagh mountains which offer firmer, less boggy high plateaux than the Comeraghs. The Araglin valley, rising from Kilbrien to the west, affords with

Seefin a lovely circuit for serious walking. Another is around the Nier valley on the western slopes of the Comeraghs opposite Coomshingaun.

Feral goats are a common sight on the mountain slopes, and ravens and peregrines and sparrowhawks above them. In the breeding season, stonechats, hooded crows, jackdaws, meadow pipits and skylarks keep up a fairly perpetual chorus. Trout are present in some lakes, and so are char (*Salvelinus alpinus*), a colourful member of the same salmon family. This species seems to have gradually withdrawn northwards in the post-glacial period, leaving colonies in the chillier and remoter highlands of these islands A Comeraghs plant of unusual distribution is the St Patrick's cabbage (*Saxifraga spathularis*), a saxifrage with pretty red-spotted white flowers and a long thin stem over a spray of leaves. It is easily confused with its close relation London pride, although, outside Ireland, it is mostly found in southern Europe.

GAELTACHT

The old Irish, or Gaelic, language, already long declining, all but disappeared during and after the 1840s famines when hundreds of thousands of Irish speakers died or emigrated. Local conditions kept it going in a few places, mostly in the far west. Newly independent Ireland in the 1920s took steps to safeguard its survival. Irish was named first of the two official state languages, and although in practice the use of English far outweighs that of Irish, the native tongue is aired a good deal in schools, on radio and television, in the Dail, the civil service and many homes. The Government also declared those areas where Irish had hung on as first language to comprise the official Gaeltacht, subject to certain rules and concessions designed to encourage the inhabitants to keep their language alive.

BEFORE YOU GO
Maps: OS half-inch map of Ireland No. 22.

GETTING THERE
By car: from Clonmel on the N24 take the R678 (east) to just past Rathgormuck, then the R676 (south) towards Lemybrien. Alternatively, take the R671 west from Clonmel and bend south with it. There is access to the mountains from all these roads.
By rail: the nearest station is Clonmel, where direct services run between Rosslare Harbour and Limerick Junction twice a day, changing at Waterford.
By bus: the Tuesday-only Clonmel–Dungarvan Bus Eireann service runs to the east of the mountains. A Bus Eireann service from Dublin stops at Clonmel, as do Expressway Services between Kilkenny and Cork, and Limerick and Waterford. Kavanagh's, T:(062)

51563, operates services between Cashel and Clonmel, and Princes Coaches operates a once-a-day service between Clonmel and Dublin, T:(052) 31389.

WHERE TO STAY
Hotels: there is a good selection of bed and breakfasts and a few hotels in Clonmel.
Outdoor living: the nearest camp-site to this mountain range is The Powers the Pot Caravan and Camping Park in Clonmel T:(052) 23085, open May–Sept.

ACTIVITIES
Walking: there are some good trails across these sandstone hills. Good maps, compass and other equipment for mountain treks are essential. For further information contact Galtymore Adventure Holidays in Cahir, who offer one-day guided hill-walks of the mountains and can arrange guided and independent walking

holidays for groups and individuals, T:(052) 41314/41047. Independent walkers should contact the tourist board at Clonmel or Dungarvan for details of guides and maps.
Riding: hacks and treks are available at Melody's Riding Stables, Ballymacarbry, near Clonmel, T:(052) 36147, open Mar–Nov.
Fishing: there is good trout fishing on the Rivers Nier, Anner and Tar, and salmon fishing on the River Suir. Contact the Southern Regional Fisheries Board in Anglesea Street, Clonmel, for further information, T:(052) 23971.
Cycling: bikes can be hired from T. and T. Cycles in Cahir, T:(052) 25322.

FURTHER INFORMATION
Tourist offices: the Bord Failte tourist office in Clonmel is open June–early Sept, T:(052) 22960.

Slievenamon

The home of the legendary Finn McCool provides an easy climb and spectacular views

Before the invention of electronic guitars young maidens fell collectively in love with handsome youths who hunted wild boar and formed armies to raid other armies in pursuit of blood feuds, lands, princesses with prospects and so on. No young man was quite so appealing in these and other respects as Fionn Mac Cumhail, or Finn McCool as his name is usually presented in English, doughty warrior and unrivalled hero of the Fenian cycle of legends, giant of the Giant's Causeway and Fingal of the famous cave on Hebridean Staffa. Finn came from Slievenamon and was here hounded by bevies of desirous young women. The wise King Cormac Mac Art of Tara, whose somewhat cynical remarks about women have come down to us ('arrogant when called on, lewd when neglected, silly ... greedy ... hating ... tedious' and so on) devised a plan. All the women who wanted Finn should race up the mountain's side; Finn would be the winner's prize. Slievenamon means, in fact, mountain of the women. Being in love with Cormac's daughter Grainne, Finn tipped her news of a short-cut. She won, though she quickly regretted it and eloped – fatally, as it turned out – with the younger Diarmuid. The lovers are commemorated in place-names all over Ireland.

I doubt if my way up the mountain is in Grainne's footsteps. It is not the shortest route but it is easy because the road above Kilcash, which is unlikely to have existed in her day, gives you a good start. A track to the summit is signposted from this road. I like on the way to go and glimpse the old Butler castle of Kilcash – this was a Roman Catholic branch of the powerful clan – a mile below the village, festering handsomely under ivy in a private field beside its ruined church.

Slievenamon has little in common with Everest apart from the fact that, in Mallory's phrase, it is there. It is a domed quartzite peak rising to 2,368 ft (719 m), splendidly isolated, rich in myth, a bit spoiled by flanking forestry and a television mast near the top. The ascent is too much of a doddle for anyone to climb it for the sense of physical achievement. You go up for the view, which is spectacular: to the north the plains and hills of Tipperary and Kilkenny, the Galtees to the west, and the marvellously enticing, smooth silhouette of the Comeraghs, over the Suir in County Waterford. Down below is the Suir valley, a long cushion of fertility and ancient demesnes on either side of the pretty river. Not all it used to be, I suppose it goes without saying. The main road, which used to induce a leisurely pace in drivers, is now wide enough for serious speed but too narrow for safety, and you can see some of the factories that have been allowed to take theirugly places on either side. There has also been a progressive prairifying of the landscape as hedges continue tobe ripped out, making big fields for big-money crops. There are shocking industrial gashes among the green. But if you do not look too close, you can still see Arcadia smiling up sunnily.

The hooded crow, whose head plumage can make it resemble a bewigged judge, is common in all parts of Ireland; a familiar, raucous omnivore, it is very closely related to the British carrion crow (they are both sub-species of the same species).

Before you go *Maps:* OS Discovery Series maps Nos 67 and 75.

Getting there *By car:* from Clonmel follow the N24 and N76 (east). The N76 passes to the east of Slievenamon.

By rail: the nearest station is Clonmel, where services from Rosslare Harbour to Limerick Junction stop twice a day, once in the morning and once in the evening.

By bus: plenty of Bus Eireann local and Expressway services stop at Clonmel, including the Expressways between Kilkenny and Cork and Limerick and Waterford. Princes Coaches, T:(052) 31389, operate a single daily service between Clonmel and Dublin, while Kavanagh's, T:(062) 51553, operate several services between Cashel and Clonmel.

Where to stay: there is a good selection of bed and breakfasts and a few hotels in Clonmel, and camp-site, The Powers the Pot Caravan and Camping Park, T:(052) 23085.

Activities: mountain-climbing and forest walking south of Clonmel, and hiking up the 719-ft (216-m) Slievenamon itself.

Further information: there is a seasonal tourist office in Clonmel, T:(052) 22960.

Blackstairs Mountains

A 15 mile (24 kilometre) range with broad views from Mount Leinster

The relatively uncomplicated ridge which takes in Mount Leinster and the Blackstairs mountains is a kind of Sunday-afternoon extension of the Wicklows. Geologically they are parts of the same thing: a core of Caledonide granite rising above shoulders of quartzite and other hard, metamorphosed rocks, though these – in the case of the western edge of the Blackstairs – have been hidden under the widespread, sedimentary limestone of the central plain. A 15-mile, north–south silhouette (tipped a little clockwise) of long gentle slopes, cones and curves, it rises to 2,610 ft (783 m) at the summit of Mount Leinster in the north and 2,409 ft (723 m) at that of Blackstairs mountain in the south. And it fills what would otherwise be a gap in the almost continuous line of highlands which occupies Ireland's south-east periphery. Actually it leaves County Wexford, whose boundary with County Carlow it forms, on the outside of the rim – the reason, perhaps, why richly agricultural Wexford has been noted in the past for both a rather British feel to the landscape, and a fiery Irish patriotism.

The ridge provides a natural archive of startling panoramas, requiring very little exertion to be enjoyed. Robert Lloyd Praeger, who probably knew better than anyone, said that the road crossing the northern shoulder of Mount Leinster commanded a wider view than could be seen from a car almost anywhere else in the country. He also thought that walking the range from end to end made a good day's outing. It undoubtedly did, but taking in the distance, all the ups and downs, some squishy bog and punishing scree, would require a body in the kind of trim and training which seems to have been his for over eighty years and few others' for a quarter as long. For most it is probably more satisfactory to take a round walk from road to peak (Leinster or Blackstairs) and back. These do not have to be tame. The walker and writer David Herman's suggestions in the *New Irish Walk Guides* all involve climbing to 2,000 ft (600 m) or more, and occupy four or five hours of steady and just occasionally strenuous going. Mount Leinster, north of the Scullogue Gap (the only road that takes traffic across the range), is gentler than Blackstairs to the south, which is sprayed thinly with boulders and granite outcrops. The time could be prolonged in early summer by picking bilberries (*Vaccinium myrtillus*), common among the heather on the upper slopes, and one of Ireland's neglected wild harvests.

Before you go *Maps:* OS half-inch map of Ireland No. 19. *Guidebooks: New Irish Walk Guides – East and South* by David Herman and Miriam McCarthy (Gill and Macmillan, 1991).

Getting there *By car:* from Enniscorthy, take the R702 through Kiltealy. This road runs right through the middle of the Blackstairs mountains. *By rail:* the nearest station is Enniscorthy, where services between Rosslare Harbour and Dublin stop three times a day. *By bus:* a Bus Eireann service from Waterford to Dublin stops at Bunclody, just north-east of the mountains, and at Enniscorthy.

Where to stay: there are a handful of bed and breakfasts and one hotel, Murphy-Floods, T:(054) 33413, in Enniscorthy.

Activities: the Wicklow Way passes to the north. For those who like a challenge, Mount Leinster makes for a good hike.

Further information: the nearest Bord Failte tourist office is in Enniscorthy, T:(054) 34699/35926, and is open June–Aug.

Waterford Harbour and River Barrow

An estuary teeming with bird life; the great auk was last seen here

For the most part the south-east of Ireland consists of the basins of four big rivers, their drainage areas like four segments of a sliced-through orange, centring roughly on Carnsore Point. The Slaney rises in the Wicklow mountains and flows through the pastoral undulations of central Wexford to merge with the sea at Wexford harbour. The other three unite in their final reaches and come to the sea as one. The Barrow runs 120 miles (190 km) north to south, dividing (roughly) Counties Laois from Kildare and Kilkenny from Carlow. Just above New Ross it is enlarged by the waters of the Nore,

whose 90-odd miles (140 km) have brought it south-eastward from the slopes of the Slieve Bloom. A few miles below New Ross both are joined by the Suir (pronounced just about as the word 'sure' is) which, having risen not much more than a stone's throw from the Nore's source, has incorporated a big southerly bulge in its 115 or so miles (185 km). Together, they now make Waterford harbour their estuary.

Each river negotiates most of its vertical descent within a few miles of its source, and from then on coils lazily through valleys of rich farmland and woods based on the carboniferous limestone that covers much of the Irish interior. There are some grasslands that flood and provide wintering grounds for waterfowl: greylag geese on the Suir between Carrick-on-Shannon and Coolfin; and others on the lower Barrow floodplain. It is lush green countryside, this, interspersed with big old estates, recognizable – if the big house is hidden or gone – by the grandeur of perimeter walls and park trees. Such estates have bred and nourished some of the world's finest racehorses and are often enhanced by a backdrop of mountain – Comeraghs or Blackstairs or an extended

Bog cotton and other acid-dependent plants colonize the slopes of the Blackstairs mountains, overlooking Carlow's farm lands.

frieze of Wicklows. Wild is not the word this area brings to mind, but there are thin threads of a kind of wildness and the best of these runs up through the harbour, parts of which in summer evenings lose their human associations and become – through sight and sound – a twilight kingdom of touchy, raucous, gradually settling birds. The threads continue into the Barrow, whose lower section lies, exceptionally, in the foundering granite of the Leinster chain and has carved deep wooded gorges where its pace is quickened by the narrowness of the channel.

Waders are drawn to the west side of Waterford harbour by several miles of mudflats, and over 2,000 regularly winter here, so that you can feel aggrieved if you miss the piping of oystercatchers, the unvarying beep of ringed plover, or the curlew's bubbling dirge. There are redshanks, bar-tailed godwits, a lot of common gulls, some dabbling ducks (mainly wigeon), geese (brent) and grebes (great crested). There are also turnstones, wintering here (and on many Irish and British coasts) after breeding in Greenland and the northern limits of Scandinavia. Seen in poor light or at a distance they are often confused with their plover cousins, grey or ringed, but in flight they display a unique and distinct pied pattern of black and white. Their short bills are slightly *retroussé*, and they twitter, but not helplessly. Ringing has shown they can cover 500 miles (800 kilometres) in a day. They are seen in small groups, often riffling through seaweed for almost anything (they are the least fussy of eaters). To the same end they justify their name by turning over stones. Sometimes several join forces to turn over a big one. A relief sculpture of a turnstone on a house in Dublin's Lower Bagot Street (I think) made me link them for ever with Ireland, and I always feel absurdly cheered by the sight of them.

The Barrow connects Waterford harbour with the Grand Canal extension at Athy (pronounced 'a thigh'), whence a small boat can be got, by canal or navigable river, to any region of Ireland. Commercial traffic still plied the river in the 1950s. Now it is mostly converted barges, launches, rowing boats and canoes. The Barrow is tidal as far as St Mullins and thereafter the river is often accompanied by a tow-path. Although many of the interesting and pretty sights along this walk are man-made – houses, locks, lock-keepers' cottages, bridges and towns of mellowed prosperity – nature plays the lead. When the view is clear, Mount Leinster and the Blackstairs show to the east and the graceful line of Brandon Hill (1,703 ft/511 m) to the west. Trees and shrubs support the homelier birds; a streak of blue may signify a kingfisher. The malefactor mink makes appearances. In the water itself there are rudd, perch, bream, pike and trout, and on the bank, at appropriate times, the raptor man spreads the green umbrella which thinking fish probably take to be his wings, and casts his barbed enticements.

BEFORE YOU GO
Maps: OS half-inch maps of Ireland Nos 19 and 23.

GETTING THERE
By car: from Waterford, follow the N5 (north-east) towards New Ross, in the Barrow valley. To reach Waterford harbour, follow the R733 (south) to Arthurstown. To reach Graiguenamanagh, take the R700/R705 (north) from New Ross.
By bus: Bus Eireann services from all over Ireland stop in Waterford, and most of these also stop at New Ross. A Waterford–Dunmore East service is operated by Suliway, T:(051) 82209.

WHERE TO STAY
Hotels: there is plenty of bed and breakfasts and hotels to choose from in Waterford and New Ross, and a handful in Arthurstown, Fethard-on-Sea, Dunmore East and scattered in rural locations.
Hostels: there is an An Oige hostel in Arthurstown, T:(051) 89411, and independent hostels including the Dunmore Harbour House in Dunmore East, T:(051) 83218, and Mac Murrough Farm Hostel in New Ross, T:(051) 21383.
Outdoor living: among the several camp-sites in the area are the Dunmore East Caravan and Camping Park, T:(051) 83174, Fethard Caravan and Camping Park, T:(051) 97123, and the Ocean Island Caravan and Camping Park, Fethard-on-Sea, T:(051) 97148.

ACTIVITIES
Cycling: bikes can be hired from Wright's Cycle Depot, T:(051) 74411, in Wexford and from Edward Prendergast, T:(051) 21600, in New Ross.
Sailing: available in Waterford harbour, near Dunmore East, and also on the River Barrow, just outside New Ross.
Walking: the South Leinster Way runs through Graiguenamanagh, just north of Waterford harbour.

FURTHER INFORMATION
Tourist offices: the Bord Failte tourist office in Waterford is open all year, T:(051) 75788.

A year-round resident of Irish coasts, the ringed plover checks the flat sands and pebbles for small prey at low tide, uttering its bland, flutey call.

South Wexford and Saltee Islands

A fertile loamy county whose exhilarating outliers provide a bird-breeding success story

Unlike the high rock-dramas of the north-east, north-west and south-west corners of Ireland, the South-East ends in a whimper of sand and boulder clay. The coast is mostly low and soft, and, out to sea, a *cheval de frise* of sand reefs lies in wait for incautious shipping. ('If a ship grounds,' Praeger tells us dispassionately, 'the tide digs a deep hole on the downstream side, into which the vessel topples, and in a surprisingly short time disappears completely.') There are miles of dunes, sometimes sheltering lagoons and inland lakes. An air of haunting ghostliness can hang over the sites of sunken causeways, townships and buildings buried or half-buried by sand. There are sandy bays and banks of wiry marram, broad quiet estuaries and, of course, there are birds. The case for calling Wexford the most important county in Ireland for birds is a strong one. Where there are visible rocks – and there are, in fact, plenty of black granite rock capes

and islets – they lie low, as if undermined by their age, for they are among the oldest rocks in the country.

The area is dotted with ruins. This is the coast that was captured by Normans from Wales, the first toehold in the fateful colonization by Ireland's eastern neighbour. Cromwell was here, too, his divine angel inspiring him to horrors of what he saw as just retribution. The 1798 rebellion was as determined and bloody in County Wexford as anywhere in Ireland. Yet, in many ways, Wexford is the most English-seeming of Irish counties: green, wooded and pastoral with a loamy fertility like the English shires. There was a time when the Wexford gentry went to Bristol and London sooner than to Dublin for special shopping. Perhaps some still do.

This southern coastal strip is an exception on any score. Beyond Carnsore Point, where the tide-race and reefs have always dragged down the unwary, the confluence of currents makes for rich fishing. The Saltee Islands, biggest in the region, have their own royal family; the owner refers to himself as Prince Michael, and had himself crowned on a throne of limestone. The islands also have heady populations of birds on passage.

Generally speaking, this southern Wexford coastline is made up of two crescent bays. The larger, westerly bay curves from Hook Head to Crossfarnoge or Forlorn

RIGHTS OF WAY

In Northern Ireland (as in England and Wales) most rights of way are marked on Ordnance Survey maps, and in some cases signposted. Public libraries have comprehensive and up-to-date maps. In the Republic the legal right to cross land is in the main confined to national parks and long-distance walks.

Restrictions on walking rights have not been a problem in the past. Irish landowners both north and south have been sublimely tolerant of walkers crossing their land. The advice has always been to seek a farmer's permission, which will almost always be charmingly given, if you think you are close to him or his house. The Irish are proud of these gentle conventions, and it is a great pity that they have begun to wear thin. On popular tracks and sites litter-leaving tourists and landowners' fears about legal claims for compensation if people hurt themselves have brought about a reduction in this Irish charm quotient and an increase in the use of electric wire and impenetrable fences. These fences, with a strand of sharply barbed wire along the top, are subsidized by the EC, and may also result from the sub-division of land previously held as commonage on mountains. They are not always successful at containing the movements of sheep and have substantially reduced the national acreage available to walkers. On recent walks I have had to pass uncomfortably close to electric wire at Loop Head, the Bridges of Ross and elsewhere. I have torn my trousers on wire on Rathlin Island; found that walks described in detail in a book on Sligo had been disallowed by angry landlords; been snarled at by bright red 'Keep Out' notices in the Suir valley; and time and time again been prevented by fences from going where I was free to go only a few years ago.

Point, whose rock, after dipping underwater, re-emerges a few miles south as the Saltees; the easterly bends gently round to Carnsore Point. The one sizeable inlet is Bannow Bay, estuary of the Rivers Owenduff and Corock. For the rest, the inland waters – Lady's Island lake, Tacumshin lake and the Cull behind Ballyteige Bay – are almost entirely bounded by bars of shingle thinly capped by sand. Wind blows the sand back into the lake where it accumulates and continually, though infinitesimally, widens the bar. Wind is not the only unsettling agent. Burrowing rabbits break up the sand further and deeper. In the past, people cut such vegetation as there was for thatching and mattresses. What they removed was marram grass, the most effective answer to these disruptive influences, for its stems and long rhizomes tether and firm the sand into dunes. On this basis, other plants can settle and so, in due course, can the animal life that depends on them and on the sea's resources. Then, cyclically, rabbits arrive and spoil it all again. Some say it was the Normans who introduced rabbits to Ireland, but there is, so far as I know, no proof of this.

An auk with a comically colourful bill, the puffin breeds at a number of coastal and island sites, mainly on the west coast, nesting in disused rabbit burrows and often quite unafraid of human admirers.

There are, all the same, rich and sometimes rare plants here: wild asparagus (*Asparagus officinalis*), sea stock (*Matthiola sinuata*), viper's bugloss (*Echium vulgare*), bee orchid (*Ophrys apifera*) and cottonweed (*Otanthus maritimus*), which is found on only one beach in the south of the county, though common in the west of France and in Portugal. Bird's foot trefoil (*Lotus corniculatus*) and other quite widespread plants like seaside pansy (*Viola tricolor* ssp. *curtisii*) and lady's bedstraw (*Galium verum*) form huge carpets. Colonies of wild thyme (*Thymus drucei*) and eyebright (*Euphrasia nemorosa*) can also be seen as well as that familiar (in the south of Ireland) shrub trio: gorse, fuchsia and escallonia. Butterflies and rabbits are conspicuous by their presence, foxes less so.

Carnsore Point offers the sight of many birds, including some as small as meadow pipits and skylarks, on passage between North Africa and Atlantic destinations such as Iceland and Greenland. Lady's Island lake has several islands, one of which, Inch Island in the southern sector, supports a colony of terns, mainly of the Sandwich variety (*Sterna sandvicensis*) but including some of the increasingly rare roseate terns (*Sterna dougallii*). Several kinds of gull breed on the same island, and elsewhere on and near the lake are seen a wide variety of duck, both dabblers and divers, as well as grebes and many different waders. The movable population of Tacumshin lake is on similar lines but in greater numbers. There are large winter flocks of Bewick's swans, brent geese and numerous ducks. Further west, the long thin inlet known as the Cull has a decent winter population. A certain ingenuity is required of the bird-watcher at Bannow Bay, because the birds' daily movements carry them to pastures and havens miles apart; in addition, they may only come close enough to the shore for a reasonable inspection at high tide, or an hour or two either side of this.

Summer is not the best time for the bird-watcher on the mainland but you are never going to be without some good subject matter. For a change, you can bathe from lovely sandy beaches, turn your attention to plants or butterflies, or take a boat from the pretty fishing village of Kilmore Quay to Great Saltee Island. (Little Saltee, with no cliffs and little cover, is far less rewarding.) May, June and July are the best months, when parts of the island become a frenetic, raucous, avian maternity ward. Thousands of gulls of several kinds nest on the open ground, in fields not farmed in decades, among bramble and bracken, and on the shore. Kittiwakes, guillemots and razorbills, also in their thousands, occupy their customary shelves on vertical cliffs on the western and southern coasts. Puffins nest in burrows above them, along with Manx shearwaters, seen, or more likely only heard, by those who stay overnight.

The extinct great auk, cousin of the guillemot, puffin and razorbill, was last recorded in Ireland not far from here, in Waterford harbour, in 1846. Its disappearance heralded an era of decline for birds which gets more acute each year. More recently the nightingale gave its last Irish recital on the Great Saltee. Now and again, though, a species runs against the current of decrease. Only a few gannets bred here in the early 1930s, but numbers rose over the years, gradually but fairly steadily. Over a thousand pairs breed now, mainly on cliffs at the island's southernmost tip.

BEFORE YOU GO

Maps: OS Discovery Series map No. 77 (available in 1995); OS half-inch map of Ireland No. 23.

Guidebooks: *The Saltees, Islands of Birds and Legends* by Richard Roche and Oscar Merne (O'Brien Press, 1977).

GETTING THERE

By car: to reach the Saltee Islands follow the R739 (south) from Wexford to Kilmore Quay, the nearest village on the mainland. The R736 runs west from Rosslare, near the coast of south Wexford, to Wellington Bridge. Lanes from this road lead down to Carnsore Point, south of Rosslare harbour.

By rail: trains travelling from Rosslare Harbour to Waterford stop at Bridgetown and Wellingtonbridge, both near the south Wexford coast, twice a day, mornings and evenings.

By bus: a Bus Eireann service

runs from Wexford to Kilmore on Wednesdays and Saturdays, and a once-a-day Bus Eireann service between Waterford and Wexford stops at Wellington Bridge, on the south Wexford coast. Bus Eireann services from all over Southern Ireland terminate in Rosslare.

By boat: local boatmen can take you to the Saltee Islands. Try Willie Bates, T:(053) 29644, Declan Bates, T:(053) 29684, or Tom O'Brien, T:(053) 29727, who leave from Kilmore Quay. For more information on crossings contact the Wexford tourist office.

WHERE TO STAY

Hotels: there is no accommodation on the Saltee Islands, but there are a handful of bed and breakfasts and one hotel, Hotel Saltees, T:(053) 29601, in Kilmore Quay. There is a wide choice of hotel accommodation in Rosslare Harbour, several bed and breakfasts at Fethard-on-Sea and others scattered about the area including Mrs Breen-Murphy, T:(051) 61354, at Ballylannon.

Outdoor living: although camping on the privately-owned islands is allowed throughout most of the year, it is discouraged while the owner is in residence (generally the summer). There are four camping parks in and around Rosslare Harbour including the Rosslare Caravan and Camping Park, T:(053) 32427/45720. Among those on the south coast is the Ocean Island Caravan and Camping Park, T:(051) 97148), at Fethard-on-Sea.

Hostels: there is an independent hostel in Kilmore village, the Kilturk Hostel, T:(053) 29883, and an An Oige hostel in Rosslare Harbour, T:(053) 33399.

ACTIVITIES

Bird-watching: the Saltee Islands support puffins, guillemots, razorbills, cormorants, shags, kittiwakes The best time to visit is during the spring and early-summer nesting season and the spring and autumn migrations. Ask the warden at Wexford Wildfowl Reserve, T:(053) 23129, about arrangements. Carnsore Point, to the south of Rosslare harbour, sees a wide variety of migratory birds.

Fishing: rock and beach fishing for bass and tope. Grey mullet off Kilmore Quay. Deep-sea fishing trips for pollack, flatfish, wrasse, ray, dogfish and conger can be arranged from several of the local quays.

FURTHER INFORMATION

Tourist offices: the nearest Bord Failte tourist offices are in Wexford, T:(053) 23111, open May–Sept, and Rosslare Ferry Terminal, T:(053) 33622, open all year.

A pattern of pines looms through fog in Knockaun Forest, on the west side of the Comeragh mountains.

Wexford Slobs

Home to huge populations of geese, these mud-flats are protected by extensive wildfowl reserves

Now and again the Celtic genius for lilting place-names gives out. Ballyhooly, Tristernagh, Nahanagan and Derravaragh make way for the bog. Or the slobs. Both of which are, if not lyrical, at least onomatopoeic. Slobs are mud-flats, with perhaps admixtures of sand-dunes, inclined to be wet and pliable and, in dry weather, friable. Soppy, perhaps. Or sloppy. Slobs. In this case reclaimed from the sea in the middle of the nineteenth century and preserved by dykes for use as farmland. Birds use them, too, in colossal numbers. There would be little purpose in anyone not interested in birds visiting these slobs.

Wexford harbour, which is the estuary of the River Slaney, forms a square whose east side is a long thin promontory, which provides the harbour wall, and whose north and south sides bound, respectively, the north and south slobs. The sea along this coast is relatively shallow, streaked with shoals and reefs, submerged sandbanks and the strands of mud which, when the tide is out, emerge to offer their content of burrowing crustaceans and molluscs to the waders which depend on them. Sea movements cause low, flat, sandy islands to come and go. Up to twenty years ago Wexford harbour contained the largest colony of terns in Ireland (about 2,500 breeding pairs) but the island they bred on was slowly washed away and they moved elsewhere.

More than half the world's population of Greenland white-fronted geese spend their winter on the slobs. Numbers have reached about ten thousand, but early this century the most numerous species of goose to winter here was the greylag. They were present in Scotland too. After the Second World War Scottish farmers raised their production of root crops, a move which attracted the Irish greylags to join the Scottish. Brent geese, who find the mud-flats more to their liking, moved in. Other changes, notably drainage schemes carried out by farmers who own all the land outside the nucleus belonging to the Irish Wildbird Conservancy and National Parks and Wildlife Service, have seemed more menacing, but in the event numbers remain more or less stable.

There are plenty more birds. Maverick geese of several species get caught up with the huge white-front and brent populations. Several hundred Bewick's swans (named after the great wood-engraver when found to be a species distinct from whoopers) winter here. There are also large numbers of resident mute swans. Among the ducks are large populations of wigeon and mallard (as there are all along the south coast) and a dozen other species. Common scoters float in extensive rafts out at sea in the winter, a few metallic divers and flamboyant grebes in their midst. Waders include several hundred black-tailed godwits and good numbers of lapwing, golden plover and curlew. Amid such rich pickings the presence of birds of prey – hen harriers, peregrines and merlins

The Greenland white-fronted goose has a conspicuous patch which seems to connect the bill with the head. Traditionally a goose of bogs and wet grasslands in the midlands and west, it increasingly chooses intensive farmland, and the largest flock is based in the Wexford Slobs.

in winter, kestrels and sparrowhawks 'throughout the year – is not surprising.

Spying on the huge geese populations resident in winter can be far more exciting than anything in the novels of Le Carré. The little loyal family groups of brent geese muster together and rise, their individual flappings making a huge, collective cloud of shimmering silver, turning black and then silver again as they wheel and turn and slowly descend to a further reach of pasture, or to the sea.

ROADS, MAPS AND SIGNS

Major roads in the Republic were in the past prefixed by the letter T (for Trunk) and minor roads by the letter L (for Local). Major road numbers are now prefixed by the letter N (for National) and minor roads with the letter R (for Regional). The numbers that follow these letters have also changed in most cases. Thus the main road from Galway to Sligo used to be known as the T11 and is now the N17. In many cases an old road number may have have been replaced by up to three new numbers; similarly, one new road number may have superseded several old ones.

The Department of the Environment have replaced all the old T road signs with N signs, but they have not yet finished taking down the old L signs on back roads which are being changed to R numbers. This gradual process

means that even recent editions of the OS *Road Atlas of Ireland* are out of date. The Department advises bemused road users to rely on place-names on signposts more than road numbers. Most road signs are in English only or in English and Gaelic. To confuse matters, OS maps do not always provide both versions and signs in the Gaeltacht tend to be in Irish only. In this way what appears on most maps as Burtonport (on the Donegal coast) is announced on the road sign as *Ailt an Chorrain*, while Dunglow is *An Clochan Liath*. A driver may not be aware that *Giell Sli* is Irish for the instruction 'Yield' and that 'Danger' is rendered *Dainseas*.

In Northern Ireland road numbers are prefixed by the letters A and B as in the rest of Great Britain.

Before you go *Maps:* OS Discovery Series map No. 77; OS half-inch map of Ireland No. 23.

Getting there *By car:* from Wexford, take the R741 (north), then the R742 to reach the Wexford Slobs nature reserve. *By rail:* the nearest station is Wexford, where services between Dublin and Rosslare Harbour stop three times a day. *By bus:* Bus Eireann services stop at Wexford from all over Ireland. A Monday- and Saturday-only Bus Eireann service from Wexford to Gorey stops at Curracloe, about 3 miles (5 km) from the nature reserve.

When to go: a good time to visit

is Oct–Apr when geese and other wintering species are resident.

Where to stay: there is a wide choice of hotels and bed and breakfasts in Wexford, and a few camp-sites, including Ferrybank Caravan and Camping Park, T.(053) 42611/44378. O'Gorman's Camping and Caravan Park is just north of the nature reserve, near Curracloe, T:(053) 37221.

Activities *Cycling:* bikes can be hired from The Bike Shop, T:(053) 22514, and Hayes, T:(053) 22462, in Wexford. *Bird-watching:* within the north slobs there is a public reception area, with a permanent collection of pinioned birds,

indoor displays, and an observation tower from which some of the current populations of pasturing birds can be seen. Well designed and well run, the whole makes an excellent learning centre. The local bird population can be viewed all year round; species include Greenland white-fronted, brent, Canada, pink foot and other geese, pintails, Bewick's swans and black-tailed godwits. For further information call the Wexford Wildfowl Reserve, T:(053) 23129.

Further information: the Bord Failte tourist office in Wexford is open May-Sept, T:(053) 23111.

CHAPTER 6

Wicklow and the East

A t the head of broad inlets on the east coast of Ireland, separated by about a hundred miles, stand the two Irish capital cities, Dublin and Belfast, accounting between them for half the island's population. Across the Irish Sea are the coasts of England, Wales and Scotland, and upon the dividing water sails a lot of traffic between Clydeside, Stranraer, Merseyside, Fishguard, Milford Haven and other ports on the British side, and Rosslare, Wexford, Dun Laoghaire, Drogheda, Belfast, Carrickfergus, Larne and others on the Irish. Ireland's east coast is populous and busy. Many of those stretches of it not dedicated to people's work and homes are given over to people's play: resorts, golf courses, marinas and the like. It is not likely ground for that human neglect which permits the survival or development of wildness.

The wild, however, has, if it ever needed to, learned to co-exist with humans. `Clinging to the inaccessible edges of human dominion, sea-birds nest on promontories such as Bray Head, Wicklow Head or Howth; or they settle to pasture or roost in their thousands beside the golf course on the Bull or peck nourishing molluscs from miles of mud-flat and sandy beach.

Even in the centre of the east coast and within a stone's throw of Dublin, there are a couple of wild places to match the best the West can offer. Ten miles (16 kilometres) north of the capital you can cross three miles (five kilometres) of sea from Rogerstown, near

A winding, rock-lined creek leads down to Lough Tay from Sally Gap, in the heart of the Wicklow mountains.

Rush (having obtained permission by post from the owner's steward), and visit Lambay, an important bird reserve. The island is all that remains of an extinct volcano and, in marked contrast to the low-lying mainland shore, contains cliffs up to 400 feet (120 metres) in height, obvious home to a full complement of sea-birds. It is rich in igneous and metamorphic rocks, although one former resident would not have held with such data. The seventeenth-century Archbishop Ussher dated the origin of the universe – the Genesis creation – to the year 4004 BC, a masterfully precise claim widely accepted well into the present century. Ireland's Eye, a little island to the north of the Howth promontory, and so even closer to the city centre and more easy to get to, is also rich in sea-birds.

The River Boyne winds through the rich farming and hunting county of Meath. Demesnes of great mansions and castles and ancient royal burial grounds come down to its banks, and beside it, in 1689, a battle decisive in Irish and English history was fought. Every inch of its borders shows the influence of humans. Rivers are still wild, though, and for the most part unseen by humans. None of us can share the trout's view of the shadows he haunts, the pike's view of the trout, eyes peering from tangled roots or dense packs of reeds, the kingfisher skewering his prey, the walk of the dipper or the skimming passage of whirligig and water-beetle across the surface above. Even the patient angler is working on extrapolation and hunch, not knowledge of facts. But we see more than we otherwise would if we sit in a long smooth hollow of wood or fibreglass gliding noiselessly over the surface. A canoe is the discreetest, as well as the most enjoyable, means of spying on the wild.

The best area of wilderness around Dublin is the closest. No other capital city in Europe lives so genially cheek by jowl with a mountain range of great size, variety and beauty. The Wicklow mountains, taken with the coast beside them, offer examples of almost all that is best of wild Ireland: miles of blanket bog interspersed with monumental peaks and deep, steep-sided mountain corries; waterfalls streaming down rocky defiles to flow into the broad lakes of the big glens; cliffs crammed with nesting birds, good walks, good climbs; pastoral scenery that seems to belong to another age; a rich flora and fauna. An hour or so (much depending on traffic in the city) from the hurly-burly of Georgian squares, Trinity College or the nation's parliament in Leinster House, you can, in a manner of speaking, go wild among features that have changed little in ten thousand years, and almost forget the frenetic pursuit of difference and development continuing without pause a few miles over the hills.

GETTING THERE

By air: Dublin is the country's major airport and can be reached from airports around the world. Airlines which fly to Dublin from the UK include Aer Lingus, T:(01) 705 2222, Ryan Air, T:(0171) 435 7101 in the UK, British Midland, T:(0171) 589 5599 in the UK, and British Airways, T:(0181) 897 4000 in the UK.

By boat: Stena Sealink, T:(01233) 647047, sails from Holyhead, North Wales, to Dun Laoghaire, just outside Dublin. B&I, T:(0151) 227 3131, sails from Holyhead into Dublin. The crossing takes about 3 hours.

By rail: the Irish rail network radiates from Dublin. Different parts of the Wicklow mountains can be reached from Bray and Wicklow and other stations on the Dublin–Rosslare Harbour line. To explore the River Boyne, take the Dublin–Belfast link to Drogheda, T:(01) 366222.

ACTIVITIES
Walking: the Wicklow Way was Ireland's first officially signposted long-distance walk and is 82 miles (132 km) long. It follows a series of rough tracks from the outskirts of Dublin across the Wicklow mountains towards Wexford. For an information booklet contact COSPOIR, The National Sports Council, Hawkins House, Dublin 2, T:(01) 873 4700.
Climbing: the Wicklow mountains offer routes of up to 3,000 ft (900 m) around Glendalough. There are sea cliffs at Bray Head. Dalkey Quarry, 10 miles (16 km) from Dublin, is a training ground for climbers with many excellent short climbs.
Fishing: Tinnehinch Fly Angling Centre on the River Dargle can provide year round fly-casting instruction and more advanced fly angling on a 1-mile private stretch of river.
Cycling: Bord Failte recommends a rugged route which takes in the scenery of the Wicklow mountains. Details from Bord Failte's *Cycling Ireland* leaflet.
Sailing: Dun Caoghaibe Sailing School offers a full range of tuition, T:(01) 323938. Fingall Sailing School, T:(01) 451974, is only 9 miles (14 km) from Dublin and offers sailing and board-sailing. Dolphin Offshore Sailing Group, Shankill, T:(01) 323938, has a five-day yacht master course.
Riding: the area is dotted with riding centres which can offer trail riding, hacking, trekking or elementary tuition. Details from Bord Failte's *Equestrian Ireland* booklet.

FURTHER INFORMATION
There are Bord Failte tourist offices in Dublin city centre, 14 Upper O'Connell Street, T:(01) 747733, and Dublin Airport, T:(01) 844 5387. There is also an office in Dun Laoghaire, T:(01) 280 6984.

Wicklow Mountains

Extensive, granite range with spectacular walks and views beginning just 12 miles (17 kilometres) from the centre of Dublin

First place in the natural record of the Wicklow mountains is occupied by a blackbird. St Kevin, a recluse of the early Celtic church, came to a breathtaking gash of a glen, now known as Glendalough, to escape the sinful world. He built a cell, prayed, fasted, ate, slept, studied. One day he sat reading so intently in the cell, with the elbow of his spare arm resting on the window-stone, that he failed to notice a blackbird alight on his open hand. It lay a clutch of eggs. Such was the holy man's Celtic sensitivity and tenderness to nature that he remained quite still until the eggs were hatched. Stories like this abound in the lives of saints. There is always a deep empathy with animals, though not always with other humans, and never with humans having sexual motives. A seductive girl who followed Kevin to the glen was picked up by him and dropped into the lake, where she drowned. St Brendan beat and sent packing a girl who showed a similar attachment to him.

It is not difficult to feel in tune with Glendalough, a deep and lovely valley close to the centre of the Wicklows, holding two lakes (hence its name, two-lake glen) and a cluster of monastic ruins – for, in time, Kevin's cell attracted a large religious settlement. But this is only the most beautiful scene in a galaxy of beauties. The closeness of the range to the capital city is astonishing. The dozen miles that lie between the centre of Dublin and the nearest peaks and valleys – known as the Dublin hills because they fall within the county of that name – can seem like a thousand when you begin to breathe deep draughts of mountain air, look at broad vistas without sight of man, or wait in your car for the lane ahead to be cleared of a herd of cows.

This is not a genteel country park, placed conveniently for the delectation of towns-people, though, of course, townspeople come, in ever-increasing numbers, and some of them leave a great deal of sordid detritus behind them. It is a sizeable range of mountains, the highest reaching 3,039 feet (926 metres), higher than any in Ireland outside County Kerry. It covers an area about 30 miles (48 kilometres) north to south by 15 miles (24 kilometres) east to west, set back from the coast by a strip of lowland farm and parkland, and incorporating the largest spread of surface granite in Ireland or

Britain. This rugged wilderness has been a threat as well as a source of recreation to the capital for centuries. Tudor armies were beaten here. Rebels found sanctuary. Native O'Tooles, O'Dwyers and Byrnes periodically provoked the authorities, and there are many relics of nervous government precautions from the 1790s, when the ideas behind the French Revolution were taking seed in Ireland, to blossom, fall and moulder in the agonies of the 1798 rising. The remains of a chain of barracks and other defensive buildings, as well as the Military Road – now in use as one of the main highways – all date from this period.

It was the crust-crushing convulsions of 500 million years before, consequent upon the infinitely slow collision of the American and European tectonic plates, which first created the Wicklows. The newly bunched surface consisted of a variety of slates and shales, rock layers formed from sea sediments compacted by the weight of water during former aeons. The peaks they formed were more than a thousand feet (300 metres) higher than they are now, further raised by the irruption from far below of a mass of molten magma, which cooled into granite. Down the centre of the range, exposure to periods of violent weather slowly eroded the slaty overlay, leaving exposed the long granite core which still forms most of the mountains' heartland. Slate remained on the sides, and here and there other sedimentary rocks were metamorphosed by heat and pressure into a harder consistency. The resilient quartzite that makes up the two tall, conical Sugar Loaf mountains near Enniskerry is the most conspicuous result of these processes.

Further weathering and slow corrosion worked by a gentler climate through unimaginable spans of time, made the granite summits big, rounded, and so set, in looks anyway, for eternity. Later the traverses of heavy trains of ice polished this work. The metamorphic slates and schists on either side were more spiky, angular and sharp than the central heights. Ice nevertheless squeezed into and through the several defiles and ravines, leaving them deeper, wider and smoother and sometimes floored with lakes.

But an angularity remains to this day in the short steep glens of the west and the long – many miles long – broader valleys of the eastern scarp. Ice has left other distinctive features apart from the cones of quartzite at Enniskerry already noted: the sharp features of the Bray Head escarpment, raised riverbeds, waterfalls and several examples of a type of channel caused by the uneven melting of glaciers. As the climate warmed, the highest ice melted quickly. When the process reached the rock valleys and lowlands, the shade and colder ambient temperature greatly slowed things down. At this level the ice became a kind of extension of the lower mountain. Water flowing from the great uplands melt would be checked by its mass and forced to turn to right or left or both. The resultant churning and turning carved out what was to become – and remains – a mountain lake. The escaping overflow, still prevented from descending down the valley by the ice-sheet, excavated a sideways channel, known as a glacial spillway, across the mountain ridge. Here and there – at the Scalp, and Glen of the Downs near Enniskerry, at Piperstown glen below Killakee mountain, and down to the south of the Poulaphuca reservoir above Hollywood – these cross-ridge channels survive, dry, covered by vegetation, and betraying little sign of their icy origins.

Some of the glen rocks contain minerals in quantities once thought worth exploiting. Lead was mined in Glendalough, Glendasan and elsewhere in the nineteenth century, and there are the ruins of miners' cottages, smelting houses and slag heaps to show it. In the south, on the side of Croghan mountain, there is gold. Somewhere, it seems, there may be quite a lot of gold, in a mother lode buried, perhaps, under hundreds of feet of rock. What has come to light has been in tiny quantities, though enough to set off a couple of gold-rushes – in 1795 and 1935 – and probably to provide the material for large numbers of very beautiful, ancient gold decorative objects, of which many superb examples are in Dublin's National Museum. If you are determined to build your fortune on Irish gold, take your pan to Woodenbridge and progress up Gold

Mines river. Or better, catch a leprechaun and squeeze the secret out of him.

There are no surprises among the more accessible fauna. All the birds here are well represented in other parts of Ireland but, if you parcel the adjoining coast with the mountains, there is quite a wide variety. The rocky faces of Wicklow Head and Bray Head provide nesting space for the standard company of Irish sea-birds: guillemots, razorbills, kittiwakes, fulmars, herring gulls, great black-backed gulls, shags. The increasingly rare grey partridge may still occur, though there have been no officially accepted sightings recently. For the ravens and peregrines which nest here, the mountains are hunting grounds, though peregrines may spend a day in Wales, or the North, or the West, for variety. Ravens are quite often seen, scouring the hillside for carrion or prey or simply playing in the winds. They seem to become more common each year, sensitive, perhaps, to the more tolerant feelings of humans, who used to persecute them. They also do extremely well out of the European Union sheep headage subsidy, which has encouraged farmers to run more sheep than the land can nourish. The result is a plentiful supply of carrion.

Ravens are favourites of mine: grand, handsome, with the sinister aura Poe exaggerated, and very clever – they have always been thought that. You may have heard the account of one raven which came on a dead deer on a mountainside. As it began its lone feast a whole flock of ravens appeared and approached. Suddenly the single bird rolled over and lay still, done for, it seemed, by the poison some farmer had put in the carcass. The other birds looked at the meat, strutted over to the body and looked at that, drew their conclusions and flew away. Intelligent, certainly; but ravens can be more intelligent still. As soon as they had gone the original bird got up, shook out his feathers, and resumed his meal.

Wicklow has the usual repertoire of ling (*Calluna vulgaris*), bell heather (*Erica cirerea*) and – on wetter ground – cross-leaved heath (*Erica tetralix*) together with upland grasses found in other acidic Irish ranges. It also has its share of conifer plantations. As they reach maturity the evergreens black out

A cross-marked standing stone survives from a past age on the west of Tonelagee mountain, in the middle of Wicklow: an ancient way-mark, perhaps, on an old pilgrimage route.

almost all subsidiary life-forms; but here and there are good broadleaf woods, among them the old oak stands of Glen of the Downs and the Vale of Clara, and the mixed woodlands of Glendalough, Devil's Glen and Shillelagh (which gave its name to the famous Irish oak cudgel), where a lot of small birds breed. Pied flycatchers, which hunt by casting themselves into exquisite aerial loops, breed here, as do monotonously chiffchaffing chiffchaffs, some wood warblers, blackcaps with their lovely choirboy voices and occasional redstarts. On the sparser parts of the uplands you might glimpse whinchats, stonechats, linnets, meadow pipits, and those aristocrat assassins the hen harrier, merlin and kestrel – the last being the only true hoverer occurring in these islands, steadily holding its exact position in the air (as you can see if there is a backdrop of hill or tree to check by) with no more than a corrective tremor of its wings.

Deer are here: red (introduced in 1920), fallow (introduced by the Romans, it is thought), sika (escaped from the spectacular gardens of Powerscourt, near Enniskerry), but mostly sika-red crosses. One October in Wicklow I heard what I took to be a pig grunting but saw no sign of beast or sty or pen or paddock. The noise kept recurring, and then I realized it must have been something I had seldom heard before: a concealed fallow buck, with its deep grunt (what a 32-foot organ pipe would sound like, perhaps, if it were able to belch), soliciting female company and warning rival stags at the beginning of its rut, a season of several weeks during which it does not even feed.

Of other sizeable mammals, badgers are about, and by no means always at night, as is so often claimed. There are foxes, feral goats, rabbits, hedgehogs, pygmy shrews, rats – whose numbers in some years disconcert – mice; and there are Irish mountain hares (*Lepus timidus hibernicus*), a native subspecies of the blue hare (*Lepus timidus*), found in Scotland and other parts of Europe. Unlike blue hares, the Irish animal does not normally turn white in winter. It can be distinguished from the brown hare (*Lepidus capensis*), which is common in Britain, by its shorter ears and pale tail and by its reddish coat, which fades and goes patchy during winter moults – that of the brown hare tends to be dark on top. But 'reddish' will not really do. Hare colours have the rich complexity of a much-used palette, a palette of reds, browns, buffs, chestnut, cinnamon, russet, creams, whites and beiges. It is this, along with their effortless zigzag run and skill at concealment, that has led them to be endowed, in all national myths, with mystical, magic powers. Time and again, a seemingly blameless wife turns out to be a part-time witch, speeding off to covens and other diabolical assignments in hare form, and given away by a graze or

bruise in a part of her body corresponding to the wound on a hare the farmer-husband has shot or snared.

If not all things to all men, the Wicklows are quite a lot to quite a few. They are a quick breather, or a day out, for a million Dubliners, a place the visitor landing at Dublin or Rosslare may well take in before heading west, a mighty and magnificent obstacle for midland Irish needing to reach the Wicklow coast and Wicklow coast Irish needing to reach the midlands. For many, they are the site of week-long or longer rambles, hikes and climbs. There is, of course, an ancient picnic tradition, by Loughs Tay or Dan or Luggala or by the Powerscourt waterfall, leading to tales of old-school dons and writers being nasty about each other over Thermos tea and cucumber sandwiches. One Trinity teacher, as Oliver Gogarty records, complained that since a colleague of his had given up preaching sermons he had suffered insomnia in church. And Yeats remarked that the worst thing about a particular compatriot was that when he was not drunk he was sober.

The plurality of Wicklow's roles makes any prescription of route unnecessary. Certainly it would be a pity to miss many of the grandest scenes: the Wicklow Gap, Glendalough, the Sally Gap, the Meeting of the Waters, the Vale of Avoca, the Vale of Clara, Glenmacnass, Glenmalure, Powerscourt and Enniskerry, Roundwood (the highest village in Ireland), the Avondale forestry park, the Glen of Imail. But all the main through-roads, as well as the official long-distance Wicklow Way from Dublin's outskirts to Clonegal, include some of these attractions and most illustrate the varied immensity of the range: the heady rise and fall of the pass-roads, with broad, sweeping valleys narrowing to rock-crimped woody cuts; the accompanying streams or torrents; the stately beauty of the lakes; and a thousand more enclosed and intimate scenes, revealing hill, wood, waterfall, rock feature, gold glinting like good intentions in a stream, bright green hags (as moist enclaves in the bog are called) and that impressive boulder on a hill above the Vale of Avoca, the Motte Stone. Left precariously perched by a receding glacier, the stone is said in the fast-fading local folklore to roll downhill every May Day (a time electric with magic potential) to the Meeting of the Waters for a long draught of water, and thereafter to roll up again.

BEFORE YOU GO
Maps: OS Discovery Series maps Nos 50, 56 and 62. OS half-inch maps of Ireland Nos 16 and 19.
Guidebooks: *Hill Walkers' Wicklow* and *The New Irish Walk Guides: East and South-East* by David Herman (Shankshare, 1989 and Gill and Macmillan, 1991). See also *The Complete Wicklow Way: A Step by Step Guide* by J.B. Malone (O'Brien Press, 1988) and *The Wicklow Way, from Marlay to Glenmalure* by Michael Fewer (Gill and Macmillan, 1988).

GETTING THERE
By car: from Dublin follow the N82 to Tallaght, the N81 (south) to Hollywood, then the R756 (east) to Laragh. This takes you right through the middle of the Wicklow mountains. The R115 from Dublin to Laragh (along the old Military Road) is another scenic traverse.
By rail: Bray, Wicklow, Rathdrum and other stations on the DART (Dublin Area Rapid Transport), south-eastern (red), suburban line provide starting points for eastern and southern approaches to the mountains.
By bus: a local Bus Eireann service running from Dublin to Waterford stops at Wicklow and Rathdrum, towards the southern end of the mountains. Another Dublin–Waterford local Bus Eireann service stops at Tinahely, further south.

WHERE TO STAY
Hotels: there is a huge selection of bed and breakfasts and hotels in Dublin and plenty more in Bray, Wicklow, Rathdrum, Glendalough and the surrounding area.

Outdoor living: the Shankill Caravan and Camping Park, T:(01) 282 0011, is just south of Dublin and is open all year. Nearer the mountains in Redcross, campers can stay at Johnson's Caravan and Camping Park, T:(0404) 48133, which is open 17 Mar–24 Sept, or at the River Valley Caravan and Camping Park, T:(0404) 41647, open 17 Mar–18 Sept. Also nearer the mountains is the Redwood Caravan and Camping Park, T:(01) 281 8163, open 31 Mar–25 Sept.
Hostels: there are about six independent hostels in Dublin, including Goin' My Way, T:(01) 878 8484, and Marlborough House, T:(01) 874 7629. The An Oige hostel is the Dublin International Youth Hostel, T:(01) 830 1766. Rathcoran House, T:(0508) 81073/81222, is in Baltinglass just south of the mountains, and there are An Oige hostels in Glendalough, T:(0404) 45342, and Bray, T:(01) 2864036 or (01) 2864037.

ACTIVITIES
Climbing: Glendalough is the main centre for climbing, with routes up to 3,000 ft (900 m) on sound granite. Most climbs are in the Severe and Very Severe grade, though there are a few Difficults and Extremes. Luggala is another big granite crag with many fine routes. A climbing guide is available from Joss Lynam, T:(01) 288 4672.
Walking: 1,000 square miles (1,600 sq km) of granite domes make up the mountains, so there is plenty of scope for walkers, with trails offering great distances and good views. Particularly fine walks run from Glendalough, including the hike up Camaderry, which starts at the entrance to the Upper Lake car park. The Wicklow Way, which is 82 miles (132 km) long, goes from Dublin to Clonegal and offers wonderful views, some tough walking, and in poor conditions, the possibility of getting lost. Dress appropriately and take

The red grouse may be seen in uplands in several parts of the country, breaking cover in boglands or heathery moors – the various parts of the heather plant form its favourite food – but its numbers have been steadily declining for some years.

compass, map, whistle and some food. See Bord Failte information and map sheet 26B. For accommodation details see the Bord Failte *Accommodation Guide for Long Distance Walking Routes*. For more information contact Wicklow County Council, County Buildings, Wicklow, T:(0404) 67324. The Tiglin Adventure Centre will organize a walk through the mountains for you, T:(0404) 40169.

Riding: Calliaghstown Riding Centre, T:(01) 589236, runs horse-trail rides over the mountains.

FURTHER INFORMATION
Tourist offices: the Bord Failte office in Wicklow, T:(0404) 67904, is open all year, as is the Bord Failte tourist office in Dublin, 14 Upper O'Connell Street, T:(01) 747733, and the head office of the Tourist Board, T:(01) 676 5871.

Ireland's Eye

Insular nature reserve a few minutes' boat trip from Howth

Islands, islets, sea-girt rocks – even tight-necked peninsulas – are rarities on Ireland's east coast. Lambay, opposite Rush in County Dublin, is the biggest of them. It consists of ancient volcanic and sedimentary rocks, and its cliffs and rock stacks support a good population of sea-birds. It is, however, closed to the public. Dalkey Island, opposite Dalkey at the southern extreme of the capital, is relatively featureless but is an important roost for post-breeding terns in late summer. Other east coast islands include Rockabill, with its lighthouse, which hosts the most important colony of roseate terns in Western Europe, and three low-lying islands, also off Skerries in north County Dublin. The merits of the only other island of substance, Ireland's Eye, are that it is just a mile off the mainland, that boat owners from Howth can usually be hired in summer to take visitors around it, and that it offers a home, particularly on its north-eastern cliffs, to thousands of sea-birds.

There are nearly a thousand nesting kittiwakes, almost as many guillemots and over 150 pairs of razorbill on the Eye, besides fulmars, black guillemots, both great and lesser black-backed gulls, a sprinkling of puffins, and those evil-smelling denizens of guano-spread rock roosts to north, south, east and west of Ireland, the cormorants and shags. Both birds are black almost all over, but the cormorant is distinguished by

Wicklow and the East

Key
— Exploration zones.
— Roads.
-- Footpaths.
(i) Points of interest.
---- Regional boundaries.

2000 and over
1000 - 2000
200 - 1000
0 - 200
metres

to Castleblaney · Warrenpoint
CAVAN · Cootehill
Kilkeel
Carlingford
Dundalk
Carrickmacross
LOUTH · Dundalk Bay
Ardee · Irish Sea
Kells · Slane · Drogheda
Navan · Julianstown
River Boyne · Balbriggan
Athboy · Trim · MEATH · Skerries
DUBLIN · Rush
Portrane · LAMBAY ISLAND
Donabate
WESTMEATH · Kinnegad · Malahide
Dublin Airport · Ireland's Eye
Maynooth · Howth
Edenderry · Dublin · Dublin Bay
KILDARE · Dun Laoghaire
Naas · Shankill
Droichead Nua · Enniskerry · Bray
Kilcullen · Greystones
Lough Tay · Glen of the Downs
Dunlavin · Lough Dan · Roundwood
Wicklow Gap · Glendalough
WICKLOW
LAOIS · Wicklow Mtns · Wicklow
Athy · Baltinglass · Rathdrum
Vale of Avoca
Carlow · Woodenbridge
Tullow · Tinahely · Arklow
-N-
CARLOW · Gorey
0   5   10miles
0   5   10   15Km.

white cheeks and somewhat slower wing-beats. There are also Manx shearwaters nesting in burrows in the ground during the breeding season, uttering shrill, late-night cries. 'Daemonic' is the word often used, but I have heard comparisons with a donkey's bray and a manic mating cat.

And there are gannets, an ornithological success story in an age when there are all too few. None bred here until 1988; there were 27 pairs by 1990 and there are well over 50 pairs now, making the usual reeking bedlam of their nesting sites, bickering, posturing, squawking throughout the period of breeding, yet converting on their fishing expeditions into elegantly streamlined aerial torpedoes, plummeting through the air at 30 miles an hour to impale and carry away some unwary mackerel. The founders of this colony came from St Kilda in the Hebrides, far to the north, where 60,000 pairs breed.

Before you go *Maps:* OS Discovery Series map No. 50, OS half-inch map of Ireland No. 16.

Getting there *By car:* from Dublin city centre, follow the road along the sea-front north-east to Howth, the nearest mainland point to Ireland's Eye.
By rail: take the DART suburban (green) line to Howth.
By boat: boats can be taken from Howth to Martello Tower, on the island. Contact Frank Doyle, T:(01) 831 4200, who runs boats every half hour during the summer. It is possible to book.

Where to stay: there is a vast choice of accommodation of every kind in Dublin, including bed and breakfasts, hotels and hostels. There are also a few bed and breakfasts in Howth, including Saint Lawrence, T:(01) 832 2643, and Mrs Hobbs, T:(01) 839 1391. There is an An Oige hostel in Dublin, the Dublin International Youth Hostel, T:(01) 830 1766, and a camp-site at Rush, up the coast opposite Lambay Island, the North Beach Caravan and Camping Site, T:(01) 843 7131, is open all year.

Access: Lambay Island is private property and landing is not allowed without permission from the owners. Visits to Ireland's Eye are usually restricted to the summer months by the weather. No unauthorised visitors are allowed on Rockabill during the breeding season.

Activities *Fishing:* sea-angling in Howth includes pier and boat fishing for pollack, coalfish, codling and mackerel, and deep-sea fishing for tope, ray, pollack and conger.
Bird-watching: Ireland's Eye is a sea-bird sanctuary where visitors can see kittiwakes, razorbills, cormorants and shags.

Further information: the nearest Bord Failte tourist office is in Dublin, 14 Upper O'Connell Street, T:(01) 747733.

BIRD-WATCHER'S CODE OF CONDUCT

1. The welfare of birds must come first.
2. Habitat must be protected.
3. Keep disturbance to birds and their habitat to a minimum.
4. When you find a rare bird think carefully about whom you should tell.
5. Do not harass rare migrants.
6. Abide by the bird protection laws at all times.
7. Respect the rights of landowners.
8. Respect the rights of other people in the countryside.
9. Make your records available to the local bird recorder.
10. Behave abroad as you would when bird-watching at home.

Perched on a rock, pole or branch and spreading its wings to dry, or flapping energetically a few feet above the surface of the sea, the cormorant is familiar along the whole of Ireland's coastline; increasingly in recent years it has been found on inland waterways and lakes.

River Boyne

A cross-section of County Meath, taking in Navan, Slane, Drogheda and the Boyne estuary

I once canoed down the Boyne from source to sea. My first canoe journey of any length, it was 60 downstream miles (100 kilometres) and could have been done in a day; but I span it out to five, stopping to see Newgrange and the burial mounds in the great, prehistoric royal graveyard of Brugh na Boinne, as well as the site of the battle which finally saw James II off British and Irish soil and marked the end of Roman Catholic monarchy. I watched birds and fish for hours on end. There is no way of intruding so silently on nature as in a canoe (except, I suppose, by balloon). Once a kingfisher almost parked on my head; it panicked about a yard away. Even herons

192

took my arrival calmly and paused to look before making unflustered ascents.

Committing myself, the boat and my possessions packed into two dustbin bags and stowed within the fibreglass prow to each weir as it came, I thought I was worth a medal for valour, though I soon learned it was not me but my almost weightless shiny craft that guided us. Sharp rocks shaved the paint as we careered through the frothing white water, twisting and turning at what seemed (there is the same illusion in surfing) like a hundred miles an hour. Had death come then I should have gone happy. I have loved few experiences in my life as much as those. The only grating thing was an occasional curse or threat from a fisherman who feared, I suppose, that I would foul his line. If I am truthful, something else pained me, but retrospectively. I read later that if the aggregate of an Irish river's dangers is put on a scale of ten, the Boyne's total amounts to one. So much for medals. So much for a glorious death.

Being in a boat on the river is the only way of seeing it all. You and your boat have to be brought to the highest navigable point, of course, which is at the Boyne Aqueduct, carrying the Royal Canal high over the river's channel, and you have to be collected at the mouth, if that is where you finish. The smooth, reedy waters of the elevated canal almost lured me away at the start – it could have taken me to the Shannon, the country's central artery, from which at Leitrim there is now access to Lough Erne by way of the restored Ballinamore and Ballyconnell canal; but I deferred that pleasure till later. The River Blackwater, which slams head-on into the Boyne at Navan, causing it to slew right and north-eastward towards Slane, is another enticing detour. It comes from Lough Ramor in the south of County Cavan.

Best of all, though, is the estuary. You emerge from Drogheda, whose vertiginous quays and hulls impart a pathetically Lilliputian and crushable feel to the toe-high canoeist, into a weird reach of broad river hemmed by nineteenth-century walls with gaps through which appear bleak, high and seemingly infinite mud-flats. Cormorants stretch their wings to dry on the navigation posts, as if crucified. The tide ripples in, with whatever breeze the eastern seaboard can muster. The atmosphere is surreal. The mud here is rich in mussels, and it is worth seeing the passion with which oystercatchers attack boats loaded with a new cargo of the shellfish. Turnstones may join in. Large flocks of golden plovers and brent geese may be seen from close to. Avocet and little egret are among the many recorded rarities.

The estuary broadens to a width of a mile, then narrows to a neck less than half a mile long and a hundred yards or so wide. I remember my elated arrival here with special warmth. An old man picking cockles from the sand as I paddled by asked where would I be going. To the sea, I said; I just want to finish canoeing the river.

'The whole river?'

'The whole river.'

'Sure, there's madder folk about than I thought there was.'

On my return journey he helped me lift the canoe out and hide it. Halfway through, alarmingly, he called out: 'Amn't I a man as had three heart attacks?' Then he gave me a lift – a rather juddering, halting lift in his small car – to a small hotel a few miles away, talking about local history and his state of health. I approached the beauteous brunette at the desk feeling self-conscious: in shorts, more or less soaked from head to foot, my luggage in two black dustbin bags, sunburnt

Found in or beside – often standing motionless at the edge of – almost all the rivers, lakes, ponds, canals and estuaries in Ireland, the grey heron, often called 'crane' by the Irish, breeds in colonies of flat twiggy nests on the top of tall trees.

skin peeling prolifically. Two ladies, genteelly dressed, and a fully togged priest passed me on their way out.

'Excuse my appearance,' I said to the reception girl.

'You're very welcome,' she said. 'Wouldn't it be a fool would judge a feller by the way he looked?'

And she gave me a heavenly room overlooking beach and sea.

BEFORE YOU GO

Maps: OS half-inch map of Ireland No. 13.

GETTING THERE

By car: to follow the river inland from Drogheda, take the N51 (west) to Navan and then the R161 to Trim.

By rail: the nearest station is in Drogheda, with DART services from Dublin Connolly on the northern suburban line (blue).

By bus: a local Bus Eireann service from Athlone to Dundalk stops at Trim, Navan and Drogheda.

WHERE TO STAY

Hotels: there are bed and breakfasts in Trim, Slane and Navan, and a handful of hotels. The choice in Drogheda is slightly better.

Outdoor living: Bettystown Caravan and Camping Park, T:(041) 28167, is open Easter–Sept.

Hostels: in Drogheda, the Harpur House Tourist Hostel, T:(041) 32731.

ACTIVITIES

Cycling: bikes can be hired from Clarke's Sports Den in

Navan, T:(046) 21130, and from P.J. Carolan in Drogheda, T:(041) 38242.

Riding: is available at the Castlehill Equestrian Centre, in Julianstown, just south of Drogheda, T:(041) 29430.

Fishing: the Boyne has good trout and salmon fishing; contact the Eastern Regional Fisheries Board, T:(01) 379209.

FURTHER INFORMATION

Tourist offices: the Bord Failte in Trim, T:(046) 37111, is open in the summer, as is the office in Drogheda, T:(041) 37070.

CHAPTER 7

Northern Ireland

Northern Ireland is much misunder-
stood. People abroad consider it
dour, industrial, industrious, fanatic,
joyless, gratingly masculine. They think
of it as full of tough, Bible-belt funda-
mentalists calling down the wrath of
God on a minority of libertine
Catholics. Or vice versa. There are little
corners of the North where these ideas
have a certain validity. Mostly they are
wrong. When I go to the North I expect
to be cheered up and almost invariably
am. I have wished my life would allow
me to live in Belfast, the most buoyant-
ly cheerful, kind, intelligent and alive
city I know. I have the greatest difficulty
getting people to believe me.

I tell them of the Northern sense of
humour, a commodity many think does
not exist, of the friendliness and help-
fulness you will meet as a traveller –
quite as much in the North as in the
Republic. People are surprised to hear
that outside touchy areas Catholic and
Protestant are, and as often as not have
been, neighbours, and good neighbours
at that. Of course Ulster retains its
strong Scottish connection. It would be
curious if things were otherwise, for if
you look east from the North's east
coast, Scotland is the only country you
see, as close as 12 miles (19 kilometres)
away. The important role played in the
history of America by the Scots-Irish of
Ulster is often ignored: they provided
several presidents and hundreds of
thousands of less highly placed immi-
grants.

Ulster has often led the rest of Ireland,
as far back as history takes us. It piloted

Slopes of debris running down to the sea skirt the
sheer basaltic cliffs of Fair Head, topped by a fresh-
water lake, at Ireland's north-east corner

violent bids for independence in the sixteenth, seventeenth and eighteenth centuries, and it has given Ireland many of its heroes, ancient and legendary, modern and real. Not that Ulster and Northern Ireland are quite the same thing. The latter consists of six counties retained within the United Kingdom in 1921 when the rest of the country achieved independence. The ancient province of Ulster comprises these six and a further three – Donegal, Cavan and Monaghan – which, being essentially Catholic, were allowed to go with the South.

The greatest misconception of all is that the North is dull and plain to look at and travel in. For its size it has a variety of scenic beauty that few similar areas can boast. You could walk out of the sea, up the Mourne mountains, and down to the bird-haunted dunes of the Murlough reserve in an afternoon. An hour's drive in a car could show you the yo-yo undulations of Antrim's east coast; views of Rathlin, the Mull of Kintyre, Islay and the distant Scottish highlands over the water from the dizzying heights of Fair Head; the broad fertile gashes of the Glens; a bleak brown and purple plateau of Antrim moorland and the out-of-kilter architecture of grey basalt hexagons that form the Giant's Causeway.

Not all these items pass as true wilderness. In the North, even more than in the Republic, defining what is wild is difficult. Both countries have cultivated and grazed every inch they can. As in the South, the wild consists in the main of cliffs, sand, rivers, lakes and mountain tops. But here the problem is a little more acute. Because it is richer, because it wants to show off the merits of its system, because it is less content than the Republic to leave things that are doing no great harm as

they are, because it has less room, because it is more provident – for whatever reason, the government of the North tends to look after both the external and visible elements of the land better than that of the South.

You notice this at its best and most obvious in the state of road surfaces, the durable solidity of road signs, the neat cleanliness of the houses, castles and other sites open to the public. On the other hand, this dedication to the spick, span and explicit assorts ill with wildness. There are just too many signs, too many nanny hands reaching down to take us along the mountain walk, to the bird-watching hide, or the rocky beach.

There is no need to dwell on this tendency to domesticate, or reduce to human dimensions, because so much of the North is not conducible to this end. The inland lakes – Neagh and Upper and Lower Lough Erne – do little more than nod acknowledgement of the human presence. Neagh, the biggest sheet of water in Ireland, needs getting to know. On a grey day it is no more than a wet grey carpet in the plain. Bit by bit it reveals its charms: the Oxford Island bird reserve or the park at Shane's Castle are the obvious points of access, but innumerable little lanes lead to countless little bays in its fish-rich, bird-frequented periphery. The two Lough Ernes are a pattern of islands – 57 in the upper, 96 in the lower – and form part of the longest navigable stretch of water in Ireland. Exploration calls for a boat. Their surrounds are beautiful and they are rich in birds and plant life.

There are two big mountain ranges in the North. Of the two, the Sperrins are the less dramatic: gentle slopes for the most part, and some broad mantles of forestry, but never crowded. The

Mournes, of course, draw the crowds. They are an easy drive from the most populous parts of the province. To my taste, these relatively recent extrusions of granite have made one of the most fetchingly shaped ranges in Ireland. In their roll down to the sea they add another jewel to the North's coastal treasury. The deeply penetrating sea loughs (Belfast, Larne and island-studded Strangford); Antrim's climbs and cliffs; the great flawed Causeway set down for Finn the giant to march to Staffa and the land of Argyll; Sheep Island with its wing-spreading cormorants and Rathlin Island with its avian opera-house and the descendants of the spider that spurred a king to glory – all these are the North. There is nothing dour, dull or humourless about them.

GETTING THERE

By air: hourly flights from Heathrow to Belfast International Airport, and four flights per day from London Gatwick to Belfast City Airport. Regular flights from Luton and UK regional airports to Belfast City; from Glasgow and Manchester to Derry; and from Jersey to all three airports in Northern Ireland. Direct flights to Belfast International Airport from Paris, Amsterdam, Frankfurt, New York and Toronto.

By boat: the only crossing from England is operated by Norse Irish Ferries, T:(01232) 779090, from Liverpool to Belfast, taking 11 hours and running once a day. From Scotland there is a choice of three routes: Stranraer to Belfast, operated by SeaCat, T:(0345) 523523, leaving up to five times daily and taking 90 minutes; Stranraer to Larne, operated by Stena Sealink, T:(01233) 647047, leaving eight times daily and taking 2 hours; Cairnryan to Larne, operated by P&O European Ferries, T:(01581) 200276, leaving six times daily and taking 2 hours. It is also possible to sail from the Isle of Man May–Sept; ferries go 2–4 times per week and are operated by Man Steam Packets Company, T:(01624) 661661.

By rail: in Northern Ireland, local services are run by Northern Ireland Railways, T:(01232) 230310, who offer a seven-day unlimited travel Runaround ticket.

By car: if you are travelling to Northern Ireland by car from the Republic, be sure to cross the border only at officially recommended points, marked on road maps.

By bus: the local bus services are run by Ulsterbus, T:(01232) 333000.

WHERE TO STAY

For lists of self-catering accommodation send an s.a.e. to Northern Ireland Self-Catering Association, Carlton Cottage, Belleek BT93 3FX. To obtain a youth hostel accommodation guide contact YHANI, T:(01232) 324733. NITB (see below) publish an accommodation guide, *Where To Stay*.

ACTIVITIES

Walking: the Ulster Way makes a 560-mile (896-km) circuit of the six counties and is divided into 32 stages; for further information see *The Ulster Way* by Paddy Dillon (Walking World Ireland, Dublin). NITB publish *An Information Guide to Walking in Northern Ireland,* or see *Ulster Walk Guide* by Richard Rogers (Gill and Macmillan, 1994), or *Ulster Rambles* by Peter Wright (Greystone Press, 1993).

Climbing: contact Ardelinis Activity Centre, 1 High Street, Cushendall, Co. Antrim BT44 0NB, T:(012667) 71340.

Adventure: contact Northern Ireland Centre for Outdoor Activities, T:(01232) 381222.

Riding: Northern Ireland offers marvellous rides, including hunting. NITB Bulletin 19 lists approved stables.

Fishing: information from Fisheries Conservancy Board, T:(01762) 334666, Department of Agriculture (Fisheries), T:(01232) 76393, Ulster Coarse Fishing Federation, T:(01662) 245433. Licences and permits can be obtained from NITB (see below), T:(01232) 246609, Lakeland Visitor Centre, Enniskillen, T:(01365) 323110, and local tackle shops.

Bird-watching: useful contacts include RSPB, T:(01232) 491547, and the National Trust, T:(01238) 510721. For bird-watching facilities and accommodation contact Lough Neagh Tourism, T:(01849) 463113, and Strangford Lough Tourism, T:(01247) 812215. Bird-watching package holidays in the region are organized by Murphy's Wildlife Tours, 12 Belvoir Close, Belvoir Park BT8 4PL, T:(01232) 693232.

FURTHER INFORMATION

Tourist offices: The Northern Ireland Tourist Board is at 59 North Street, Belfast BT1 1NB, T:(01232) 246609.

The Mournes

Picturesque mountain range in south-east County Down, rising from the sea between Dundrum Bay and Carlingford Lough

The rewards of climbing Slieve Donard, the highest of the Mourne mountains, are quite out of proportion to the effort involved. You ascend from the exhilaration of Newcastle's sandy beach to an intoxication of mountain air, and to views over the Mull of Kintyre, the Isle of Man, Lough Neagh and County Down. This is accomplished in a climb of just a couple of hours, yet when you come down you may look back with satisfaction at what is without doubt a serious, steep-sided, cone-shaped mountain that looks as if it would not be out of place in the Alps or the Himalayas. Few other peaks give such a ready, if only illusory, sense of achievement.

The effect is enhanced if you approach the Mournes from Belfast and the north. Much of the road is through drumlin country, a Lilliput of toy-town hillocks and villages and clean low bungalows. Always ahead is this fine dark silhouette of story-book mountain shapes: up-dome-down, up-cone-down, up-dome-squiggle-dome-down, getting bigger and bigger every mile. That is, of course, on clear days. There are plenty of days on which the peaks fail to emerge at all, as if the weather were affording them beauty treatment: a mudpack of mist, a massage by hail and sleet, a wash of rain, a tonic blow of wind and snow, from which they emerge, a day or week later, in incomparable bright splendour.

The range lies on a diagonal south-west to north-east, but the twelve highest peaks stand close to each other, in a rough circle, at the north-east end. South-east of the mountains the foothills level out for a few miles until they meet the sea or Carlingford Lough. This insulated lowland enclave is known as the Kingdom of Mourne, and consists of good farmland divided by the most impressive dry-stone walls in Ireland. These are constructed not from the slabs or variegated jigsaw blocks of the West, but from balls of stone the diameter of a fore-arm, some of them flattened at the top to make a perfectly level surface. They, and the mountains from which they are sprung, are composed of granite.

It was not a straightforward spew of molten lava that made the Mournes. The main transference was, in fact, contained underground, a mighty displacement caused by the dropping into the earth of a huge volume of shale – all this in the Tertiary epoch, some 65–50 million years ago. A covering of shale remained, so the risen granite was contained within the original outer shell. Since then almost all the shale has been eroded away. Exposed to the range of climates that followed – from tropical to Arctic – the uncovered granite cracked and split into characteristic rectangular blocks. It was these which, weathering and wearing at the corners, became the innumerable rock spheres which still hang around the heights or, having slid to the foothills, have been so skilfully cleared and piled into walls. The last stages of their downward progress were effected by ice, which dragged them along the deep wide valleys carved by its slow movement, whose river names are often repeated in the seaside towns at which they end: Kilkeel, Annalong, Bloody Bridge.

A long periphery of sandy beaches, with water of a green-blue clarity seen less and less in Europe's purlieus, hems the area. To the north, beyond Newcastle, begins a long broad spit of sand-dune, the Murlough National Nature Reserve, rich (and far richer than the mountains) in bird, plant and insect life. South of the Mournes lie the ten miles (16 kilometres) of Carlingford Lough, a varied and islanded sea inlet with the long wall of Carlingford mountain on the far side and wintering brent geese, ducks and waders.

Yet the Mournes are under an hour's drive from the nearly half a million inhabitants of Northern Ireland's capital, Belfast. As resource, natural sanctuary and source of recreation, it is not to be expected that they have been neglected. In high summer they are noisy and crowded and the roads can choke with traffic. Newcastle has more yardage of amusement arcade – 'the machines' – than any town of like size I know. The mountains attract many, but as the air gets thinner the number of people reduces drastically. To throw them off altogether requires great effort and a good deal of luck, and the best hope lies among that exclusive brotherhood of peaks which rise close to Newcastle.

Most of these peaks are linked by a great wall, 22 miles (35 kilometres) long by six feet (two metres) or more high and a yard or so wide. It was built early this century to enclose the so-called Silent Valley, which was then dammed to create the reservoir which supplies most of the county's, and much of Belfast's, water needs: an artefact, but a beautiful one, reflecting the reeds and shrubs and steep mountain-sides as they slide into its depths. But the finest sights come high on the mountains themselves. There are cliffs and chimneys and natural keeps of broken granite, easy slopes and demanding climbs, including sheer rock faces for those who cannot resist them, and stunning views which change rapidly from seascape to landscape, from rock to pasture, from Scotland to what seems like an unfurled map of all Ireland.

'Men of wisdom love the sea,' said Bertrand Russell; 'men of virtue love the mountains.' With a shore like that of the Murlough reserve nearby, I find my virtue soon crumbles and I am down at sea-level, standing or crouching to look at the flurry of bird life along the beaches and within the dunes. The population changes markedly with every season, for an enormous number of birds, from swans to midget passerines, breed or winter or pause for breath here on long migrations. The regular sandpipers, dunlins, scoters, mallards and others have often seemed to me to share local qualities. Quick, smart, clean-living, hard-working, they flock and bustle over sand and water with what seems like a palpable, Protestant sense of purpose.

THE CATTLE RAID OF COOLEY

The beautiful, red-cloaked and rather martial Maeve was married to King Ailill of Connacht, whose palace was at Rathcroghan in County Roscommon. She and her husband kept separate herds of cattle and one day her famous white-horned bull, unwilling to belong to a mere woman, abandoned Maeve's herd for her husband's. She decided to make good the loss by acquiring the peerless Brown Bull of Cooley (or Cuailgne, now known as Carlingford, in County Louth). She asked the owner for it, offering to sleep with him in return. He turned her down and she went to war. The consequent prolonged invasion was known as the Cattle Raid of Cooley, or *Tain Bo Cuailgne*. It is considered the *Iliad* of Irish myth.

When Maeve's Connacht forces invaded, the men of Ulster were laid low by a mysterious, recurrent sleeping sickness. Only the youthful Cuchulain was fit to fight, but he was remarkable even by heroic standards. To cool his ardour, for instance, three tubs were filled with ice-cold water and he was placed in each consecutively. The first burst asunder. The second boiled. The third got hot. He could contort his face into almost any shape. He could turn around within his skin, so that his feet and hands were behind and his back and buttocks before him. In the war in question he took up position in strategic places and killed a hundred and more invaders a day. But such efforts took their toll. Even when he was covered with so many wounds that there was not a needlepoint of intact skin left on him, he propped himself up on a pillar-stone, strapped himself to it and fought on. Before the Connacht men killed him the other Ulstermen rallied from their torpor, and took on the fight. The image of Cuchulain dying for freedom remains potent, and was an acknowledged inspiration to those who rose against British rule in 1916.

BEFORE YOU GO
Maps: OSNI Discoverer Series map No. 29.

GETTING THERE
By air: nearest airports are Belfast International and Belfast City.
By car: take the A24 to Dundrum and then the A2 to Newcastle. To skirt the mountains, follow the coastal route along the A2. To enter the range, drive through Tollymore Forest Park or Dollard Wood.
By rail: to Newry for Carlingford Lough. Belfast–Newry service runs 5–6 times per day Mon–Sat and takes 1 hour. Sunday service is very limited.
By bus: frequent service to Newry on weekdays, very limited on Sunday; journey time 1 hour 10 mins. Buses to Newcastle are more frequent and take 1 hour 20 mins.

WHERE TO STAY
Hotels: free accommodation booking service for any of the numerous bed and breakfasts is available at Newry Tourist Office, T:(01693) 848666. Hotels include the Glassdrumman Lodge at Annalong, T:(013967) 68451, the Portaferry Hotel, which overlooks Strangford Lough, T:(012477) 28231, and the Strangford Arms Hotel, Newtownards, T:(01247) 814141.
Outdoor living: for caravan-site bookings at Rostrevor, Newcastle or Castlewellan call the Forestry Division, T:(01232) 520100
Youth hostels: Newcastle Youth Hostel, T:(013967) 22133.

ACTIVITIES
Walking: abundant, all levels of difficulty. For guided walks June–Aug, T:(013967) 24059, or try the Burrendale Hotel at Newcastle, T:(013967) 22599. See also the NITB walking guides Nos 3 and 6.
Fishing: there are coarse-angling events in May at Newry Canal, which has bream, perch, pike and roach (bank-side fishing only). For group bookings contact Newry and Mourne District Council, Greenbank, Warrenpoint Road, Newry BT34 2QU, T:(01693) 67226.
Sailing: the Carlingford Lough Regatta is in Sept; contact local NITB for further information.
Bird-watching: contact Lough Neagh Tourism, T:(01849) 463113, and Strangford Lough Tourism, T:(01247) 812215; Ebbtide Bird-watching Breaks, T:(01247) 883348, organize short breaks, staying in farm and country houses.

FURTHER INFORMATION
Tollymore Forest Park, Tullybrannigan Road, Newcastle, T:(013967) 22428, has wildlife and forestry exhibitions, and organized walks. Newry Tourist Office, T:(01693) 848666, at the BP Service Station, is open in summer.

Lough Neagh

The largest lake in Ireland and the UK, much exploited for private and commercial fishing along its usually low and often marshy banks

Lough Neagh jangles with records and distinctions like a banana-state field-marshal with medals. It is by far the largest lake in Ireland or Britain, about ten miles by six (sixteen kilometres by nine), receives the flow of six major rivers, drains 42 per cent of Northern Ireland's surface. Rich in plants, animals and birds, it provides up to 100,000 wildfowl with winter quarters, and yields 700 tonnes of eel to fishermen every year: the biggest eel-haul in Western Europe. Nearly a third of Northern Ireland's homes get their water from it. The water it contains could fill somewhere in the region of seven million swimming pools.

You may glimpse or come on Lough Neagh from all over the place. A bit east of centre of the province, it adjoins five of the six counties: a huge flat sheet filling the hole left – so the myth says – by the handful of mud Finn McCool, in a rage, grabbed and threw into the sea, to form, as it happened, the Isle of Man. Geology tells a different story. Repeated disgorgements of molten basalt from the depths of Northern Ireland up to about 50 million years ago left huge cavities below. The crust sagged and slowly sank, in all by some 1,200 feet (350 metres). As it did so the resultant depression was partially filled by clays, sand and plant debris brought in by rivers. Surveys of recent years have shown that much of the plant matter has been converted into lignite, a form of fuel that could be described as peat on its way to coal; consequently the lake is under threat from proposed surface mines and power stations, with the pollution these would involve. The overlying water of the lake is relatively shallow: on average about 30 feet (9 metres) and nowhere deeper than 100 (30 metres).

Lough Neagh scenery is not sensational. Engaging with the lough always means focussing down from its broad national significance to little intimate encounters. It can be approached from any number of places and almost everywhere, in mild weather, there will be trees, pasture, marsh, reedy shallows, tethered boats and the slap and slop of desultory water toying with the shore. At Shane's Castle in the north-east corner there is a medieval keep and a row of cannon on the terrace over the water, bird-watching from battlements, and a narrow-gauge steam railway running through lakeside woods. At Gartree to the east is a lone and ancient church, marooned on an airfield. To the west, Ardboe offers a 30-foot (9-metre) rise, pleasant views, and a village of charm. You can swim anywhere.

The true wildness of Lough Neagh is, of course, inaccessibly on or invisibly under the water. A rich growth of algae supports all the teeming life, which in turn feeds a large population of fish. Eel – poor reward for their toiling from the Sargasso – are caught, on autumn nights, on mile-long, thousand-hook lines. Pollan (*Coregonus pollan*), fresh water cousin of the herring, is unique to the lake, while rudd, roach and perch abound, as do pike, those stubborn gourmands that have been seen to swallow fish of their own

A summer visitor from Africa, the common tern breeds in colonies on little islands all round the coast of Ireland, as well as in some inland waters, its excitable screeching belying the exquisite grace of its form and flight.

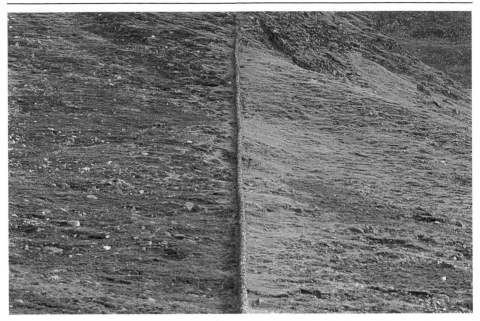

The massive 22-mile (35-km) dry-stone granite wall bounding the catchment area of the Silent Valley reservoir was built early in the twentieth century to keep out animals. Grazed and ungrazed land displays conspicuous differences, despite incursions by some persistent, gap-searching sheep.

size and take three days doing it. A particularly giant variety of greedy pike is found in nearby Lough Beg. But the stars of the lake, as so often in Ireland, are the birds. Oxford Island National Nature Reserve is one of several well placed for sighting great rafts of diving ducks in winter. Abundantly present throughout the year is that flat-capped dandy the great crested grebe, who despite his rakish appearance becomes a dedicated feeder of his family as they grow. Three kinds of swan frequent the lake, and in winter graze on neighbouring pastures. From a distance they can look like flocks of sheep.

BEFORE YOU GO
Maps: OSNI Discoverer Series maps Nos 14, 19 and 20.

GETTING THERE
By car: for access to Shane's Castle and the north-east side of the lough, take the M2 from Belfast to Antrim. For access to Oxford Island and the south-east of the lough take the M1 out of Belfast to junction 10.
By rail: frequent weekday and limited Sunday service from Belfast Central to Antrim, journey time 45 mins. Trains to Lurgan are frequent throughout the week.
By bus: Goldline Express Service runs buses to Antrim (journey time 35 mins, every hour except on Sundays). A slower, stopping bus runs more frequently throughout the week. All buses go from Oxford Street Bus Station. There is also a Goldline Express service to Lurgan which takes 40 mins. Before setting off, beware the infrequency of late-evening buses, and be sure to check return times.

WHERE TO STAY
Numerous bed and breakfasts in Antrim, Moneymore and Moira, as well as caravan parks. Forest Caravan Park at Drum Manor Forest Park, Cookstown – contact Forest Service for details, T:(016487) 62774 – and lakeside caravan sites at Antrim, Oxford Island and Ballyronan.

ACTIVITIES
Fishing: game fishing, especially bream and pike in rivers; eels at Toomebridge. Coney Island on south side of lough good for angling and canoeing. Seagrove Cup fishing festival held Nov. Kinnego Marina best May–July for bream, hybrids, perch, roach and rudd. Contact Paddy Prunty at Craigavon Borough Council, T:(01762) 327573.

Walking: the shores of Lough Neagh are sedgy and wooded. You should park and approach the shore on foot.
Boating: boats can be hired from Oxford Island, T:(01762) 322205, Antrim (contact Tourist Office, The Forum, T:(01849) 463113), Coney

Island and Ballyronan.
Bird-watching: from Shane's Castle and Lough Beg. Great crested grebes, herons, breeding corncrakes and a large variety of other water and land birds, along with hides, information and audio-visual displays, at Oxford Island National Nature

Reserve, T:(01762) 322205.
Riding: facilities at Richill Riding Centre, Course Lodge, 38 Annareagh Road, Richill BT61 9JT, T:(01762) 871258.

FURTHER INFORMATION
Tourist offices: at the Forum, Antrim, T:(01849) 463113.

Strangford Lough

This sea lough, sprinkled with drumlin islands, is of enormous importance for wildlife both within its waters and along its mostly flat and muddy shoreline

Strangford Lough is a sea lough but, instead of opening into the sea by means of a broad splay of estuary, it is connected by a long and relatively thin neck, some five miles (eight kilometres) long and at one point only 500 yards (460 metres) wide. Twice a day, when the tide has started moving in, the level of water in the sea is higher than that in the lough. Twice a day it is the other way round. Either way the pressure on the water to even up the levels is immense. On its way in it charges through – all 400 million tons of it – and only gradually, as it spreads along the 15 or so miles (24 kilometres) of the lough proper, rounding islands and filling channels and bays, does it settle to serenity. In next to no time it is moving out again.

The wash of water over any particular corner of the lough is likely to be different in force and effect from that in another. That is one of the factors giving Strangford Lough its enormous biological variety. Another is the fact that, although most of its bed and shores are based on carboniferous limestone, the erosion of other kinds of rock, mainly at the northern end, feeds the waters round about with a varied diet of minerals. More comes from the rivers it receives, the Quoile, Comber and Blackwater. In spite of the million or so people living within a few miles, the lough has not been irredeemably exploited or polluted.

The lough bottom tells much. Unlike the bed of the sea, scraped, grazed and heavily depleted by fishing, it teems with life. Huge carpets of stationary horse mussels provide a firm foundation for other species to settle on, a weird tapestry of things that squirt or sting or squelch: sea anemones, sea squirts, sea gooseberries, scallops, feather stars, sponges, worms, snails, crabs, sand-eels, jelly fish. The intertidal edge is rich in bladderwrack, tangle and other seaweeds. As often, the main and most visible beneficiaries of this abundance are the birds. Like so many of the waters of Ireland, Strangford supports crucial populations of certain species. Most of the world's pale-bellied brent geese pass through Strangford on their way to other coastal sites in Ireland, and the long shoreline and wealth of islands encourage waders and dabblers. The lough is never without great numbers of birds. Not the least conspicuous are the four species of breeding tern: common, sandwich, arctic (the bird world's longest distance migrant, from Arctic to Antarctic) and roseate. With their long wings, split tails and balletic motions – for fishing or display terns are among the world's most graceful birds, though they leave a different impression when they dive at humans who get too close to their barely concealed eggs, and warn them off with Billingsgate menaces.

Common seals breed on Strangford Lough in large numbers – possibly the largest numbers in Ireland. Grey seals and porpoises are here too. The surrounding countryside is flat and heavily cultivated, but there are fine houses and estates and remains (Castle Stewart, Castleward, Killyeagh, Grey Abbey), and associations with St Patrick at and around Downpatrick. Saul, a mile or two to the east, is held to be the place the saint landed to begin the conversion of Ireland to Christianity in AD 432.

The curlew may be seen – and its plangent call heard – in any part of Ireland, summer and winter. Most of its food is worms, taken from deep in the sand or soil by its extraordinarily long bill.

BEFORE YOU GO
Maps: OSNI Discoverer Series maps Nos 15 and 21.

GETTING THERE
By car: from Belfast take the A20 to Newtownards and on down the east shore to Portaferry; or the A22 to Comber and Downpatrick.
By rail: the nearest station is Bangor, Co. Down. You then have to catch a bus.
By bus: frequent bus services run to Newtownards and Comber throughout the week. Services are less frequent to Downpatrick (especially Sundays). Change at Newtownards for Portaferry.

WHERE TO STAY
Portaferry Hotel, T:(012477) 28231. Self-catering is available at Bangor, Killyleagh, Portaferry and Downpatrick. Barnholm Youth Hostel is in Portaferry, T:(012477) 29598.

ACTIVITIES
Walking: an organized 34-mile (55-km) route called Lecale Trail starts in Downpatrick. For details call Down District Council, T:(01396) 610800. The NITB guide to walking contains a 7-mile (11-km) walk along St Patrick's Way starting and ending in Saul village.
Bird-watching: there are well-placed hides around the lough; contact Castle Espie Wildfowl Centre, T:(01247) 874146.
Riding: try Leitrim Farm Stables, Loughries Road, BT23 3RN, T:(01247) 811935, as well as Saintfield, 126 Monlough Road, BT24 7EU, T:(01238) 510141.
Sailing: Galway Hookers Regatta is held in Portaferry, end of June, and features traditional boats.

FURTHER INFORMATION
Tourist offices: NITB have lists of approved accommodation. Try Bangor, T:(01247) 270069, Newtownards, T:(01247) 812215, or Newry, T:(01693) 67226.

Glens of Antrim

Series of nine glens cutting seaward and mostly eastward across the high plateau of north-east Antrim, containing several large nature reserves. Linked by a spectacular coast road

Here and there the narrow road rises and falls like a roller-coaster, though to drive as if it were one would be foolish because cars come the other way too. At its highest points the road comes level with the boggy plateau of heather and grass that sprawls over much of north-east Antrim.

The dips cross the coastal outlets of glens which have run down, west to east, from plateau to sea. The up-down succession, all the way along the east and north coasts of County Antrim, offers, on a good day, some of the grandest scenery in the world. Scotland, as little as 12 miles (19 kilometres) away, contributes the changing facets of the Mull of Kintyre, the Paps of Jura, the island of Islay and some smaller islets. Off Antrim's north coast, Rathlin Island is another landmark whose aspect changes as you go. Near you, on the mainland, cliffs and slopes jagged like broken glass tumble to a sea that matches sunshine with a rich turquoise smile. At times I feel that at some undiscovered phase of our evolution we were giants with a highly developed frolicsome side, because rolling down the curved hills or pirouetting on the pinnacles or plunging into the blue seems such a desirable and obvious thing to do.

The Scottish connection – the accent, the strong Presbyterian presence (about 50 per cent in this part), the traditional thrift and homely virtues – is a physical presence here. A boat and a breeze would see you in Scotland sooner than a horse and cart could take you to Belfast. Every inch of this territory has a historic or mythical link with Scotland: royal incursions, clan vendettas, marriages, treaties, conquest. As long ago as the Roman withdrawal from Britain the Irish established toeholds in Scotland, as they did in Wales and on Man, set up colonies, and energetically evangelized the local populations.

But that was in the recent past. The first people arrived as soon as the last mile-thick blanket of ice receded and melted. Innumerable remains found at the base of bogs show that Mesolithic hunters were here 12,000 years ago, before the peat even started to form. There is something tremendously ancient and seasoned in this countryside, and every bank, ditch, runnel and tussock may be a clue to some past human activity, the way life was lived, animals killed, habitations built, food prepared.

Ancient is a relative term. Ireland's oldest rocks have been in place 250,000 times longer than the period of human occupation. The rocks of Antrim include the country's youngest but they are also the most varied – possibly the most varied in Europe – and for the geologist as well as the traveller the place is a paradise. The bed-rock of most of the county is basalt (see Giant's Causeway, p. 210) but along the coast, and especially in the north-east corner, landslips and settlements have exposed carboniferous sandstones, shales, old red sandstone, broken seams of trias and lias, and chalk. There are curious tree fossils from the Carboniferous period, layers of coal, boulder clay smeared by the ice across the basalt blanket, and flints, contained in the chalk and formed from silica. These were of great use, as innumerable remains show, to our earliest ancestors.

Such rocks underlie also the soils of the glens, with their broad scooped floors and steep hanging sides. Formed first by rivers wearing through surface basalt, these descending valleys were expanded and rounded by the slow and intransigent dynamic of the glacial ice into their present dimensions. Narrow, wooded (sometimes with forestry Sitkas) and cut by thin white waterfalls in their upper reaches, they unfurl lower down to provide rich alluvial soils for farmers and to frame rounded views of Scotland beyond the sea. But the glens themselves, for all the attractions of sheep, tufted banks, gurgling rivulets, lichened stone walls and evocative abandoned farmhouses beside their protective groves of pine and beech, are not wild. The wilderness is on the inland heights.

It is unfortunately hard to resist the suspicion that the Garron plateau, some 50 undulating square miles (130 square kilometres) spreading south-west from Garron Point, is the largest area without tracks in Northern Ireland because there is little reason, certainly in the aesthetic line, for crossing it. Wild ponies do, and they are interesting. There are a lot of birds. But these occur elsewhere. Romantics might see a kind of Wuthering Heights appeal in ominous weathers, but even they will recognize that the Antrim uplands tend to be desolate and featureless, hard and soggy by turn, unrewarding. They are seriously upstaged by the dramas of the nearby coast.

Even here, by the sea, there are problems. Indeed, the better the scenery the worse the problem. Murlough Bay is one of the great sights of the north coast, but it is the fate of great sights, especially those consigned to the National Trust, to be tamed to order and predictability. So this steep, bumpy terrain, bristling with rocky outcrops, and falling to a beach in a bay with stony islands, is impaled on a zigzag road which swells into a car park halfway down. The custodian's cottage is suburban-neat. You might have to meet deer and other wildlife by appointment: there is no other way. Individuals and traffic need control. By and large the control is sensible. I am standing aside and moaning for a world gone by.

It is, besides, only in the best-known sites

that the intrusions are seen and felt. Apart from Murlough and Fair Head and the world-famous spectacles to the west of Ballycastle, you can walk the whole coast of Antrim with scarcely more than a signpost to tell you humans have passed this way before. Knocklayd, a mighty if slightly bland mountain south of Ballycastle, is an easy climb with colossal views accumulating as you go. For the bird-watcher the whole daunting stretch of uplands can make walks worthwhile. Curlews nest there, along with a few, a very few, golden plovers, red grouse, black-headed gulls and redshanks. At Fair Head, to match its awesome structures, several birds of prey have bred in recent years: sparrowhawks, kestrels, buzzards, but also the rarer peregrine falcon.

BEFORE YOU GO
Maps: OSNI Discoverer Series map No. 9.

GETTING THERE
By car: the A2 from Belfast to Ballycastle runs along the coast as far as Cushendun and crosses the seaward end of all the glens. For a sampling drive, go up Glenarm and come down Glenariff a few miles north. The coast road beyond Cushendun, passing Torr Head and Fair Head, is not too wide and very steep and bendy but provides breathtaking views.
By rail: there is no train to Ballycastle, but there are regular trains to Ballymena, Larne, Portrush and Coleraine.
By bus: there is no direct bus to Ballycastle from Belfast; change at Ballymena. The Belfast–Ballymena service is frequent but the link to Ballycastle is very limited and should be checked in advance. Call Belfast Bus Station, T:(01232) 337015. Alternatively you could catch an Antrim Coaster bus which runs along the scenic coastal route, T:(01232) 333000 for inquiries. This service does not operate on Sundays and is very often restricted during the rest of the week.

WHERE TO STAY
Hotels: the Londonderry Arms at Carnlough, Harbour Road, BT44 0EU, T:(01574) 885255; Magheramorne House, Larne, BT40 3HW, T:(01574) 279444.
Outdoor living: details of caravan parks are available from tourist information centres.
Youth hostels: Cushendall Youth Hostel, T:(012667) 71344.

ACTIVITIES
Fishing: Fair Head to Garron Point for plaice and dab. Sea- and river-angling at Ballycastle: codling, plaice, small coalfish and whiting. Sea-fishing boats, tackle and bait at Red Bay Boats, Coast Road, Cushendall, T:(012667) 71331.
Walking: in order to walk round Fair Head (Walk No. 9 in the NITB guide), park at Murlough car park.
Bird-watching: at Fair Head there may be buzzard, kestrel, peregrine, sparrow-hawk, chough and twite. At Murlough Bay there are eider, fulmar and buzzard. At Larne Lough/Swan Island there are pale-bellied brent geese in the winter and common and Sandwich terns in the summer, along with red-breasted merganser.

A sunset silhouette of muscular oak branches stands out against the lake in Castlewellan Forest Park a few miles north of the Mournes.

Riding: Watertop Trekking Centre, 188 Cushendall Road, Ballycastle, T:(012657) 62576. At Islandmagee (Larne), try the Ashfield Riding Centre, 9 Middle Road, T:(01960) 372609.

FURTHER INFORMATION
Tourist offices: Larne Tourist Information Centre is at St Thomas Dixon Buildings, Victoria Road, Larne BT40 IRU, T:(01574) 260088; Moyle District Council, Ballycastle, T:(012657) 62024, can also supply information on accommodation. Glenariff Forest Park is on A43 Ballymena–Waterfoot road, T:(012667) 58232.

Rathlin Island

The shape of an inverted 'L', its cliffs and stacks are important for breeding sea-birds

Crossing to Rathlin you can feel you are within a Gaelic archipelago, with Scotland on the right, Ireland behind and the island ahead. Kintyre, Islay, Jura, and Argyll, kingdom of the eastern Gael, are out of sight to the north. There to your left is the Giant's Causeway, which (in legend at least) carries on submerged to Scotland, where it re-emerges as Fingal's Cave. You hear Scottish accents. And you recall Robert the Bruce, pondering his defeats and exile in a cave in the north-east of the island until the famous imperturbable spider he observed repeatedly trying to spin a web inspires him to go back and fight his English enemies.

I do not know whether arachnologists make pilgrimages to the place, or whether Rathlin spiders are otherwise special. There are plenty of caves. There are delightful plants: various of the more common orchids, thyme, broomrape (*Orobanche alba*), and the arum-like fern Adder's tongue (*Ophioglossum vulgatum*). Most of all there are birds: on occasion distinct rarities like golden eagles and sea eagles. Peregrines have bred in recent years. The general run of sea-birds is well represented. Even on the journey across the water (which, by the way, is noted for turbulence, with currents and winds funnelled through the sound) there may be Manx shearwater, and there are certainly common scoter and velvet scoter. Sometimes gannets – another Scottish connection – make a day trip from Ailsa Craig in the Firth of Clyde. The best, however, is yet to come.

Rathlin is a fine, hilly island with a bloody history and interesting remains, including a Neolithic factory for making tools out of porcellanite, a rare mineral of extreme hardness. It is four miles (six km) long and one mile and upwards wide, the shape of a sock, as someone pointed out in Tudor times, with the toe on the east, pointing at Ireland. Most of it is rich pasture, the soil based on the same basalt that covers the mainland opposite, though the underlying chalk is exposed on the south coast, around the harbour. About a hundred people live here. Vast and beautiful views open out to Malin Head (in Donegal), Fair Head, Torr Head and Scotland. The seas yield crayfish and lobsters to the two families that live by them, and a great deal more fish to big trawlers from Killybegs and from Scotland. But you would need to be a keen ornithologist to make the forty-minute crossing from Ballycastle.

In spite of the shearwater and scoter, and the ducks on scattered lakes, nothing is quite as spectacular as the stacks. A five-mile (eight-kilometre) walk or (in summer) bus-ride west along the bending, winding road from the harbour brings you close to Bull Point. Here there is a sudden cessation of green field and a plummeting drop to, on one side, a lighthouse, and on the other, what suggests to me an avian opera house in perpetual, chaotic rehearsal for the big night. Far below is this huge, sheer, three-walled natural auditorium facing the sea. Countless sea-birds are tucked into niches, ledges, shelves and hollows, sometimes watching the activity in front of them, sometimes turned to the wall as if to protest at the prima donna. Others are speeding here and there with or without the appearance of a sense of purpose. The composite noise is of a high-decibel level, and much of it comes from what might be seen as the stage, two huge cylinders of black basalt diminishing in girth by stages as they rise from the sea, like tiered wedding-cakes, on which perch and screech and fidget and ovulate and defecate thousand upon thousand of the birds which always make such formations their own: gull, kittiwake, puffin and fulmar but predominantly razorbill (up to 9,000 of them) and not dissimilar guillemot (up to 40,000 in total), whose formal black coats and white waistcoats are very suggestive of a smart but anarchic orchestra. There is no conductor. Nothing seems to begin or end. To me and innumerable others this is, notwithstanding, one of the greatest shows on earth.

Along about two and a half miles (four km) of cliffs stretching north from the stacks (and managed and owned by the RSPB) there are breeding black guillemot, puffin, Manx shearwater, fulmar and five kinds of gull. Eider duck breed in the south-east of the island, and the meadows, marshes and lakes support good populations of characteristic birds.

Before you go: OSNI Discoverer Series map No. 5.

Getting there: daily crossings from Ballycastle, all year round, 10.30 am returning at 4 pm, T:(012657) 63934.

Where to stay: Rathlin Guesthouse, T:(012657) 63916; Manor House, T:(012657) 63920. Camping in demesne on Mill Bay just to right of harbour, past post office. Nearest youth hostel is Whitepark Bay, T:(012657) 31745.

Activities *Bird-watching:* the island's cliffs are home to tens of thousands of sea-birds. Best place to see them is the Kebble Nature Reserve (also known as Rathlin Island Bird Sanctuary) at the west end of the island, near lighthouse, T:(012657) 63935. Manor House (see above) runs nature and bird-watching breaks.

Scuba-diving: is possible off the coast of the island, where there are many wrecks and scenic drops; contact Richard Branson Activity Centre, T:(012657) 63971.

Fishing: for conger eels in Church Bay, around wreck of WWI cruiser *The Drake*; pollack at Rue Point. Off-shore good for cod, haddock, skate and other big fish. Sharks have been reported north of the island. Deep-sea angling boats can be hired at Ballycastle (see below for NITB phone number), Portrush and Portstewart.

Further information: Ballycastle Tourist Office is at 7 Mary Street, Ballycastle BT54 6QH, T:(012657) 62024/62225.

THE IDEA OF THE WILD

Until three centuries ago a publisher would have had what some Ulster Irish call 'a wee bit of a want' to attempt to market books about the wild. Wilderness was the enemy, the abode of the evil, weird and scary. If demons did not get you, highwaymen would. It was the tamed things like gardens that were lovesome. Landscapes painted by Poussin and Claude bathed their mountains and forests in ethereal light and garrisoned them with columned temples and vigilante statues. The Picturesque – an orderly marriage of nature and art – held sway through much of the eighteenth century. Towards the end, romance and gothicism were moving into art and literature. In stories and painting the appeal of the untamed, the farouche, the unexplained and unamenable continually grew. Thunder, lightning and clouds splashed landscapes; a sea was not a sea if breakers were not hurling ships against rocks. People loved all this. But they tended to love it only within book covers, or in oils and on their drawing-room walls.

The Lake poets – Wordsworth and Coleridge above all – are credited with making the wild physically desirable at the beginning of the nineteenth century. They actually climbed the Westmorland hills and wrote prose and poetry that reproduced nature's effects in a wholly attractive and appetizing way. Already people were dunking themselves in the sea (albeit from wagon-style bathing machines) for pleasure. The formation of a national police force reduced outdoor risks from cut-throats and robbers. Other aspects of the great outdoors became apparent. The English, leading the movement, discovered the Alps and started inventing things to do on them. They and others penetrated deep into regions of Africa, Asia and America, finding infinite reserves of what seemed to them exotic wilderness, even if to native populations they were just home. Back in Europe, trains enabled people to get out of grimy cities for therapeutic sojourns on coasts, islands, rivers and mountains. Bicycles have made wild nature more accessible still. Advances in geology and biology added intriguing dimensions to the elements of the wild.

Nowadays things have come full circle. Humanity builds, bombs, lays roads, drains here and floods there, leaves empty cans and cigarette packs on the summit of Carrantuohill, and discards bags, clothes and even corpses on the side of Everest. Instead of our cowering at the thought of the wild, the wild has good reason to fear humanity and its insouciance.

Giant's Causeway

On the north coast of County Antrim, thousands of hexagons, a foot or two across, of columnar basalt, form an uneven floor under tall cliffs

This is nature's work; no doubt about that. But wild it is not allowed to be. It is far too grand and strange to be passed by, yet the effect it had on travellers up to fifty years ago and less is not to be had now. The main road you arrive by is so luxuriously tarmacked it feels sprung. By the car park (and thus close to the causeway display centre, the bookshop, the cafeteria, the hotel, the school museum) a National Trust notice pithily spells out your options: 'Starting here, you may choose from four

---

A trefoil flourishes beside a stream in Glenariff Forest Park, County Antrim. A number of trefoils and other plants have been claimed as shamrock, but since the word simply means clover without identifying a particular species, any could be worn without fear of error on St Patrick's Day.

walks along National Trust paths.' No more, you understand, and no less. There is also a National Trust bus that runs along the National Trust road every ten minutes in season. Here and there, National Trust notices deflect, warn, prohibit, advise. You cannot hope to experience the sense of the sublime our ancestors felt two hundred years ago, once they had overcome the fear of coming here at all. They were thrilled and chilled. They painted pictures which exaggerated the dramas, steepened the cliffs, enlarged the bluffs, puffed up the overhangs, raised the waves, darkened the skies, deepened the sunset, dropped in a shipwreck or two. We go the other way, making so much of the artificial that nature pales into the background, or staying timidly within the frame of a bus or café window.

All the same, more here was made by nature than by the National Trust. The so-called causeway, and the coast to the east of it, round Benbane Head, consist of a series of rocky bays with steep grassy or rocky slopes on the landward side, and, every so often, what seems like an inner skeleton of dark bones showing through. These are more or less vertical clusters of rock piping, each pipe usually of six sides and fitting, as in a honeycomb, tightly against its neighbours. At Benbane Head itself these shafts are fully exposed and rise to the full height of the cliffs. On the seaward side irregular tracts of worn or crushed columns jut out into the water, forming pavements of six-sided flagstones you can walk on. The biggest of these is the Giant's Causeway. The myth says that it was built by Finn McCool, one of the towering heroes of Irish myth, and

continued (and still does, underwater) as far as Fingal's Cave on Staffa, off the Scottish coast, where the columns reappear.

In fact, the causeway is the result of the welling-up of basaltic lava, which overran the prevailing limestone and has in time been eroded, split and stripped by slips and by the relative changes in the levels of land and sea. The hexagon is the form the lava takes on cooling; the slower the cooling, the broader the column. Horizontal stripes of paler rock show that long periods of slow sedimentary rock-building intervened in the build-up of basalt, which lasted in all some 15 million years, coming to an end 50 million years ago.

Before you go *Maps:* OSNI Discoverer Series map No. 5.
Getting there *By car:* from Coleraine take 129 to Portrush, A2 through Bushmills and then B146.
By rail: change at Coleraine for Portrush.
By bus: direct summer service to Portrush.
Where to stay: Auberge de Seneirl, T:(012657) 41536, Bushmills Inn, T:(012657) 32339. Caravan sites and self-catering in Bushmills and Portrush.
Activities *Walking:* NITB guide suggests walk from Portballintrae to Carrick-a-Rede.
Fishing: game fishing on local rivers.
Bird-watching: buzzard, kestrel, peregrine, sparrow-hawk, occasional black and common guillemots, razorbill, eider duck, chough and twite.
Horse-riding: at Ballymoney, T:(012656) 65500.
Further information: available from Portrush Countryside Centre, T:(01265) 823600; also Causeway Safari Park, Ballymoney, T:(01265) 741474.

Sperrin Mountains

A sprawling mountain range of forest and wild moorland; wooded plains and innumerable streams attract fishermen and gold prospectors

Halfway up the glen, between sea and an endless plateau of moorland, the Glenariff Forest Park is a kingdom of steep, lush and copiously watered woodland.

The Sperrins, in Tyrone, which is probably Ireland's least-known county, are, I suspect, the country's least-known mountain range. The highest peak, Sawel, is at 2,240 feet (670 metres) only two-thirds the height of Ireland's highest, and close to what Lloyd Praeger called, with crisp disparagement, 'the usual Irish height'. There are no spiky cones or vertical rock-sheets or leprous crags or deep dark corries, and hardly any lakes. Mountains have assumed the genteel shape of the open umbrella, more or less. But there are towering views from the heights, and long picturesque rambles (the walkers and writers Wilson and Gilbert offer an 18-mile/29-kilometre route that stays above 1,000 feet/300 metres) and pretty, peripheral wooded glens. Sawel's summit presents you, for the small cost of turning full circle, with the highlands of Donegal, Fermanagh, Cavan, the Mournes, the Antrim plateau and the steep escarpment of the Binevenagh range to the north. There is a great deal of blanket bog, above what might be called the farmhouse line.

The Sperrin mountains occupy a slightly curved area (swelling southward) about 30 miles (48 kilometres) west to east and 10 (16 kilometres), more or less, north to south. They consist in the main of schists and gneisses, ancient metamorphic rocks blown apart by eruptions of igneous matter which has since eroded away. The River Glenelly, with a good road beside it, forms a rough southern boundary. Neat and kempt and steep-sided, with the odd wooden house, it looks rather Swiss. To the east, between Draperstown and Dungiven, there are dull dark miles of forestry plantation. The western edge slides down to the Mourne river, which runs into Lough Foyle at Derry, and

the northern edge is broken by streams and wooded glens. It all makes for a quiet landscape in which to take a quiet pleasure.

The kestrel, hen harrier, peregrine, raven, long-eared owl and low-flying woodcock are sometimes to be seen in the Sperrins, and curlews and a very few golden plovers breed here. Waders winter on the flood plains to the north of Strabane. There is also a plant which occurs nowhere else in Ireland, although it abounds in parts of England, Scotland and Norway: the cloud berry (*Rubus chamaemorus*). Found in a few scattered patches of the high moorland, it is an arctic plant, with a distinctive orange fruit formed like that of its cousin the blackberry. It seems to have thrived during Ice Ages. For some centuries it has survived more by vegetative than sexual reproduction, a sign, perhaps, that it is out of kilter with the climate. The fruit, consequently, is even rarer than the plant.

There is gold in them thaar hills. Not much, and very localized, but there nevertheless, among the head-waters of the Foyle system near Plumbridge. Gold helped to make Ireland rich 2,000 years ago and more. It was made into brooches and other ornaments and exported to Rome and its empire, along with dogs and pottery. Wicklow was the main source (see pages 186–87) but some may have come from Tyrone.

Locals have gone a long way to augment the appeal of their mountains. There are centres with all the usual aids for taking in the nature and culture of the Sperrins and their surrounds; being so out of the way, the area is relatively rich in folklore. Over the years turf-cutting has exposed innumerable remains of Mesolithic and Neolithic inhabitants. At Beaghmore, on the western slopes of Beleevnamore mountain, south of the Glenelly valley, finds have been particularly rich. They include, from the 1930s, a series of seven stone circles, most of the stones being two or three feet tall.

For visitors to the Sperrins, places to stay are plentiful but distant, most of them in the surrounding towns of Dungiven, Draperstown, Cookstown, Strabane and Omagh. Earlier in the century, Praeger had to share a five-foot bed with his botanical colleague, both of them over six foot, with their feet sticking out of the window, in the only cottage with rooms to hire. In the morning hens were roosting on their toes.

BEFORE YOU GO
Maps: OSNI Discoverer Series maps Nos 7, 8, 12 and 13.
Guidebooks: *The Big Walks, Challenging Walks and Scrambles in the British Isles* by Ken Wilson and Richard Gilbert (Diadem, 1981).
GETTING THERE
By car: take the M2 out of

Other birds try, and up to a point succeed, but the kestrel is the only bird in Ireland that has mastered the art of hovering, while it quarters the ground for prey. It is found year-round in all parts of the country, and is no stranger to towns. It sometimes nests on tall buildings.

Belfast, join the A6 and then the A31 for Magherafelt. From Magherafelt you can drive straight through the Sperrin mountains on the B40, B41 and B47.
By rail: there are no trains to either Magherafelt or Cookstown. The nearest station is Portadown.
By bus: you can get a bus to Magherafelt or Cookstown, remembering that the Sunday service is limited.

WHERE TO STAY
There are bed and breakfasts in Cookstown, Omagh, Strabane and Draperstown.
Self-catering: Lough Beg Coach Houses, Ballyscullion Park, Bellaghy BT45 8NA, T:(01648) 386235.
Youth hostels: Glenhordial Youth Hostel, near Omagh, T:(01662) 241973.
Outdoor living: there are forest caravan parks at Learmount, Parkanaur and Drum Manor.

WHERE TO GO
En route from either Cookstown or Magherafelt it is well worth stopping at Slieve Gullion, a beautiful mountain surrounded by smaller hills which are collectively known as the Gullion Ring Dyke. If you take the B162 from Cookstown you will pass the outer ring of mountains and can drive straight on to the Sperrins. Slieve Gullion Forest Park is on T:(016937) 38284. Sperrin Heritage Centre, Cranagh, at which you can pan for gold, is on the B47 towards Plumbridge, T: (01662) 648142). On the B48 from Gortin to Omagh, the Gortin Glen Forest Park is on the left and the Ulster History Park on the right, with Stone-Age houses and round towers, T:(01662) 648188.

ACTIVITIES
Fishing: Moyola and Ballinderry rivers for trout and salmon, and local loughs for brown trout.
Bird-watching: breeding golden plover, peregrine, raven and red grouse mainly to the north of the B47.
Riding: Marsh Kyse Riding School, 19 Hospital Road, Magherafelt, T:(01648) 33332, and the Edergole Riding Centre, 70 Moneymore Road, Cookstown, T:(016487) 62924.

FURTHER INFORMATION
Tourist offices: at Magherafelt, T:(01648) 32151, and Cookstown, T:(016487) 66727.

Lough Erne

Two lakes formed by massive broadenings of the River Erne, occupying central County Fermanagh and divided by Enniskillen and a narrower section of the river

Lough Erne and Marble Arch

Key
- National Park.
- - - Footpath.
- Exploration zone.
- ● Points of interest.

Most of the land around Lough Erne is used for farming, as are many of the islands. One island on the upper lough offers bed and organic breakfast. This is smart country, with the prosperous market town of Enniskillen dividing the two lakes. Wildness is usually out of sight or distant, on or in the water. Large numbers of great crested grebe (about 400), mute swan (400) and whooper swan (800) winter on the upper lake. The hundred or so pairs of 'common' scoter which used to make the lower lough the birds' main breeding ground have dwindled to under ten, perhaps due to the introduction of roach (brought primarily as live bait), which disastrously reduced the scoters' food, or perhaps to numbers of mink. There are also regular alignments of human anglers under large green umbrellas. People swim, boat and water ski, for as well as fulfilling other functions the loughs are human playgrounds on the grand scale.

This is an area of great

historic interest. Enniskillen was virtually a Protestant frontier town in the seventeenth century, providing two regiments for the British crown, the Fusiliers and Dragoon Guards, a contribution matched by no other town in Britain or Ireland. The remains of many great Ascendancy estates rim the lakes. Some of

these have found modern roles: in particular, Castle Archdale is now a country park, with a National Nature Reserve and arboretum, while Castle Caldwell has a timber forest and RSPB reserve of wooded islands on which a dwindling population of common scoters breeds. Both of these estates are on the lower lake. So are the

The Irish or fastigiate yew, of upright habit, is a variety of the common yew. All Irish yews trace their ancestry to a single, female tree found in the eighteenth century on a mountain close to Florence Court in County Fermanagh.

cliffs of Magho, dramatically overlooking the north-west corner, and, further along the west coast, Ely Lodge Forest, where fine old woodlands have been allowed to survive. These are in contrast to the miles of conifer plantations on the lake-studded highlands to the west, contained within the bounds of Lower Lough Erne, Lough Melvin and Lough Macnean.

The upper lake is really a dense pattern of islands, like Lough Oughter, from which it is scarcely separated. They used to say that Lough Erne was in Fermanagh except when Fermanagh was in Lough Erne, and before drainage and hydro-electric dams controlled the water levels there was much flooding of the abundant drumlin islands and surrounding coast. It is not always easy for visitors to reach the shores because so much land is private and deterringly fenced. Great numbers of birds, including the great crested grebe and swans already mentioned and innumerable other winter visitors, have no such problem. Various waders breed in the prolific reed-beds lining the inlets, islands and lagoons. The corncrake – a symbolic victim of new farming methods (see p. 146) – is more likely to occur in the marshy lands of this area than elsewhere in Northern Ireland, but even here it is verging on extinction.

Before you go *Maps:* OSNI Discoverer Series maps Nos 17 and 27; OSNI Lough Erne 1:25,000 (2 sheets).

Getting there *By car:* take the M1 out of Belfast and then the A4 to Enniskillen.
By bus: Goldline Express buses run to Enniskillen from Belfast (journey time 2 hrs). These operate hourly Mon–Sat, with only three buses on Sundays.

Where to stay *Outdoor living:* Enniskillen, Castle Island Camp Site, T:(01365) 324250; Irvinestown, Castle Archdale Caravan Park, T:(013656) 21333; Lisnaskea, Mullynascarthy Caravan Park, T:(013657) 21040. Also see NITB's *Camping and Caravan Parks.*
Youth hostels: Castle Archdale Youth Hostel, T:(013656) 28118. For more information, see ÑITB's *Northern Ireland - All the Places to Stay.*

Activities *Bird-watching:* large populations of birds both summer and winter on Lower Lough Erne include breeding great crested grebes, several ducks, and many warblers

The most notable curiosity of the Giant's Causeway is the series of irregular pavements formed of the tops of basalt columns cooled to hexagonal shape from the molten liquid of ancient volcanic flows.

including Irish garden warbler. Common scoter is no longer abundant. RSPB reserve at Castlecaldwell in the north-west corner. Upper Lough Erne offers a great variety of habitat and accommodates among many others large winter populations of great crested grebe, mute and whooper swans.

Fishing: coarse fishing on Ballinamallard river, pike and roach all through Upper and Lower Lough Erne. Coolyermer Lough for brown and rainbow trout. Lower Lough Erne for brown and sea trout and salmon, especially good at Lusty Beg, Lusty More and Hill's Island.

Riding: at Ashbrooke Equestrian Centre, Ashbrooke, Brookeborough, T:(013655) 3242; Drumhoney Riding Centre, Castle Archdale Country Park, Irvinestown, T:(013656) 21892.

Further information: contact the Fermanagh Tourist Information Centre, Wellington Road, Enniskillen, T:(01365) 323110, open all year.

Marble Arch

An underground complex open to the general public since 1985, consisting of subterranean waterways, lakes and caves.

Cuilcagh (pronounced something like queelca) mountain, whose summit (2,188 ft/798 m) straddles the national border, is divided between Counties Cavan and Fermanagh. Its surface is mainly sandstone with patches of millstone grit above, but the bulk of its body is of limestone. Time, water and the porous nature of lime have caused parts of it to become riddled with holes like a Gruyère cheese.

The mountain offers a good tough climb from the north side, way-marked from the road between Florence Court and Marble Arch. There are other attractions lower down: Lough Macnean Lower, the ash trees of Marble Arch wood, the mixed woods of Spring Grove. Florence Court itself is a grand mid-eighteenth-century mansion, home of the Earls of Enniskillen and now owned by the National Trust.

In 1780 a nearby farmer found two attractive upright yew trees on his land. He gave one to the Earl. Yews are either one sex or the other and in this case both specimens were female. Breeding true was therefore impossible, but cuttings were taken and the variety spread – always by that means – all over Britain and, in due course, much further afield. Indeed, all the world's fastigiate yews (*Taxus baccata fastigiata*) trace their ancestry from the Florence Court specimen.

A natural freak is found at Marble Arch, west of Florence Court. The arch is a natural, double-arched limestone bridge, and the water moving under it has just emerged from a network of underground channels and caves, through which it has flowed, concealed, down the mountainside. Or mostly concealed: sometimes the ground has given way and a subterranean stream is exposed. From the arch onwards, the water flows above ground to the River Arney. The caves by the arch have now been opened to the public, who can visit various illuminated examples, complete with waterfalls and stalactites. The tour is conducted partly in boats with guides aboard. Higher up the mountain, pot-holers – who are very unwise to go without local guides – can explore the swallow-holes. R. Lloyd Praeger, who was among the team which explored and charted the caves in 1907–8, wrote of his experiences in a way that will not induce everyone to venture underground: 'The water is cold and as black as ink, the candle stuck in your hat is inclined to be extinguished if the roof gets too low or if owing to a blunder your head goes under, parts may be too narrow for swimming with the arms, and from the unplumbed bottom knife-edges of limestone may rise ...' But of course it is not candles these days.

Before you go *Maps:* OSNI Discoverer Series maps Nos 17 and 26.

Getting there *By car:* from Enniskillen take either the A4 to Blacklion or the A32 to Florence Court. Parking at Florence Court and Marble Arch. *By bus:* there are good local bus links to the area from Enniskillen.

Activities: from mid-March to Sept every day there are tours around the caves, running from 11 am until 4.30 pm and lasting one hour. For information about tours and facilities call Marble Arch Caves, T:(01365) 348855. For Florence Court, T:(01365) 348249, and for Castle Coole, T:(01365) 322690.

Where to stay: for bed and breakfasts close to Marble Arch and Enniskillen, see NITB's *Northern Ireland – All the Places to Stay. Outdoor living:* Florence Court Forest Park, T:(01232) 524456. *Youth hostels:* Castle Archdale Youth Hostel, T:(013656) 28118.

USEFUL ADDRESSES

An Taisce (National Trust), Tailors Hall, Back Lane, Dublin 8, T:(01) 541786.

Bord Failte Eireann, Baggot Street Bridge, Dublin 2, T:(01) 676 5871.

Central Fisheries Board, Balnagowan House, Glasnevin, Dublin 9, :(01) 379206.

Coillte Teoranta (The Irish Forestry Service), Leeson Lane, Dublin 2, T:(01) 763636.

ENFO (Environment Information Service), 17 St Andrew Street, Dublin 2, T:(01) 679 3144.

Federation of Pike Angling Clubs, 19 The Grove, Kingswood Heights, Dublin 24, T:(01) 520072.

Forest Service, Department of Agriculture, Dundonald House, Upper Newtownards Road, Belfast, BT4 2F, T:(01232) 650111.

Irish Association for Sail Training, Irish Federation of Marine Industries, Kildare Street, Dublin 2, T:(01) 779801.

Irish Wildbird Conservancy, Ruttledge House, 8 Longford Place, Monkstown, Co. Dublin, T:(01) 280 4322.

Irish Yachting Association, 3 Park Road, Dun Laoghaire, Co. Dublin, T:(01) 280 0239.

Irish Yacht Chartering Association, Irish Federation of Marine Industries, Kildare Street, Dublin 2, T:(01) 779801.

National Coarse Fishing Federation of Ireland, Blaithan, Dublin Road, Cavan, T:(049) 32367.

National Parks and Wildlife Service, Office of Public Works, 51 St Stephen's Green, Dublin 2, T:(01) 661 3111, or 16 Eyre Square, Galway.

National Trust for Northern Ireland, Rowallane House, Saintfield, Ballynahinch, Co. Down, BT24 7LH, T:(01238) 510721.

Northern Ireland Tourist Board, 48 High Street, Belfast, BT1 2DS, T:(01232) 231221.

Royal Society for the Protection of Birds, Belvoir Park Forest, Belfast, BT8 4QT, T:(01232) 491547.

Shannonside Activity and Sailing Centre, Killaloe, Co. Clare, T:(061) 376622.

Sports Council, House of Sport, Malone Road, Belfast, BT7 1RU, T:(01232) 661222.

Youth Hostels Association (YHANI), 56 Bradbury Place, Belfast, BT7 1RU, T:(01232) 324733.

FURTHER READING

Bellamy, David: *Bellamy's Ireland: The Wild Bog-lands* (Country House, 1986)

Crawford, Peter: *The Living Isles, a Natural History of Britain and Ireland* (BBC, 1985)

De Buitlear, Eamon: *Ireland's Wild Countryside* (Boxtree, 1993)

Dempsey, Eric and O'Clery, Michael: *The Complete Guide to Ireland's Birds* (Gill and Macmillan, 1993)

Feehan, John: *The Landscape of Slieve Bloom* (Blackwater Press, 1979)

Fewer, Michael: *Irish Long Distance Walks: A Guide to the Way-Marked Trails* (Moorland Publishing Co., 1993)

Herman, David: *Great Walks: Ireland* (Ward Lock, 1991)

Herman, D. and MacCarthy, M.J.: *New Irish Walk Guides – East and South* (Gill and Macmillan, 1991)

Hickin, Norman: *Irish Nature* (O'Brien Press, 1980)

Hutchinson, Clive: *Where to Watch Birds in Ireland* (Gill and Macmillan, 1994)

Lehane, Brendan: *Companion Guide to Ireland* (Collins, 1985)

Mersey, Richard: *The Hills of Kerry and Cork* (Alan Sutton and Gill and Macmillan, 1987)

Mills, Stephen: *Nature in its Place, the Habitats of Ireland* (Bodley Head, 1987)

Mitchell, Frank: *The Way that I Followed* (Country House, 1990)

Mitchell, Frank: *The Shell Guide to Reading the Irish Landscape* [incorporating *The Irish Landscape*, 1976] (Country House, 1990)

Nelson, E. Charles: *The Burren* (Boethius Press, 1991)

O'Suillebhain, Sean: *New Irish Walk Guides – South-West* (Gill and Macmillan, 1991)

Praeger, Robert Lloyd: *The Way that I Went* (Figges, 1937)

Webb, D.A.: *An Irish Flora* (Dundalgan Press, 1977)

Whilde, Tony and Simms, Patrick: *New Irish Walk Guides – North and West* (Gill and Macmillan, 1991)

Whittow, J.B.: *Geology and Scenery in Ireland* (Penguin, 1975)

INDEX

ACKNOWLEDGEMENTS

For much help and kindness, the author and editors would like to thank John Lahiffe and Katrina Flanagan of Bord Failte's London office, and staff at the London and Belfast branches of the Northern Ireland Tourist Office, among them Joris Minne and Stewart Hanscombe. Swansea Cork Ferries generously provided sea passages between their two ports, Norse Irish Ferries a passage from Liverpool to Belfast and SeaCat a crossing from Stranraer to Larne. Eleanor Mayes provided not only the benefit of her knowledge as a consultant but also hospitality. Monica Duckworth was very generous with hospitality. Advice and facts came from innumerable people all over Ireland and in Britain: in particular Dr John Akeroyd, Alan Dalton, John Feehan, Rosemary FitzGerald and Matt Murphy.